Paging New Jersey

11/5/03

To Andrea and Harry,
It was nice meeting you both —
Hope you enjoy the book!

all the best —
J.F. Brodie

PAGING NEW JERSEY

A Literary Guide to the Garden State

JAMES F. BRODERICK

RUTGERS UNIVERSITY PRESS

New Brunswick, New Jersey, and London

LIBRARY OF CONGRESS CATALOGING-IN-PUBLICATION DATA

Broderick, James F., 1963–
   Paging New Jersey : a literary guide to the Garden State / James F. Broderick.
     p.   cm.
   Includes bibliographical references and index.
   ISBN 0-8135-3290-6 (alk. paper)
     1. American literature—New Jersey—History and criticism.   2. Authors, American—
Homes and haunts—New Jersey.   3. Literary landmarks—New Jersey.   4. New Jersey—
Intellectual life.   5. New Jersey—In literature.   I. Title.
PS253.N5 B76 2003
810.9'9749—dc21

                                                    2002152304

British Cataloging-in-Publication data for this book is available from the British Library.

The publication of this volume has been made possible, in part,
by a gift from Nicholas G. Rutgers IV to support books about New Jersey.

Manufactured in the United States of America

Contents

Acknowledgments   vii

Introduction   1

PART ONE   **THE WRITERS**

Philip Freneau   7
James Fenimore Cooper   12
Mary Griffith   17
Walt Whitman   20
Mary Mapes Dodge   27
Thomas Nast   32
Mary Wilkins Freeman   37
Stephen Crane   41
Albert Payson Terhune   46
William Carlos Williams   50
Joyce Kilmer   53
Allen Ginsberg   58
Mary Higgins Clark   62
Toni Morrison   65
Amiri Baraka   71
Joyce Carol Oates   76
Peter Benchley   79
Anna Quindlen   84

PART TWO   **THE BOOKS**

Cheaper by the Dozen   91
Goodbye, Columbus   95
The Pine Barrens   99
Eddie and the Cruisers   104
Jersey Luck   109
Rosamund's Vision   112

Laying Down the Law   116
One for the Money   120
Our Guys   123
Lost Legends of New Jersey   127

PART THREE   THE HISTORY

Searching for Captain Kidd's Treasure   135
Burr, Hamilton, and the Duel of History
    in Weehawken   141
The Lindbergh Baby Kidnapping   148
The *Hindenburg* Disaster   155
The Trials of Rubin "Hurricane" Carter   162

PART FOUR   A LITERARY MISCELLANY

Mobbed in New Jersey   171
On the (Paper) Trail of the
    New Jersey Devil   179
Dodge Poetry Festival   185
The New Jersey Literary Hall of Fame   190
Stages of Greatness: A Survey of the
    History of Theater in New Jersey   194
Reaching Critical Mass
    in the Garden State   200
Stoned in New Jersey   207

Index   211

Acknowledgments

From the beginning of this project I have benefited greatly from the generous counsel of many friends and colleagues. I wish to thank Bruce Chadwick for his assistance in every phase of this book's preparation. I was always grateful to have the ear of this gifted writer and teacher.

I'd also like to acknowledge my debt to the following people: Helen Beckert of the Glen Ridge Public Library for her help in locating source materials; William Fullerton for sharing his knowledge and remembrances of New Jersey detective Ellis Parker; Mrs. Bobbie Fettinger for pointing me to research materials about the Lindbergh baby kidnapping case; Betsy Carpenter, supervisor of public programs for the Pine Barrens Commission, for her overview of the history of the Pinelands preservation efforts; and James Osbourn of the Newark Public Library, James Lewis of the New Jersey Historical Society, and Barbara Moss of the *Newark Star-Ledger* for their assistance in locating photographic materials. My mother-in-law, Maria Ascarelli, saved many useful books from an inglorious end in the recycling heap and sent them my way. I wish to thank her for all her help and support. Leslie Mitchner, my editor, has been a steadying influence during the past two years as this book came together. Her early support of this book and her invaluable course corrections are deeply appreciated.

I wish to thank my father for sharing his deeply informed perspectives on American history and offering his thoughts on a wide variety of subjects that made their way into this book. His encyclopedic knowledge of history could fill a dozen such books. And I cannot omit my debt to my mother, whose unwavering belief in me has always given me the confidence to take on new challenges.

And then there is Miri, an extraordinary writer, editor, sounding board, and wife. But for her, we never would have come to New Jersey, and this book—as well as lots of other wonderful things in my life—would never have come to fruition. It is to her and to my daughters, Olivia and Maddy, that I dedicate this book.

Paging New Jersey

Introduction

Joann Carlino and I cruised out of the Holland Tunnel and once more through that weird, fallen landscape which Eddie had loved. The Pulaski Skyway carried us over the refineries and marshes he celebrated. The turnpike and then the parkway led us south along the tawdry, half-romantic shoreline where his voice still reached the corners of a hundred common bars.

> — P. F. Kluge, *Eddie and the Cruisers* (1980)

When came I first to Paterson
(Full twenty years ago)
I hied me to its market place
With joy and wonder in my face
To gaze upon the show:
But should you go to Paterson,
Things are no longer so.

> — Ruth Guthrie Harding,
> "The Old Wagon-Market" (1916)

Sitting there in the park, I felt a deep knowledge of Newark, an attachment so rooted that it could not help but branch out into affection.

> — Philip Roth, *Goodbye, Columbus* (1961)

Philip Roth's youthful narrator is only one of the many prominent literary voices that has expressed a love of the Garden State. New Jersey's place in the pages of our national literature is secure and singular. From the Revolutionary War lyrics, which stirred Washington's Morristown-based troops, to contemporary romance novels, which unfold along the Boardwalk, New Jersey remains the focal point of a literary crosscurrent—and the home of some of today's best-known and most important writers.

No single book, however comprehensive, can claim to tell the whole story of New Jersey's literary connections. Just the biographies of the state's well-known authors would fill the reference room of many local libraries. And then there are those authors who have set their stories in New Jersey, given their characters a

Jersey hometown, or made one of the state's institutions (Princeton, a Jersey diner, even the N.J. Turnpike) a marker of significance. How to handle the vast trove of Revolutionary War literature: patriotic poems, diaries, letters, and first-hand accounts of the fighting? There's also folklore and legend to contend with; the New Jersey Devil alone has inspired several books and dozens of articles. Finally, how can one write about New Jersey's literary legacy without accounting for such oft-recorded events as the Burr-Hamilton duel, the Lindbergh baby kidnapping, the rise and fall of the Mafia, or the strange case of Rubin "Hurricane" Carter?

The collection of such a disparate body of work seems to beg several questions. Beyond spending a portion of their writing energy here, are these writers really *connected* to New Jersey? Do they reflect a New Jersey consciousness? Can the state's collective artistic output be reduced to a set of New Jersey–influenced themes? In a state with such diverse populations and a variety of regional economies (working farms abut industrial highways, world-class casinos illuminate pristine ocean beachheads), the answer seems clear. No single animating idea, from the noble ("Crossroads of the American Revolution!") to the ephemeral (summer weekends "down the shore") can represent the whole.

That is perhaps the fittest justification for this compendium. Only a multiplicity of Jersey voices can help clarify the Garden State's kaleidoscopic literary artistry. When Benjamin Franklin half-derided New Jersey's position between New York and Philadelphia as "a barrel tapped at both ends," he unwittingly captured the state's flavor: a fluid concoction, fermented by history, varietal, at times even intoxicating—though, for some, it remains an acquired taste.

Let me clarify, briefly, the criteria for selection of the material in this present volume. The writers, books, and events included in *Paging New Jersey* are connected to the state in some arguably meaningful way. In the case of an individual writer, it might be through birth, attendance at one of the state's colleges or universities, or perhaps simply as a temporary port in the storm during a critical time in a writer's career. An author can claim multiple residences, each of which might have left an imprint on the intellect or imagination. No one could claim, for example, that Walt Whitman is exclusively a "New Jersey writer." His connections to other locales, especially New York City, are legendary. The same could, of course, be said of Allen Ginsberg, James Fenimore Cooper (who, after all, hails from the eponymous municipality in New York State), Toni Morrison, and Amiri Baraka. These writers' imaginations are large enough to absorb multiple geographic imprints. "I am vast," Whitman announced. "I contain multitudes." The literary connections I've traced are significant and demonstrable—but by no means exhaustive.

Some features, however, of the Garden State appear singular in their contribution to the literary and cultural landscape. Joyce Carol Oates's jaw-dropping productivity has been fueled for decades by Princeton's intellectual fervor. Thomas Alva Edison was attracted to northern New Jersey's energy. Alexander Hamilton was drawn to the blank slate of Paterson, etching from his imagination the blueprint for America's first "planned city." And the list of the many rock-and-roll poets inspired by the decadent charms of the Jersey Shore is too long to enumerate. One can assert without fear of contradiction that the course of American literature, from the highbrow to the crassly commercial, has been deeply affected by a New Jersey state of mind.

The elusive attractions of the state were temporarily pinned down in print by John Cunningham when he wrote:

> Somehow New Jersey escapes the words that praise it (and unfortunately, most of the words that damn it). The reason is that New Jersey is more than people, more than geography, more than history, more than industry, more than agriculture. It is a flotilla of sailboats on a North Jersey lake, a picnic in a state forest.
>
> It is the old streets of Cape May, the modernity of the New Jersey Turnpike. It is the red and gold touched on North Jersey's maple leaves in the fall, the appeal of Atlantic City's casinos year round. It is the George Washington Bridge, and the wooden covered bridge at Sergeantsville.
>
> Jersey is old, Jersey is new. It struggles to be all things to all people, and both fails and succeeds. It is factory and farm; it is High Point and Cape May.
>
> Diversity—that's the spirit of New Jersey.

I've chosen to focus on those literary connections that are unusual, historically significant, unavoidable, and in some cases downright obscure (when was the last time you curled up with a copy of Mary Griffith's *Three Hundred Years Hence*?). New Jersey can lay claim to all manner of literary representation, from the sublime to the ridiculous, and I tried to capture something of that range. Additionally, while attempting to distill the opinions of a corps of literary critics who have written about our state's many authors, I've made no attempt to keep my own judgments under wraps. What drew me to this literature in the first place was my own enthusiasm for the work, rather than an encyclopedist's impulse toward objectivity. I freely offer my opinion about these books and writers in the hope that other readers will find something here that ignites a spark of interest in the literature of New Jersey.

As Henry Charlton Beck stated in the Foreword to his book *A New Jersey Reader*, published four decades ago, "There is, after all, no end to the tales that have been, or could be, written about New Jersey." This present volume, I hope, proves him right.

Part One   The Writers

BORN January 2, 1752, in New York City
DIED December 19, 1832, in Mount Pleasant, New Jersey
BEST KNOWN FOR A handful of early American romantic poems and a collection of verse satirizing the British crown.
THE JERSEY CONNECTION Attended Princeton (when it was called "The College of New Jersey") and spent the last three decades of his life on his farm in Mount Pleasant.

Philip Freneau

A critic once remarked of Freneau that his work would have been twice as good if he'd only written half as much. That sums up much of the reason Freneau is remembered by only a select few modern readers and largely forgotten by almost everyone else.

His writing—mostly poetry—is patriotic, romantic, celebratory, pastoral, jingoistic, and voluminous. Freneau never seems to have found his literary niche, yet he kept trying. Although his work is often called "admirable" and "representative of his age," it seldom lingers in either the ear or the mind. Yet, given the highly restrictive couplet form popular in his day, Freneau occasionally manages to crystallize a thought memorably, even strikingly. His work may not do much for the contemporary reader, but the late-eighteenth-century literate crowd accorded Freneau a great deal of respect, and many of his contemporaries considered him to be one of America's most important writers.

There's little doubt that his work would have been recognized by the British literati save for the fact that most his verse was aimed at excoriating all things English. When Freneau alters his focus from nationalistic battle hymns to the larger human questions, he brings to mind such great neoclassical poetic statements as Alexander Pope's "Essay on Man." In Freneau's "On the Civilization of the Western Aboriginal Country," one sees the still-dominant Augustan emphasis on natural order given a uniquely American spin by celebrating reinvention and triumph over adversity:

Two wheels has nature constantly in play,
She turns them both, but turns a different way;
What one creates, subsists a year, an hour,
Then, by destruction's wheel is crushed once more.
No art, no strength this wheel of fate restrains,
While matter, deathless matter, still remains,
Again perhaps, new modelled, to revive,
Again to perish, and again to live!

Philip Morin Fresneau (he dropped the "s" after his father died) was the first child of Pierre and Agnes Watson Fresneau. Comfortably established in the colonies by Freneau's grandfather, who prospered in commerce and land investing, the family lived on an estate at Mount Pleasant in Monmouth County, New Jersey. Freneau attended schools in New York City, where he studied Latin and Greek. His father's social circle included leaders of commerce and culture, and the young scholar had the chance to mingle with learned members of society

Philip Freneau—"Poet of the American Revolution."
From the Collections of the New Jersey Historical Society.

from his earliest days; the death of his father, however, brought about a fairly rapid decline in prosperity and ended this almost aristocratic lifestyle.

When Freneau entered Princeton (known then as "The College of New Jersey") in 1768, he intended to study for the ministry. But inspired by discussions with classmates such as James Madison, Hugh Henry Brackenridge, and William Bradford, he shifted his focus from theology to politics. As he studied the great British political thinkers and writers of the century—Alexander Pope, Jonathan Swift, Addison and Steele—Freneau began to grasp the potential for effecting political change through literature. He became determined to give voice to the emerging political zeitgeist, to become the poet of, in his words, "Paradise Anew."

He graduated in 1771 and tried (almost completely unsuccessfully) to sustain himself through the publication of poems on American themes. He worked briefly as a teacher on Long Island and in Maryland and produced his first (though little noticed at the time) important work, the pastoral poem "The American Village." In 1775, when the seige of Boston began, Freneau dashed off a series of patriotic verses—largely satiric in nature—that gained wide circulation and captured the indignation and emergent zeal of his fellow colonists; he emerged as revolutionary scribe and propagandist.

One of his more venomous—and popular—poems of that period was "A Political Litany," published as a broadside in New York City in June of 1775. Here's an excerpt:

> From the group at St. James's, who slight our petitions
> And fools that are waiting for further submissions—
> From a nation whose manners are rough and severe
> From scoundrels and rascals—do keep us all clear
>
> From pirates sent out by command of the King
> To murder and plunder, but never to swing
> From [Brit. Navy captains] Wallace and Greaves and Vipers and Roses
> Whom, if heaven pleases, we'll give bloody noses
>
> From a kingdom that bullies, and hectors, and swears,
> We send up to heaven our wishes and prayers
> That we, disunited, may freemen be still,
> And Britain go on—to be damned if she will.

On paper, Freneau found such sentiments easy to express, and he poured out a huge volume of stirring, searing, anti-British verse. However, the inescapable realities of revolution—the death, dislocation, and barbarity—caused Freneau to privately question the morality of war. Some of his work, written as early as 1776, expresses remorse for the current state of the conflict, and his poetry from this point begins to assume a less dogmatic patriotic posture. Feeling the need to distance himself from the surrounding daily carnage and brutality, Freneau suddenly fled to the island of St. Croix in the West Indies, where he found the peace and inspiration to pen such paens to nature as "The Wild Honeysuckle":

> Smit with those charms that must decay
> I grieve to see your future doom;
> They died—nor were those flowers more gay,
> The flowers that did in Eden bloom;
> Unpitying frosts and Autumn's power
> Shall leave no vestige of this flower.

In 1778, feeling increasingly conflicted at having abandoned his countrymen at a critical time, Freneau left his island sanctuary and returned to New Jersey. Outraged and disheartened by the devastation wrought by the recent battle of Monmouth, he once again embraced the cause of patriotism and enlisted in the state militia. After serving as a scout along the Hudson River shore, he was assigned to a warship, wounded in a skirmish, and taken prisoner on the British frigate *Scorpion,* where his brutal mistreatment was chronicled in the poem "The British Prison Ship." The following excerpt, from "Canto II" of the poem, introduces a series of grotesque vignettes, including torture and murder:

> Remembrance shudders at this scene of fears—
> Still in my view some English brute appears,
> Some base-born Hessian slave walks threatening by,
> Some servile Scot with Murder in his eye
> Still haunts my sight, as vainly they bemoan
> Rebellions manag'd so unlike their own!
> O may I never feel the poignant pain
> To live subjected to such fiends again,
> Stewards and mates that hostile Britain bore,
> Cut from the gallows on their native shore;
> Their ghastly looks and vengeance-beaming eyes
> Still to my view in dismal colors rise—
> O may I never review these dire abodes,
> These piles for slaughter, floating on the floods . . .
> Hail dark abode! What can with thee compare—
> Heat, sickness, famine, death and stagnant air.
> Pandora's box, from where all mischief flew,
> Here real found, torments mankind anew!

After entreaties from his well-placed friends secured his release, Freneau threw himself into journalism, first as a writer for *United States Magazine* and then as editor in chief of *The Freeman's Journal.* After four years, drained by the demands of daily journalism and growing tired of political propagandizing, he took a post as "Clerk, Postmaster General of the United States." Growing restless

---

BATTLE LINES OF VERSE

Philip Freneau may have distinguished himself as "the Poet of the American Revolution," but he was certainly not the only patriot at the time writing verse. Everyone is familiar with the poems of Francis Scott Key, whose lines in praise of the defense of Fort McHenry became our national anthem. (Of course, most people know only the first stanza of Key's poem; there are four. Whether any stanza is easier to sing than the first may never be known.) And Thomas Paine's stirring verses helped rally Washington's troops as they prepared to cross the Delaware.

But it was no less a scribe than President John Quincy Adams who produced one of the nineteenth century's most popular poems, entitled "The Wants of Man." Here's a sampling:

Man wants but little here below,
Nor wants that little long.
Tis not with me exactly so,
But tis so in the song.
My wants are many, and if told
Would muster many a score;
And were each wish a mint of Gold,
I still should long for more.

---

yet again, he soon began a new career as a brigmaster and sea captain, sailing trading vessels between Jamaica and the east coast of the United States in the 1780s. All the while, he kept on writing. After marrying Eleanor Forman in 1789, he returned to the shore for a decade, editing newspapers in New York City, Philadelphia, and, in 1795, the *Jersey Chronicle* in Monmouth County, where he became one of the first political journalists to actively support Jefferson—a bold position in the pre-Federalist era.

At the end of the decade, his life alternated between service as a sea captain and brief stints as a gentleman farmer. In 1807, he retired permanently to his farm in Mount Pleasant. In 1832, the man who had survived the American Revolution, perilous sea travel, and imprisonment on a British frigate died when he lost his way home in a snowstorm, fell in a bog, and froze to death.

It is sad that the voluminous literary output of his post–Revolutionary War years—poems, essays, travel writing—never brought much admiration, or money, to the man who, for a brief time, was considered "the Poet of the American Revolution."

Freneau's literary legacy seems to be entrusted to a handful of poems that are still anthologized in American literature textbooks. An exemplar of early American romanticism, Freneau's very best work strikes just the right notes: an exaltation of the natural world, a belief in the primacy of the self, and a dewy-eyed idealism born of revolutionary fervor:

From distant lands a thousand sails
Your hazy summits greet,
You saw the angry Briton come,
You saw him, last, retreat!
With towering crest, you first appear
The news of land to tell;
To him that comes fresh joys impart,
To him that goes, a heavy heart,
The lover's long farewell. . . .

—from "Neversink"

FURTHER READING

Books by Freneau

Poems of Philip Freneau, Poet of the American Revolution. Edited by Fred Lewis Patee. 3 vols. Princeton Historical Society, 1902.

Books about Freneau

Bowden, Mary. *Philip Freneau.* Boston: Twayne's United States Author Series, 1976.
Eberwein, Jane, ed. *Early American Poetry: Selections from Bradstreet, Taylor, Dwight, Freneau, and Bryant.* Madison: University of Wisconsin Press, 1994.
Hiltner, Judith. *The Newspaper Verse of Philip Freneau: An Edition and Bibliographic Survey.* Albany: Whiston Publishing, 1986.

James Fenimore Cooper

BORN September 15, 1789, in Burlington, New Jersey

DIED September 14, 1851, at Cooperstown, New York

BEST KNOWN FOR His series of novels (known as "The Leatherstocking Tales") depicting pioneer life on the frontier.

THE JERSEY CONNECTION He was born in Burlington, and returned to the area several times later in life.

Probably no other prominent literary career in the history of American letters has been launched in the accidental way James Fenimore Cooper's began: as a dare. The well-known anecdote that describes Cooper's wife daring him to write a better book than the one he was grudgingly reading—and loudly grousing about— has the weight of historical truth. Most biographers have accepted the tale as accurate, a curious beginning to one of the most significant writing lives in all of American literature. (Ironically, Cooper had previously shown absolutely no desire to write; he was reluctant even to write letters to his friends.)

Cooper's life is full of ironies, puzzles, accidents, and surprises, His best-known books evoke the Western frontier and all its naturalistic charm and terror, although he himself never saw the Plains. He is considered the most American of authors, but much of his life was spent in Europe—he wrote *The Prairie* in Paris, much of *The Water Witch* in Germany, and *The Herdsman* in England. He was also a relative late bloomer as a novelist. He wrote nothing his first thirty-one years, and thirty-two novels in the subsequent thirty-one years. And finally, to the list of strange dichotomies in Cooper's life must be added the critical reception of his works. No established author in the canon has been as lavishly praised and brutally excoriated as Cooper.

Some critics trace the very best strains of American writing directly back to Cooper, calling him a famous but underappreciated author whose impact is inestimable. In one of the many spirited attempts during the last two centuries to restore Cooper's critical standing, critic Donald Ringe stated in his important study, *James Fenimore Cooper* (1961):

> The number of firsts to be attributed to Cooper is truly astonishing. He created the first American Utopia and the first American novels to describe the lives of succeeding generations of characters. Among his first four books are two truly revolutionary ones, *The Pioneers* and *The Pilot*; and in *The Last of the Mohicans* he composed what is perhaps the classic tale of Frontier adventure.

Set that commentary against the famous Mark Twain review of Cooper's *The Deerslayer* and the extremes that have earmarked Cooper criticism from the start become clear:

> A work of art? It has no invention; it has no order, system, sequence or result; it has no lifelikeness, no thrill, no stir, no seeming of reality; its characters are confusedly drawn, and by their acts and words they prove that they are not the sort of people the author claims that they are; its humor is pathetic, its pathos is funny; its conversations are—oh! Indescribable; its love scenes odious; its English a crime against the language.
> Counting these out, what is left is art. I think we must all admit that.

Cooper, in the year before his death, sized up his legacy this way:

> If anything from the pen of the writer is to outlive himself, it is, unquestionably, the series of 'The Leather-Stocking Tales.' To say this is not to predict a very lasting reputation for the series itself, but simply to express the belief it will outlast any, or all, of the works from the same hand.

Cooper was born in Burlington, New Jersey, but his family relocated to Cooperstown when James was thirteen months old. James's father, William Cooper, had purchased with a fellow investor an immense tract of land—about a half million acres—during the waning days of the American Revolution. A village had since developed along the property on the shore of Otsego Lake, and, despite reluctance from the elder Cooper's wife to leave their Burlington home (reportedly she had to be lifted, armchair and all, into the wagon), the family moved to the relative untamed wilderness to begin life in the newly named "Cooperstown."

He returned briefly to Burlington to attend school during two winters when he was a boy but otherwise attended a local academy near Cooperstown and later a boarding school in Albany in preparation for Yale University, which he left after two years, when he was expelled for "misconduct." In 1806, with the hope of joining

LITERARY TURF BATTLES

James Fenimore Cooper was among the best known and most popular writers of his time, but literary historians are now inclined to bestow the title of "Greatest American Writer" of his time to Cooper's contemporary, Washington Irving. Cooper was mindful of the rivalry—and quite resentful.

Cooper's dislike of Irving was reportedly based in part on the latter's reputation as a "literary man"—in other words, a *real* writer. Cooper, though widely read and traveled, was generally considered to be more storyteller than man-of-letters. Irving was considered the "polished" writer, Cooper, merely the "hack." In a letter to a friend, Cooper once lambasted Irving as being "below the ordinary level, in moral qualities, instead of being above them, as he is cried up to be."

the Navy, he became a sailor, shipping out on a merchant vessel, *The Stirling*. He became a midshipman in the Navy in 1808. A year later his father's death left him $50,000 and much of the family's property in Cooperstown. In 1811, he married Susan Augusta Delancy; soon after he resigned from the Navy and moved to a farm owned by his father-in-law in Westchester County, New York.

His first book, *Precaution* (1820), caused little stir in the literary world. The novel is a rather pallid attempt to imitate the English "novel of manners." His second book, *The Spy* (1821), a historical novel about the American Revolution, brought him some measure of fame and profit. He relocated his growing family, which eventually numbered seven children, to New York City and dedicated himself to writing full time. It proved to be a good decision. The next year, he wrote *The Pioneers* (1823), the first of the multivolume "Leather-Stocking Tales," a phenomenally successful series of pioneer stories revolving around the exploits of a trapper named Natty Bumppo.

For the next two decades, Cooper churned out more "Leather-Stocking Tales," historical novels set in medieval Europe, several essays and volumes of social criticism, and a massive study, *The History of the Navy of the United States of America* (1839). All the while he was regularly getting himself in hot water with his tart observations about the narrow-mindedness of his countrymen.

Consequently, he spent considerable time defending himself against charges of becoming "European," "elite," and aristocratic in his politics. In fact, some of Cooper's political views were even more conservative and aristocratic than those of many of his European peers. He did not favor granting women the vote, he abhorred the excesses of a free press (and initiated a number of well-publicized and lengthy legal battles against columnists and editors who criticized him publicly), and he was blind to the hardships of slave labor (once he wrote that "physical suffering cannot be properly enumerated among its evils").

Yet, to much of the nineteenth-century English-speaking world, Cooper *was* America. He delineated the American ideological litany vividly in his fiction: freedom, democracy, self-reliance, love of nature, optimism, endurance, a rough-and-ready posture. Though Cooper's view of human nature is more nuanced than many of his critics have acknowledged—for instance, his characters debated such tangled subjects as "natural" versus "legal" rights and progress/civilization versus pristine nature—most readers still think of him as a teller of frontier tales, a man who imbued his characters with a small helping of genteel European cultivation and a large dose of Daniel Boone–like courage and cunning.

Critical estimation of Cooper's value as a writer is, two centuries later, still quite muddled. His popular "Leather-Stocking Tales" continue to sell well. Many critics generally find the works poorly wrought and melodramatic, though Natty Bumppo has his defenders, and the Tales are still widely anthologized in high school and college literary textbooks. Cooper's social criticism is considered rather caustic and reactionary, and few modern readers are persuaded by any of his arguments. However, his body of travel writing is often vivid, even lyrical, and full of surprises and well-selected details, yet these travel essays remain virtually unknown. The same fate embraced his murder mystery, his play, his novels of the sea, his utopia, and his short stories. Posterity has footnoted almost all of Cooper except for the "Leather-Stocking Tales." But do the Tales hold up? Here's a typical passage, excerpted from *The Last of the Mohicans*, with all of Cooper's glories and foibles richly displayed:

> The words were still in the mouth of the scout, when the leader of the party, whose approaching footsteps had caught the vigilant ear of the Indian, came openly into view. A beaten path, such as those made by periodical passage of the deer, wound through a little glen at no great distance, and struck the river at the point where the white man and his companions had posted themselves. Along this track the travelers, who had produced a surprise so unusual in the depths of the forest, advanced slowly towards the hunter, who was in front of his associates in readiness to receive them.
>
> "Who comes?" demanded the scout, throwing his rifle carelessly across his left arm and keeping the forefinger of his right hand on the trigger,

though he avoided all appearance of menace in the act—"who comes hither among the beasts and dangers of the wilderness?"

"Believers in religion and friends to the law and king," returned he who rode foremost. "Men who have journeyed since the rising sun in the shades of this forest without nourishment and are sadly tired of their wayfaring."

"You are then lost," interrupted the hunter, "and have found how helpless 'tis not to know whether to take the right hand or the left?"

On the debit side of Cooper's literary ledger, there's the inappropriately elevated diction, the reliance on cliché, the two-dimensional characterization, and the stilted dialogue. But, to his credit, there's also a genuine reverence for nature, a wealth of closely observed naturalistic detail, and a rapid, economical progression of plot.

Cooper knew his wilderness sagas would win him a readership, which is why he continued to return to the fictional woods throughout his career. Arcane critical disputes about the literary worth of the "Leather-Stocking Tales" are essentially irrelevant and fail to acknowledge the deep-seated appeal of the American frontier story. Readers have flocked to Hawkeye, Natty Bumppo, the Deerslayer, and lots of colorful, wayward prairie travelers for two centuries. Cooper knew his audience, and he understood its fascination and romance with the exotic American West; he wrote "westerns" before the genre was invented. In that sense he was a visionary, even if that vision was blurred by crudely drawn characters in predictable, highly charged melodramas. Like the emerging frontier whose growth he chronicled, Cooper's works are overgrown, untamed, even primitive—yet deeply rooted in the America of the world's imagination.

FURTHER READING

Books by Cooper

The Prairie. New York: Penguin, 1987.
Red Rover: A Tale. Albany: State University of New York Press, 1991.

Books about Cooper

Dyer, Alan. *James Fenimore Cooper: An Annotated Bibliography of Criticism.* Westport, Conn.: Greenwood Publishing Group, 1991.
Grossman, James. *James Fenimore Cooper.* London: Methuen, 1950.
Railton, Stephen. *Fenimore Cooper: A Study of His Life and Imagination.* Princeton, N.J.: Princeton University Press, 1978.

Mary Griffith

BORN 1800 (exact date, place unknown)
DIED 1877, in Franklin Township, New Jersey
BEST KNOWN FOR A once-important science fiction novella, *Three Hundred Years Hence.*
THE JERSEY CONNECTION Spent most of her adult life living at "Charlie's Hope," her farm in Franklin Township near New Brunswick.

Edgar Allan Poe reviewed her work for his highbrow readers in the *Southern Literary Messenger*. Known affectionately to the farmers of New England as "the first female author on tillage," Griffith wrote a science fiction novella that occupies an important place in the development of utopic fiction. She published short stories, novels, and musings on soil, light, and phrenology, and she was an early proponent of women's colleges and the extension of copyright protection. Yet even before her death, she lapsed into obscurity, remembered today only by the compilers of science fiction encyclopedias; her works are long out of print.

New Jersey's first great contributor to science fiction published her most important book anonymously. *Three Hundred Years Hence*, printed in Philadelphia in 1836, was embedded among other tales by Griffith and collected in a volume titled *Camperdown; or, News from Our Neighborhood*. Poe (in an unsigned review widely accepted as coming from his hand) called *Three Hundred Years Hence* "well conceived," and the *New York Mirror*, seizing on Griffith's call for the elevation of women's status, noted, "The Ladies will read it with delight, for our fair author loses no opportunity of advocating the position and character of the gentler portions of creation—and the gentlemen will find in her pages much that they can turn to their account."

Griffith's novella remains important for scholars of American literature as well as science fiction. The work blends an Irving-esque Rip Van Winkle motif with a European strain of social commentary and utopianism (critics have found strong borrowings from L. Louis Mercier's *L'an deux mille quatre cent quarante*, published in 1771). Additionally, horticultural asides on the development of farm technology and the geography of New Jersey testify to her strong connection to the land. Although she signed all her letters later in life with the simple return address "Charlie's Hope," no such designation exists today; local historians point to Franklin Township as the locale of the Griffith farm.

Absent much biographical material on Griffith, critics have been forced to sift for biographical nuggets in her handful of works and her few notations throughout the publications of various horticultural societies in Massachusetts and New Jersey. (The editor of the *New England Farmer*, for example, obliquely noted in one issue that Griffith was left a widowed mother "in the prime of life.")

Three Hundred Years Hence captured readers' imaginations with its curious collection of "accurate" predictions and somewhat daft exhortations: she argues for
the elimination of all dogs from society, for example. She deals with both massively problematic social issues (she envisions transplanting "the whole of the
Negro population to Liberia, and to other Healthy colonies" as a means of dealing with the emancipation question) and small, labor-saving innovations (pre-
dicting the development of the first power lawn mower). As with most
nineteenth-century fiction writers, Griffith's belief in the universal benefits of
technology belie an age of backbreaking, dangerous daily life, whereas the new
machines of the twenty-second century

> mowed the grass, raked it up, spread it out, gathered it, and brought it to the
> barn. The same power distributed it to the merchants and small consumers
> . . . the machines have done everything. They fill up gullies, dig out the roots
> of trees, plough down hills, turn water courses.

Daily life gets easier, and nightly repose becomes less anxious, where future
houses are "almost all fire proof since the discovery of a substance which renders
wood almost proof against fire."

So much for technology. Actually, in the sphere of human relations Griffith
has the most to say, and her emphasis on mutual aid and compassion for both
the poor and women elevates her book from a mere compendium of hit-or-miss
crystal-ball gazing:

FROM TIME TO TIME

In the novella *Three Hundred Years Hence*, Mary Griffith relied on what has become
a staple of science fiction writing: time travel. Everyone from H. G. Wells to Rod
Serling to contemporary screenwriters has employed the device of sending one's
protagonist into another time; almost always, the *future* is visited, not the past.

There's a good reason that most time travel is future-based. Traveling back-
wards, as many science fiction fans know, results in the paradox known as "the
grandfather problem," which goes something like this: If I travel back in time and
kill my grandfather, my father no longer exists, and neither do I. If I don't exist,
then I can't kill my grandfather, which means that my father does exist, and so do
I. So I can go back in time.

Many science fiction writers skirt this dilemma by sending their travelers
back in time, but only as observers or ghosts. They can see the world of the
past, but the people from the past can't see them (think of Ebeneezer Scrooge's
journey in the company of the "Ghost of Christmas Past," for example). Other
solutions involve letting the traveler intervene in the past and change the
course of history, but then the traveler reveals the whole episode to be either
dream or hallucination.

Well, why should not women have the same privileges as men? Do you not think that a woman had the same fears? A man married again and gave his money to strangers—did he not? The fact is, we consider that a woman has the same feelings as we have ourselves—a thing you never once thought of—and now the property that is made during marriage is as much the woman's as the man's; they are partners in health and sickness, in joy and in sorrow—they enjoy every thing in common while they live together, and why a woman, merely on account of her being more helpless, should be cut off from affluence because she survives her husband, is more than we of this century can tell. Why should not children wait for the property till after her death, as they would for their father's death? It was a relic of barbarism, but it has passed away with wars and bloodshed. We educate our women now.

An improvement, to be sure. But Griffith was also a teetotaler whose compassion did not extend to drinkers or smokers. She foresaw prohibition and seems to revel in her attack on hedonistic pleasures, as in this wry exchange between two characters traveling from Philadelphia to New York:

But what are you looking for?
"I thought I might see a cigar box about—not that I ever smoke."
A what?—a cigar? Oh yes, I know—little things made of tobacco leaves; but you have to learn that there is not a tobacco plantation in the world now. That is one of the most extraordinary parts of your history: that well edu-cated men could keep a pungent and bitter mass of leaves in their mouths for the pleasure of seeing a stream of yellow water running out of it, is the most incomprehensible mystery.

Moreover, New Jerseyans can take heart in Griffith's vision of her home state, no longer simply the nineteenth-century tramping grounds between Philadel-phia and New York. In *Three Hundred Years Hence*, the Garden State has arrived:

"What a change," said Hastings, as they returned to their car—"all is altered. New Jersey, the meanest and poorest state in the Union, is now in appearance equal to the other inland states. It was in my time a mere thoroughfare."

Griffith's profile as an important American woman writer deserves burnish-ing. In each area she turned her attention to, she made a significant contribution. Precious little is known about the personal struggles she faced as a widowed mother raising children and crops and turning out treatises on soil conservation and science fiction novellas. One can only speculate that the themes of women's economic security, universal public education, and the dream that technology would ease life's work were rooted in the first-hand travails Griffith encountered during her days at Charlie's Hope. The world that shaped her artistic vision has largely been lost to history, but the promise she saw in the future has been bestowed to readers of her engaging and thought-provoking work.

FURTHER READING

Of Related Interest

Adkins, Nelson F. Introduction to *Three Hundred Years Hence.* 1950. Reprint. Boston: The Gregg Press, 1975.

Ash, Brian, ed. *The Visual Encyclopedia of Science Fiction.* New York: Harmony Books, 1977.

Walt Whitman

BORN May 31, 1819, in Huntington Township, Long Island
DIED March 26, 1892, in Camden
BEST KNOWN FOR His collection of poems *Leaves of Grass,* an epic series of exhortations that changed the direction of American poetry.
THE JERSEY CONNECTION Spent the last nineteen years of his life in Camden.

It would be difficult to overestimate Whitman's impact on the last one hundred fifty years of American letters. His influence touched every subsequent era; each generation of poets was forced to wrestle anew with this poetic Colossus. In terms of literary style, he forged an idiom at once uniquely American yet wholly divorced from anything the country had produced. In terms of content, his frank embrace of the body would not be appreciated (or, in many circles, tolerated) until the modernist movement half a century later. In terms of politics, Whitman was an irrepressible force for equality. An outspoken abolitionist, he was also a century ahead of his time in his celebration of homosexuality. In terms of poetic aspiration, his single-handed ability to lift the poet from a mere decorator in verse to a high priest of American culture changed the place of the artist in society. And in terms of legacy, his work has gained a foothold in the lecture halls of the great universities of the world, while still selling briskly in pocket-sized editions suitable for easy transport in a lunchbox or glove compartment. If there is one literary figure who can be said to have claimed the American psychic landscape and made it safe—necessary, even—for poets, writers, pictorial artists, journalists, and novelists to gaze squarely upon, it is Walt Whitman.

Although the bulk of his groundbreaking poetic oeuvre was produced while he was working in New York and New Orleans and traveling through the Middle West, he chose to live in New Jersey during a period of almost nonstop refinement of his works. The landmark 1891 edition of *Leaves of Grass*—the one most often read and commented upon—is well known as the "deathbed edition" because Whitman continued revising the poetry until he died. Perhaps less well known is that Whitman's death occurred in Camden, in his beloved home of almost twenty years. There, he not only saw a steady stream of admirers but also perfected a first-rate, mature poetry and prose.

The general biography is probably familiar. He was born on Long Island in 1819, the son of Louisa Van Velsos and Walter Whitman, a farmer and carpenter. In 1823, the family moved to Brooklyn where young Walt attended public schools until 1830, when he left to become a printer's apprentice on the Brooklyn newspapers, the *Patriot* and the *Star.* The biographical record indicates that Whitman was an active, eclectic reader whose tastes ranged from the Bible to Homer, Shakespeare to the periodical press, Hindu poets to Sir Walter Scott. In 1841, he moved to Manhattan and began writing fiction and journalistic pieces while working at the *New World*, a daily newspaper in New York City.

Walt Whitman's home in Camden, where the elder statesman of American poets spent the last decades of his life.

From the Collections of the New Jersey Historical Society.

He also began writing poetry, and in 1842 he completed a novel, *Franklin Evans; or, The Inebriate*. Active in Democratic politics, he edited and wrote for a number of New York City newspapers during the 1840s and early 1850s. He traveled to New Orleans in 1848, where he had a short stint as editor of *The Crescent*, before taking an extended trip through Missouri and Illinois. After his return to the New York area, he founded and edited the *Brooklyn Freeman* and ran a printing and book-selling business. Whitman eked out a subsistence living through his journalism, but his literary artistry had yet to come to the fore. He wrote lots of poems and essays and continued his eclectic exploration of the literary canon, but nothing he had produced brought him acclaim or money—though that was about to change.

In 1855, Whitman published (at his own expense) *Leaves of Grass*, the work that was to secure his reputation, garnering critical kudos from Ralph Waldo Emerson and launching his literary career. Though many readers were put off by the brusque, highly charged physicality of the poems—with charges of obscenity dogging Whitman's work all of his life—the freshness of expression and bold embrace of the sensory world, with all its wonder and terror, still leaps off the printed page. How can one not be arrested by the energy and nerve of these lines from "Song of Myself":

> Stop this day and night with me and you shall possess
> The origin of all poems,
> You shall possess the good of the earth and sun . . .
> There are millions of suns left,
> You shall no longer take things at second or third hand
> Nor look through the eyes of the dead . . .
> Nor feed on the spectres in books,
> You shall not look through my eyes either,
> Nor take things from me,
> You shall listen to all sides and filter them for yourself.
>
> Clear and sweet is my soul . . . and clear and sweet is all
> that is not my soul.
>
> All goes onward and outward . . . and nothing collapses,
> And to die is different from what anyone supposed,
> And luckier.

American poetry has never really shaken the spell of such utterances. It took some time, to be sure, before Whitman's work cracked open the vault of contemporary poetic expression. In 1860, Whitman found a Boston publisher willing to issue a greatly expanded *Leaves of Grass*, which brought his work to a much wider audience. In 1862, horrified but mesmerized by the brutality of the Civil War, Whitman volunteered to work as a nurse, tending war wounded in a hospital in Washington. Whitman's experiences are recounted in the war poems, which were added to editions of *Leaves of Grass* throughout the 1860s and early 1870s.

A major boost in securing Whitman's reputation was the 1868 publication in England of selected work. Whitman became something of a father figure to a generation of English poets (among them Alfred Lord Tennyson and Oscar Wilde), many of whom made pilgrimages to meet the American icon. These visits usually occurred in Camden, where Whitman moved in 1873 when his health began to decline. He lived briefly with his brother George, at 322 Stevens Street, and then got a small house of his own at 328 Mickle Street.

One of Whitman's closest friends in Camden was author and journalist Horace Traubel. Traubel's six-volume chronicle of Whitman's life at this time— *With Walt Whitman in Camden*—provides a massive amount of minutely observed Whitmania. Here's a sampling of a typical diarylike passage (with Whitman's words in quotes):

Thursday, July 12, 1888.

Evening, 7:45. W, lying down. A good day again. Mind clear. "I cannot reasonably expect complete physical rehabilitation: but I still hope to get my head cleared up. If I can make that much gain I may be able to do my work. After the work is done I shall be willing, even glad, to resign." Read some today but wrote nothing. "A bit in the Bible. After you have got rid of all your dogmas then you can read the Bible— realize its immensity—not till then." W read something in Cooper's Pathfinder. "I never forget Natty Bumppo—he is from everlasting to everlasting. . . . I can now read a little without the terrible sensation as of the ground sinking under my feet."

Imperiled by poor health, Whitman spent the majority of his days at home, writing, revising, reading proofs for the ever-expanding

A SONG OF MYSELF.
ALSO SOME PAINTINGS,
THEATER, AND A GIFT SHOP

The Walt Whitman Cultural Arts Center in Camden offers fans of the poet a great opportunity to learn more about him in a performing and visual arts center that draws admirers from all over the world.

The center is housed in a neoclassical library building adjacent to Camden's historic waterfront. Taking seriously Whitman's call to "produce great persons / the rest will follow," the center maintains an active educational program ranging from live theater to young artists' workshops. There is an art gallery for visiting shows, a plaza featuring statuary and wading pools, and a 187-seat theater with a balcony.

Information about the center's schedule of exhibits, lectures, and live presentations is available through the center's website at *www.waltwhitmancenter.org*, or by calling 856–964–8300.

Walt Whitman.
Courtesy of the Newark Public Library.

Leaves of Grass, and entertaining friends from an intensely devoted social circle that included literary luminaries such as Oscar Wilde, Arthur Symonds, Robert Louis Stevenson, and a physician-biographer, Richard M. Bucke, who authored the first official biography of the poet in 1883. He continued to contribute essays to magazines and newspapers, wrote new poems for various literary journals, compiled prose narratives of his travels and his friendships, lectured on literary matters, and gave public readings of his work until age and increasing paralysis (the result of at least two minor strokes during the 1870s) made movement outside Camden difficult.

Biographer Phillip Callow, in his book *From Noon to Starry Night,* paints a poignant scene of the elder statesman of American letters ambling about Camden:

> Until he was stranded in his wheelchairs and beached in his bed he hobbled down to the Camden ferry on sticks and enjoyed the Delaware in all weathers—the gulls, the black ocean steamers with their arrogant hulls. He loved his communion with the moving waters, the air, the sky and stars "that speak no word, nothing to the intellect, yet so eloquent . . . and the Ferrymen—little they know how much they have been to me, day and night—how many spells of listlessness, ennui, debility they and their handy ways have dispell'd." He was on name terms with most of them . . . on spring nights, crossing over from Philadelphia after a visit, he liked to watch the fishermen's little buoy lights—"so pretty, so dreamy—like corpse candles—undulating delicate and lonesome on the surface of the shadowy waters, floating with the current."

The Whitman of the Camden years produced much work of lasting and profound importance: *Leaves of Grass,* 1881 edition; *Specimen Days* (1888);

BAY WATCHER

Whitman's affection for New Jersey wasn't restricted to his longtime home of Camden. One of his most memorable nature poems immortalized a part of the state's coastline that brought the elderly poet a rush of inspiration. These lines come from "Patrolling Barnegat," written in 1881:

> Wild, wild the storm, and the sea high running,
> Steady the roar of the gale, with incessant undertone muttering.
> Shouts of demonic laughter fitfully piercing and pealing,
> Waves, air, midnight, their savagest trinity lashing,
> Out in the shadows their milk-white combs careering,
> On beachy slush and sand spurts of snow fierce slanting,
> Where through the murk the easterly death-wind breasting
> Through cutting swirl and spray watchful and firm advancing . . .
> A group of dim, weird forms, struggling, the night confronting,
> That savage trinity warily watching.

November Boughs (1888); *Goodbye My Fancy* (1891); and the "deathbed" edition of *Leaves of Grass* (1891). He also oversaw the compilation of a 900-page authorized edition of his complete prose works and poetry before his death in 1892.

The general consensus about Whitman's Camden days usually tilts toward a lessening of poetic powers. There's no doubt the aged poet of Camden is, in his writings of the period, less energetic, less revolutionary, or less radical in his thought or expression. He became appropriately more reflective and spiritual, less dogmatic in his politics. Because of age and health, he also became less peripatetic. But it would be a grossly erroneous critical judgment to place the works issued from Camden below all of the earlier (and, it should be noted, often undistinguished) work. His poetic insights ripened, and his language achieved a burnished clarity and economy that is awesome, vintage Whitman. Consider the stark beauty of these lines from one of his last poems, "With Husky Haughty Lips, O Sea":

> Life, life an endless march, an endless army (No halt,
> But it is duly over,)
> The world, the race, the soul—in space and time the universes,
> All bound as is befitting each—all surely going somewhere.

Whitman's collected writings have been published in an eighteen-volume scholarly edition. Every piece of poetry and prose published during his lifetime, as well as much unpublished work and correspondence, can be found there. But before racing off to the library to find Whitman on the shelves, consider a last, cautionary word from the poet himself:

> If you want me again, look for me under your bootsoles.

Readers interested in making a pilgrimage to Whitman's home in Camden, which has been preserved much as it was during the poet's lifetime, should also take a trip to Harleigh Cemetery in Camden. Whitman ventured there on Christmas Day 1890, to choose the site for his tomb, the design for which the poet based on a drawing by the English poet William Blake. Whitman even superintended the tomb's construction; he often visited the site to read poetry to the workmen while they built his tomb.

Whitman's real monument, of course, is his poetry. Generations of students, from elementary to graduate school, have witnessed the ingenuity of his "Noiseless, Patient Spider," exhaled their way through "Song of Myself," and recalled the fallen Abraham Lincoln in "When Lilacs Last in the Dooryard Bloomed," an elegy worthy of Whitman's own life:

> Not for you, for one alone
> Blossoms and branches green to coffins all I bring,

For fresh as the morning, thus would I chant a song for you
O sane and sacred death.
All over bouquets of roses
O death, I cover you with roses and early lillies,
But mostly and now the lilac that blooms first,
Copious I break, I break the sprigs from the bushes,
With loaded arms I come, pouring for you,
For you and the coffins all of you, O death.

FURTHER READING

Books by Whitman

Levin, Jonathan, ed. *Walt Whitman: Poetry for Young People*. New York: Sterling Publishing, 1997.
Murphy, Francis, ed. *Walt Whitman: The Complete Poems*. New York: Viking, 1990.

Books about Whitman

Bloom, Harold, ed. *Walt Whitman: Modern Critical Views*. Broomall, Pa.: Chelsea House Publishers, 1986.
Lemaster, J. R., and Donald Kummings. *Walt Whitman: An Encyclopedia*. New York: Garland Publishing, 1998.
Reynolds, David. *Walt Whitman's America: A Cultural Biography*. New York: Vintage Books, 1996.
Schmidgall, Gary, ed. *Intimate with Walt: Selections from Whitman's Conversations with Horace Traubel, 1882–1892*. Iowa City: University of Iowa Press, 2001.

Mary Mapes Dodge

> **BORN** January 26, 1830, in New York City
> **DIED** August 21, 1905, in Onteora, New York
> **BEST KNOWN FOR** *Hans Brinker; or, The Silver Skates: A Story of Life in Holland.*
> **THE JERSEY CONNECTION** Began her writing career in Irvington, where she spent her adult life.

It's likely that Dodge's name is largely unfamiliar to most readers today, but her almost universally known creation Hans Brinker more than makes up for the author's relative anonymity. Even 135 years after publication, it remains a worldwide bestseller—quite a legacy for a woman who found herself newly widowed with two small children and no real prospects after her husband, attorney William Dodge, died in 1858.

Born in New York City and educated at home with her siblings, the young Mary Mapes got a taste of intellectual life early. Her father, a brilliant and slightly eccentric inventor, publisher, chemist, and agricultural scientist opened his home to frequent gatherings of scientists, musicians, poets, and journalists. Lizzie, as the young Mary Elizabeth was called, often assisted her father with editorial tasks related to his publishing career. She also developed a deep love of English literature.

In 1848, the family moved to Irvington, where they purchased a farm with the financial assistance of a family friend and lawyer named William Dodge. In 1851, Mary Elizabeth Mapes married Dodge and moved to New York City; the couple had two children. In 1858, Dodge, whose financial situation had been declining throughout the decade, was found drowned after he had disappeared from home several weeks earlier.

She moved with the children back to the family farm in Irvington, where her father continued his horticultural experiments and published a magazine, *The United States Journal*. Mary began writing for the magazine, discovered a talent for putting words together, and turned her attention to the writing of children's stories. *Hans Brinker* (1865), which was suggested to her after reading John Motley's *The Rise of the Dutch Republic*, both combined her interest in children's literature and her fondness for a nearby Dutch family whom she visited often and testified to the growing popularity of skating in the United States. By day Dodge worked on the book in a spartan room, and by night she read each day's output to her children.

As a result of the phenomenal success of *Hans Brinker*, which was translated into five languages and went through more than one hundred editions in the author's lifetime, Dodge began to circulate with some literary and journalistic titans of the mid-nineteenth century, such as Horace Greeley and John Greenleaf Whittier. These contacts proved especially useful after the death of her father in 1866, when she turned to editing full-time to support her two college-aged sons, her mother, and two unmarried sisters. She worked first as an assistant editor for a short-lived magazine, *Hearth and Home*. Then in 1873, publisher Roswell Smith asked her to edit a new juvenile publication, *St. Nicholas*. Backed by the highly successful Scribner's Publishing House, *St. Nicholas* quickly became a first-rate outlet for stories that offered, in Dodge's words, "a shade of grandiloquence—a little introducing of the heroic."

St. Nicholas attracted such well-established authors as Henry Wadsworth Longfellow, Robert Louis Stevenson, and Rudyard Kipling (whose *Jungle Book* was written specifically for the magazine). She became something of a hub in a circle of writers who frequented her cottage in the Catskills during annual summer retreats. Mark Twain was a regular visitor.

St. Nicholas was a remarkable success: popular, critically well-regarded, highly profitable. Its success is perhaps all the more surprising because the idea of a magazine aimed at young readers was unprecedented at the time. Dodge, it is

"GRETEL BRINKER, ONE MILE!" shouts the crier, as she dashes over the line. Page 278.

—*Hans Brinker.*

Mary Mapes Dodge's *Hans Brinker* capitalized on the growing popularity of ice skating in the nineteenth century.

said, was persuaded to accept the editorship when she realized how much her two sons would enjoy reading such a magazine as *St. Nicholas*.

Her editorial policy, published in the first issue, provides a comprehensive critical overview of the aims of nineteenth-century literature. Like Charles Foster Kane's "Declaration of Principles," Dodge's objectives reflect a time lost forever to television, movies, and all manner of digital engagement:

To give clean, genuine fun to children of all ages.

To give them examples of the finest types of boyhood and girlhood.

To inspire them with a fine appreciation of pictorial art.

To cultivate the imagination in profitable directions.

To foster a love of country, home, nature, truth, beauty, sincerity.

To prepare boys and girls for life as it is.

To stimulate their ambitions—but along normally progressive lines.

To keep pace with a fast-moving world in all its activities.

To give reading matter which every parent may pass to his children unhesitatingly.

SKATING THROUGH TIME

Hans Brinker had the great luck of appearing during something of a "skating boom" in the mid-nineteenth-century United States. Although popular in many European countries, skating as a pastime was slow to catch on in the United States.

Dodge was right to base the tale upon Dutch origins. It is believed the Dutch helped originate skating as the modern recreation it is today, although necessity birthed the invention of the modern skate. In 1512, with the Dutch fleet frozen in Amsterdam, Spanish Commander Don Frederick sent his troops out on the ice to capture the vessels. Historians of the sport proudly point out that the attackers were rebuffed by Dutch musketeers on skates, who had the advantage against their slippery-footed foes. The Spaniards were thoroughly routed and did not return to the ice-bound ships again.

By the nineteenth century, the "sport" of skating had achieved such popularity in England that instructional manuals were printed to help neophytes improve their techniques. One such pamphlet from the time advised:

Place your heels together, with the toes inclining outwards; then lift up the left foot, without bending the instep, and put it down again in the same position, with your heel facing the ball of the right foot, at six inches distance; then, with a small force throw your body forwards, bending the left knee a little more than in common walking; at the same time, you throw yourself forwards, straighten the right knee, press on the inside edge of the skate and force yourself forwards on the left leg; this method must be observed with both legs, and is called a stroke.

Dodge was the first and only editor of the magazine for twenty-two years until her death in 1905.

In addition to her editorial career, she wrote a number of other books, including *Rhymes and Jingles* (1870), *Theophilus and Others* (1876), and *The Land of Pluck* (1894); however, *Hans Brinker* ensures her legacy. The book retains a charm that seems undiminished during the passage of more than a century. In case you missed it in your childhood, here's a taste:

> Christmas day is devoted by the Hollanders to church rites and pleasant family visiting. It is on St. Nicholas' Eve that their young people become half wild with joy and expectation. To some of them it is a sorry time, for the saint is very candid, and if any of them have been bad during the past year he is quite sure to tell them so. Sometimes he carries a birch rod under his arm, and advises the parents to give them scoldings in place of confections.

Though *Hans Brinker* has remained undimmed in its burnished image of the young skater's coming of age, Dodge's book wasn't the only best-selling, world-beloved children's book written by an American woman in the mid-nineteenth century. Literary historians and critics of juvenile narrative prose love to debate who was the greater young readers' writer—Dodge or the estimable Louisa May Alcott. *Little Women,* published in 1867, has, like *Hans Brinker*, achieved a status that exceeds mere popularity. Comparisons between the two do little to illuminate either work, although they do testify to the growth of children's literature as a specific genre. Prior to the nineteenth century, most books synonymous with youth were written originally for an adult audience—for example, Mallory's King Arthur tales or Jonathan Swift's *Gulliver's Travels*. Both Dodge and Alcott helped codify a style aimed directly at youthful readers, who had been fed a steady literary diet of mostly moralistic, didactic, deadly dull "children's lit" during the previous half century.

Both Dodge's work and her famously engaging personality made her a favorite among the young and the young at heart. When she died at seventy-four, in Onteora Park, in the Catskills, her funeral procession was made up almost exclusively of children from the neighborhood. *Hans Brinker* reveals that childlike spirit and optimism on almost every page. From there New Jersey's farm-bred autodidact speaks to us today:

> Our story is nearly told. Time passes in Holland just as surely and steady as here; in that respect no country is odd.
>
> To the Brinker family it has brought great changes. Hans has spent the years faithfully and profitably, conquering obstacles as they arose, and pursuing one object with all the energy of his nature. If often the way has been rugged, his resolution has never failed. Sometimes he echoes, with his good old friend, the words said long ago in that little cottage near Broek: "Surgery

is an ugly business"; but always in his heart of hearts lingers the echo of truer words, "It is great and noble! It awakes a reverence for God's work!"

Were you in Amsterdam to-day, you might see the famous Doctor Brinker riding in his grand coach to visit his patients; or it might be, you would see him skating with his own boys and girls upon the frozen canals. For Annie Bouman, the beautiful, frank-hearted peasant girl, you would inquire in vain; but Annie Brinker, the vrouw of the great physician, is very like her— only, as Hans says, she is even lovelier, wiser, more like a fairy godmother than ever.

FURTHER READING

Of Related Interest

Egoff, Sheila. *Children's Periodicals of the Nineteenth Century.* London: The Library Association, 1951.

Gannon, Susan, and Ruth Anne Thompson. *Mary Mapes Dodge.* Twayne United States Authors Series. New York: Macmillan, 1993.

Howard, Alice B. *Mary Mapes Dodge of St. Nicholas.* New York: Messner, 1943.

Wright, Catherine Morris. *Lady of the Silver Skates: The Life and Correspondence of Mary Mapes Dodge.* Jamestown, R.I.: Clingstone Press, 1979.

Thomas Nast

> **BORN** September 3, 1840, in Bavaria
> **DIED** December 7, 1902, in Ecuador
> **BEST KNOWN FOR** Probably the modern image of Santa Claus, whom Nast immortalized in 1862.
> **THE JERSEY CONNECTION** Lived in Morristown in the last decades of his life.

A political cartoonist and one of the most widely recognized sketch artists of his day, Nast, who moved to Morristown at the height of his fame, produced a steady stream of provocative political cartoons that filled the pages of national magazines and newspapers. His lasting contributions to American culture include the first depiction of Santa Claus; the donkey and the elephant of the Democrat and Republican parties, respectively; and the caricatures of the scheming, corrupt "Tweed Ring" of New York City's Tammany Hall.

Nast was born in Bavaria. His father was a musician who joined the Philharmonic Society of New York City when the family immigrated to America in 1846. New York at midcentury provided the young artist with a wide variety of arresting vistas. The adolescent Nast—sketchpad in hand—used to dash out of the crowded row house his German Protestant family shared with Eastern European Jews and Irish Catholics whenever a fire truck raced through the narrow streets of Lower Manhattan. Biographers report that the Nast household was papered with young Thomas's charcoal drawings of scenes and people from his neighborhood.

Nast was educated in the public schools, where his artistic talent was first recognized. At fourteen, he began studying under Theodore Kaufman, a fellow German émigré and an artist of some note. In 1855 he began his first full-time professional job as staff artist for *Frank Leslie's Illustrated Newspaper,* where he illustrated stories and refined his style of cartooning mixed with social commentary. Nast's "job interview" consisted of his being sent to Christopher Street on Sunday morning to sketch the crowd boarding the ferry to Jersey's Elysian Fields; when Leslie saw Nast's drawing—the artist was waiting to show him the sketch first thing Monday morning—he hired him on the spot at a salary of $4 per week. Three years later, Nast started contributing to such high-profile publications as *Harper's Weekly* and the *New York Illustrated News,* where his pen captured the scene at the funeral of John Brown.

In 1860, Nast went to England to sketch a much-promoted international boxing match between Briton Thomas Sayers and American John C. Heenan. His drawing of the forty-two-round bare-knuckle match filled a centerfold pullout of the *Illustrated News.* He then traveled to Italy to follow Garibaldi's army in Sicily and Calabria. His scenes of the Italian general's campaign appeared regularly in the *London News.* When he returned to New York in 1861, he married Sarah Edwards; the couple had five children.

Throughout the Civil War, Nast's artistic talent, combined with his firsthand observations of military campaigns, was in frequent demand by U.S. periodicals. Nast proved adept at delineating political disputes in pictures, and even his battle scenes often had a component of social commentary. Santa Claus, whom Nast first drew in 1862, originally appeared in a Union Civil War uniform. Ulysses S. Grant, speaking of Nast's Civil War illustrations, once remarked, "He did as much as any man to preserve the Union and bring the war to an end." (Check out Nast's painting of Robert E. Lee's surrender to Grant—an excellent example of his wide-ranging artistry.)

After the war, Nast turned his talents toward the depiction of various social ills, such as the treatment of blacks during Reconstruction. Through his caricatures, Nast attacked Andrew Johnson and the Democrats, wielding his pen in favor of the Republican nominee and war hero Ulysses Grant in 1868. Nast was a zealous advocate of fiercely unrelenting politics; perhaps had he not become an artist he might well have entered the political arena in some capacity, so steeped was he in the political zeitgeist of his day. Both his own letters and his contemporaries' accounts reveal a man whose pen was always serving his personal political leanings as well as the popular themes of the day. Politics aside, his artistry has earned him his immortality.

Artist Thomas Nast used himself as the model for the cover of this locally produced cookbook.

From the Collections of the New Jersey Historical Society.

Nast's mastery of the illustrator's craft is obvious even to the untrained eye when his work is compared to the roughly drawn, rather loopy cartoon caricatures that his contemporaries drew for competing publications. His work has influenced not only subsequent generations of illustrators, but also apparently one of the greatest painters of his day (or any day), Vincent Van Gogh. The great Dutch artist is known to have collected magazine illustrations from the 1870s and 1880s, and he regularly perused *Harper's Weekly*, in which many Nast illustrations appeared. Van Gogh consciously set about to copy magazine illustrations during the early part of his career and, in a letter to an artist friend, announced his intention to make a career out of producing Nast-like drawings. The world's foremost collection of Van Gogh works, the Rijksmuseum, also has twenty-one illustrations by Nast: fifteen are from Van Gogh's personal collection, bound in a special album, which includes Nast's drawing of Jumbo the elephant, P. T. Barnum's prize pachyderm and the largest elephant in captivity, and an illustration of a large turkey confronting its executioner before Thanksgiving day.

Nast achieved his greatest fame through a series of political cartoons he drew throughout the early 1870s attacking the activities of New York City's infamous "Boss Tweed" and his cronies of Tammany Hall, who had seized control of various municipal departments and engaged in kickbacks, fraud, and corruption.

William Marcy Tweed, who had risen from Greenwich Village fire chief to commissioner of public works and state senator, was one of the most effectively ruthless political operatives in U.S. history. He and his well-placed friends in the "Society of Tammany," as he called his social club, stole millions of dollars—mostly through phony building contracts and kickbacks. Nast deeply resented this abuse of power, and for two unrelenting years he pictorially dissected the Tweed Ring (with such colorful supporting characters as "Slippery Dick" Connolly and "Elegant" Abraham Hall, the city's mayor) in a series of wildly popular editorial cartoons. The most famous illustration in the entire series portrayed Tweed as a ferocious tiger, growling in triumph over a slaughtered Lady Columbia, symbol of U.S. liberty. Beneath the image, Nast addressed the reader directly: "What Are You Going To Do About It?" So effective were Nast's sketches that the artist and his family, fearing for their personal safety, were forced to flee their New York City residence and relocate in Morristown. (Did he have valid reason to fear retribution from Tweed? Probably he did. Tweed was famously peeved by Nast's continuous attacks in caricature.)

Nast's influence as a social commentator and his popularity as an illustrator started to wane with the end of Reconstruction and the Grant presidency. In the last decade of his life, Nast produced a number of critically well regarded paintings based on historical scenes, continued drawing cartoons for various periodicals, and lectured throughout the United States. In 1902, he segued from political drawings to political drawing rooms, when Theodore Roosevelt appointed him consul to Ecuador. Although he lacked experience in diplomatic work, Nast's artistic fortunes had fallen off, and he felt compelled to take the position despite his ignorance of the language and the culture of the South American country. (He lobbied for a position in either England or Germany by claiming that he could be of greater service because he understood those cultures, but no diplomatic vacancies were available.) His arrival in Ecuador coincided with a massive outbreak of yellow fever, and within six months he contracted the disease and died.

As a pioneer in the field of editorial cartooning, Nast was an early exemplar of social commentary through art and a tireless champion of the right of the oppressed to have their voices heard. Nast's life and entire body of work ought to be as well known as his cherry-cheeked Santa drawings or the stripes he put in Uncle Sam's pants.

Nast's legacy is in the hands of several Garden State stewards: The Morristown Public Library has a vast collection of letters, original drawings, and sketches,

---

SANTA THROUGH THE YEARS

There's no doubt that Nast's rendering of Santa Claus—overstuffed red suit, long white beard, bulging toy sack thrown over his shoulder—is the predominant image of old Saint Nick. Prior to Nast's vision, however, several other images had been put before the Christmas-celebrating public.

In England, from the sixteenth to the nineteenth centuries, the figure of "Father Christmas" was always festooned with sprigs of holly, ivy, and mistletoe. In Germany, he was simply "Weinachtsmann"—Christmas Man. The Russians dubbed him "Grandfather Frost" and dressed him in a blue suit.

In 1801, Washington Irving described Santa in his *Knickerbocker Tales* as a jolly Dutchman who smoked a long-stemmed clay pipe and wore a broad-brimmed hat. In 1931, artist Haddon Sundblom was commissioned by the Coca-Cola Company to portray Santa on Coke billboards and advertisements. Haddon took Nast's Santa and added reading glasses, rosy cheeks, and a warm, infectious grin.

It probably does not need to be pointed out that none of the Santa-like depictions looks anything like the original source for the Santa figure, Saint Nicholas, a fourth-century Turkish bishop reported to have been austere as well as rather slender.

---

and various documents related to the artist's career; much of Nast's original work can also be viewed at Morristown's Maccullough Hall Historical Museum (the former residence of George P. Maccullough, the man behind the building of the Morris canal); Nast's house in Morristown, known as Villa Fontana, is a national historic landmark.

FURTHER READING

Of Related Interest

Keller, Morton. *The Art and Politics of Thomas Nast.* New York: Oxford University Press, 1968.

Paine, Albert Bigelow. *Thomas Nast, His Period and His Pictures.* New York: Macmillan Co., 1904.

Pflueger, Lynda. *Thomas Nast, Political Cartoonist.* Berkeley Heights, N.J.: Enslow Publishers, 2000.

Shirley, David. *Thomas Nast: Cartoonist and Illustrator.* New York: Franklin Watts, 1998.

Mary Wilkins Freeman

BORN October 1852, in Randolph, Massachusetts

DIED March 15, 1930, in Metuchen, New Jersey

BEST KNOWN FOR Her short stories depicting the stoic character of New Englanders.

THE JERSEY CONNECTION Moved to Metuchen in 1902 and remained there the rest of her life.

Mary Wilkins Freeman's career divides quite conveniently into two phases, the first of which could be dubbed "cloistered in New England" and the second, "freed in New Jersey." Freeman's early writing is her best-known work, represented in story collections such as *A Humble Romance* (1887) and *A New England Nun* (1891). After she moved to New Jersey, her work lost its former intensity of gaze at the Puritan ethos but gained an impressive breadth and reach that included historical novels, romances, and even ghost stories. She also shifted her sites from small, parochial New England enclaves to the relative expanse of suburban New Jersey and from the stifling insularity of a religious community to the cultural diffusion of her new locale.

The daughter of a solemn, hard-working tradesman and a devout mother, Mary Wilkins was raised with a strong religious emphasis in a tightly knit community, Randolph, Massachusetts, fifteen miles from Boston. In 1867, her family relocated to Brattleboro, Vermont, and in 1870, the eighteen-year-old Wilkins enrolled at Mount Holyoke Female Seminary. A year later, she transferred closer to home to the Glenwood Seminary in West Brattleboro.

After one more year of formal education, Wilkins left the Glenwood Seminary but continued a rigorous program of self-study, reading deeply the works of authors such as Goethe, Emerson, and Sarah Orne Jewett (who is said to have greatly influenced the budding writer). Her first literary success, publication of a short poem in the *Century* magazine, inspired her to write more. She continued to write poems, many of which were accepted by small literary or children's magazines. In 1880, the widely circulated *St. Nicholas* magazine published a collection of her poems. The *Boston Sunday Budget* published her first short story, "A Shadow Family," in 1882. The next year, *Harper's Bazaar* published "Two Old Lovers." She reached the high point of her early career with the 1884 publication in the prestigious *Harper's New Monthly* of her short story "A Humble Romance."

In that same year, Wilkins, now dedicated to writing full time, returned to Randolph to live on a farm with the family of a childhood friend. She spent her days wandering about the small town, closely studying the residents whose

Puritan-bred moral fiber impressed and intrigued Wilkins. Her stories from this period—probably her best work, most critics agree—involve the psychological dissection of these people. In print Wilkins seems to be straining to understand how the characters reconcile the Yankee-stoic-Puritan strain with the expansive, capitalist, freedom-embracing Americanism of the nineteenth century.

Although she's an acknowledged master of the short story form, most of her novel-length efforts were critical failures. Her novel *Pembroke* (1894), perhaps her finest piece of extended fiction, explores this see-saw relationship between satisfaction and self-recrimination. Here's a representative excerpt:

> A great grief and resentment against the whole world and life itself swelled high within him. It was as if he lost sight of individual antagonists, and burned to dash life itself in the face because he existed. The state of happiness so exalted that it became almost holiness, in which he had been that very night, flung him to lower depths when it was retroverted. He had gone

---

METUCHEN'S GREATEST?

Is Mary Wilkins Freeman the most notable literary figure ever to call Metuchen home? Perhaps the fans of prize-winning poet and critic John Ciardi would beg to differ.

Ciardi, born in 1916, lived in Metuchen for more than fifty years while he juggled an active work life that involved stints as writer, editor, translator, teacher, poet, critic, and children's book author. He is probably best known for his poetry, which esteemed critic M. L. Rosenthal said reveals "a mind in touch with earthy reality and even a certain redeeming crudeness, and also alive to the world of thought."

His poetry has been published internationally, and he received some of literature's highest honors, including *Poetry* magazine's Blumenthal Prize and the New England Poetry Club's Golden Rose. His translation of Dante's *Inferno* continues to be a best seller, four decades after it was first published. Ciardi is also credited with helping to raise the standards for poetry criticism in the periodical press. His 1956 piece in the *Saturday Review*, excoriating Anne Morrow Lindbergh's collection, *The Unicorn and Other Poems*, generated "the biggest storm of protest in the history of the *Saturday Review*," said the magazine's editor, Norman Cousins. But many established authors, such as fellow New Jerseyan Philip Roth, came to Ciardi's defense by applauding the reintroduction of rigorous critical standards.

His work continues to be anthologized, analyzed by critics, read in lecture halls, and embraced by adults and children alike. As Ciardi himself once explained, "Poetry is especially well designed to lead the child to recognition [of new words], for rhyme and pattern are always important clues. Poetry and learning are both fun and children are full of an enormous relish for both."

Ciardi died of a heart attack at his Metuchen home on Easter Sunday, March 30, 1986.

back to first causes in the one and he did the same in the other; his joy reached out into eternity, and so did his misery. His natural religious bent, inherited from generations of Puritans, and kept in its channel by training from infancy, made it impossible for him to conceive of sympathy or antagonism in its fullest sense apart from God.

Wilkins's work from this period not only explores the mental suffering of cloistered New Englanders, but it also addresses the poverty, meanness, brutality, and boredom of the day-to-day life in many small nineteenth-century communities. Her willingness to see beyond the veil of stoicism and to capture the telling—but easily missed—gesture or phrase earned her the reputation as the first of the "local color" writers. Implicit in all her work is a sympathy for the quiet sufferer and and important celebration of the willpower it takes to endure hardship. Critic and biographer Perry Westbrook noted her resolve in his study of her work:

> Mary Wilkins Freeman is our most truthful recorder in fiction of New England village life. In several volumes of short stories and three or four novels, she has caught the flavor of that life as no other author has . . . yet the New England of which she wrote was in the lowest ebb of its cultural history. Only the memories of its old vigor remained. The Civil War, the Westward migrations, and industry had drained the countryside of much of its population. The old Calvinist religion had yielded its hold to Unitarianism, or to indifference. But much of the old remained, too—especially in the remoter and smaller communities, and still remains, often in happy amalgamation with the new. Of this remnant, Mary Wilkins Freeman wrote; and in so doing, she described the very essence of the New England character, both in its social and individual aspects.

In the early 1890s, Wilkins met Charles M. Freeman, a physician seven years her junior. After a number of broken engagements throughout the decade, the two finally wed in 1902 and relocated to Metuchen. Both the marriage and the move had a profound impact on Mary Wilkins Freeman's life and work.

The marriage was disastrous. Charles Freeman, who had earned a medical degree at Columbia but never actually practiced medicine, became an alcoholic who had to be periodically confined to a state-run mental institution. Mary Wilkins Freeman—distraught, depressed, and feeling uprooted from the world she knew so well—became addicted to tranquilizers. The marriage collapsed, and her husband drank himself to death. Freeman endured the tumult, and she quite remarkably continued to write prolifically across a wide variety of genres.

Mary Wilkins Freeman wrote collections of short stories, novels, ghost stories, romances, essays, and sketches, and she received several prestigious literary honors for her work, including the William Dean Howells Gold Medal for Fiction in 1925. Few readers, however, would argue that her later work was as impressive or well-wrought as her earlier stories and novels. The "falling off" in the quality of her writing is difficult to quantify. Many encyclopedia and biographical dictionary entries about Freeman bluntly dismiss the post-1902 work as "far below that of her earlier work," but some readers find Freeman's later output to be profound, deeply evocative, and even spiritual. After moving to Metuchen, she developed a strong interest in mysticism and the occult, and many of her later works contain allusions to the unseen world and its influence on reality. In one of her supernatural stories, she asks,

> Who shall determine the limit at which the intimate connection and the reciprocal influence of all forms of visible creation upon one another may stop? A man may cut down a tree and plant one. Who knows what effect the tree may have upon the man, to his raising or undoing?

Probably the greatest champions of Freeman's total body of work, early and late, have been feminist literary critics, who applaud her attempt to portray the inequities of power in the larger world by focusing on the domestic gender struggles that cripple both the women and the men in her writings. Alice Glarden Brand argues in her 1977 essay on Freeman:

> Does reading Freeman make a difference? In tracing femaleness from passivity to rage or extinction, Freeman focuses on the struggles for women's identity. In tracing maleness from impotence to aggression and bestiality, she extrapolates his inhumanities. She forces the reader to confront rage and search for its genesis. She was more than didactic. She was a palatable propagandist because her messages were ulterior and multiple. Her narratives were subversive; heavy with unspoken possibilities. She was a civilized critic of destructive human behaviors and by documenting these behaviors, she pressed for their eradication.

Freeman's fiction resounds with an implicit plea for freedom from bondage— religious, social, financial—yet she never oversimplifies or demonizes any single entity. The tragedy of Freeman's characters often centers in their embrace of constraint, their anxiety at the prospect of pulling free. Her characters do have options, but, for reasons of pragmatism or Puritanism, they simply don't move. Rocklike, they weather misery and endure. She wrote of this impassiveness in the story "Criss-Cross," published in *Harper's Monthly* (1914):

> Whatever the attitude of women in the wider world might be, the attitude of the women in this little village remained, however covertly, that of a half century ago. In their innermost hearts they were not, and never could be, emancipated from the old conception of the proper estate for woman.

Freeman's life and work have benefited from a renewed interest in "neglected" American women authors. Her dramatic life and the shift from a sole preoccupation with New England village life to broader fictional explorations of religion, history, and fantasy make her an intriguing subject for reconsideration. Modern readers find no shortage of recent critical works examining Freeman's importance. Perhaps no modern critic, however, could put it better than an anonymous *Atlantic Monthly* reviewer who, in 1891, found in Freeman "a power to hold the interest to the close, which is owing not to a trivial ingenuity but to the spell which her personages cast over the reader's mind as soon as they come within his ken."

FURTHER READING

Books by Freeman

The Wind in the Rose Bush and Other Stories of the Supernatural. New York: Doubleday: 1903.

The Whole Family: A Novel by Twelve Authors (including Freeman, Henry James, and William Dean Howells). New York: Harper and Brothers, 1914.

The Heart's Highway: A Romance of Virgina. New York: Doubleday, 1900.

Zagarell, Sandra, ed. *A New England Nun and Other Stories.* New York: Penguin, 2000.

Books about Freeman

Foster, Edward. *Mary E. Wilkins Freeman.* New York: Hendrick's House, 1956.

Glasser, Leah Blatt. *In a Closet Hidden: The Life and Work of Mary E. Wilkins Freeman.* Amherst: University of Massachusetts Press, 1996.

Stephen Crane

BORN November 1, 1871, in Newark
DIED June 5, 1900, in Germany
BEST KNOWN FOR The Civil War novel *The Red Badge of Courage.*
THE JERSEY CONNECTION Raised in Newark and Paterson and got his start as a newspaper writer in Asbury Park.

Most literary critics believe Stephen Crane wrote his best work in the early part of his career. Some even suggest he spent his last few years in a period of pronounced decline, either vainly striving to repeat his earlier successes or simply doing hack writing for profit. They all seem to agree that little of literary value issued from his pen in his last years, although he was immensely prolific. Such judgments of a writer's later period are not uncommon, of course; the same thing is often said of figures as eminent as William Wordsworth, whose crotchety final decades produced little of enduring impact. But Crane's case is unusual because he was only twenty-eight when he died.

"I stood musing in a black world," Crane once began a poem. The image captures the essence of this deeply gifted, deeply troubled writer. His best work remains chillingly real and unsettling, a tribute to his ability to wed both naturalism and psychology into the fabric of his poetry and prose. His first novel, *Maggie: A Girl of the Streets*, laid bare the squalor and inhumane condition of life for tens of thousands of poor and dispossessed in Manhattan. In all of his work, including his journalistic sketches and his remarkable poetry, which deserves placement alongside the greatest American poetry, Crane delivered a vision of the world that is multilayered and infused with the irony that comes from seeing bitterness and death despoiling even the prettiest of pictures.

Crane has been claimed by a variety of literary schools: realism, naturalism, symbolism, modernism. In his most highly regarded work, the short story "The Open Boat" or *The Red Badge of Courage*, Crane paints a picture of humanity battered by cold, indifferent reality, hostile to people's dreams and aspirations of greatness. Characters hope in vain for deliverance from the forces that either thwart or destroy them. Circumstances beyond their control—war, natural disaster, and finally death—mock his characters' efforts to find joy, or at least a moment's peace. Crane's view of the mechanistic, unfeeling thrust of the modern world helped usher in the modern novel, with its emphasis on the individual and its disdain for the notions of valor or heroism.

Crane was both a skeptic and a depressive—a writer whose work was little appreciated in his own time. *Maggie*, because of its stark presentation of life on the streets, couldn't find a publisher, and when Crane brought the book out himself, fear of condemnation required him to use the pseudonym "Johnston Smith." *The Red Badge of Courage*, though now famous, earned him only $100. Generally unappreciated in his homeland, Crane eventually found some consolation among a small group of writer friends in England, including H. G. Wells, Joseph Conrad, and Henry James. His only financially rewarding success throughout his lifetime came through his journalistic work, first as a writer for a news service on the Jersey Shore and later as a foreign correspondent for New York newspapers. His short stories helped pay the bills. His poetry, which brought him no profit but apparently engaged his energy and thought at a deeper personal level than his prose works, baffled his contemporaries. The terse, idiosyncratic vignettes left many critics unsure about what Crane was trying to do. For example:

> A man said to the universe
> "Sir, I exist!"
> "However," replied the universe,
> "The fact has not created in me
> A sense of obligation."

CRANE WATCHING

Asbury Park residents in the late 1880s and early 1890s would not have been surprised, perhaps, to discover that the industrious local reporter named Crane was also a budding novelist and would one day take his place among great American writers. However, the "Crane" they would have expected to make his mark in the world was Townley Crane, Stephen's older brother, a writer who maintained an active news service—and a high profile—along the Jersey Shore. Stephen was all but unknown, a cub reporter submitting unsigned dispatches about local gatherings, well-known visitors, or vacation-season gossip to his older brother. It's not hard to understand how so formidable a talent as Stephen Crane could be eclipsed when one learns how Townley conducted himself; he adopted a public posture that was part Sherlock Holmes, part beach bum. Stephen Crane biographer Linda Davis, in her book *Badge of Courage*, says Townley was aptly nicknamed "the Shore fiend," given his reportorial doggedness and his dingy appearance: "He was a broad, bald, seedy-looking man who wore a fore-and-aft and a dirty tweed overcoat year round over a colored muffler that was tucked in and pinned in place of a shirt. Townley himself seemed pinned together, made of old neglected parts. He drank heavily—he was perhaps already an alcoholic—and his teeth were yellow and uncared for."

Yet his news service was highly profitable. Townley regularly placed articles in papers throughout New Jersey, Philadelphia, and New York, and he was well known in journalism circles.

In the decades before literary modernism, readers were simply unprepared for lines like these:

In the desert
I saw a creature, naked, bestial,
Who, squatting upon the ground,
Held his heart in his hands,
And ate of it.
I said, "Is it good, friend?"
"It is bitter—bitter," he answered;
"But I like it.
Because it is bitter,
And because it is my heart."

Modern readers and critics have responded more favorably to Crane's poetry (fellow New Jerseyan Joyce Carol Oates even appropriated the last two lines of the above poem for the title of one of her novels). But in his time, Crane's poetry was considered quite odd. Poet Amy Lowell was one of the first public readers to puzzle out Crane's work. In an essay written a quarter century after Crane's death, she wrote,

Crane saw life through individual eyes, and he dared write as he pleased; therein rests his abiding merit. So short a time as twelve years after his death, a type of poetry extremely like his came suddenly into being. By all rights, he should have been its direct parent, but he was not, simply because most of the practitioners of it had based themselves upon French precedent and William Blake before they knew anything of Crane. In the decade which began with 1912, Crane would have been in his element, perfectly understood, widely praised, forced to take the position of leader. He died too soon. He did much, but the temperature of the world he lived in was unsuitable. He ranks in America somewhat as Chatterton ranks in England. A boy, spiritually killed by neglect. A marvelous boy, potentially a genius, historically an important link in the chain of American poetry.

Born in Newark, Stephen Crane was the youngest of fourteen children. His father was a Methodist minister, his mother a leader in the Christian Temperance movement. When Stephen was three, his family moved first to Paterson and then Port Jervis, New York. The family moved back to Newark in 1880 after the death of the father, and in 1883 they moved to Asbury Park; there, as a teenager, Stephen worked as a reporter/writer for both a local newspaper and his brother Townley's news service that provided dispatches to the New York newspapers, including the *New York Tribune*, about life along the resort belt of the Jersey Shore.

One of Crane's most accomplished pieces of journalism for the service was a series of feature stories that focused on the people and sites of Asbury Park. Already the novelist's mix of reportorial detail, dramatic irony, and psychological insight are fusing into mature style:

> The average summer guest here is a rather portly man with a good watch chain and a business suit of clothes, a wife and about three children. He stands in his two shoes with American self-reliance and, playing casually with his watch-chain, looks at the world with a clear eye. He submits to the arrogant prices of some of the hotel proprietors with a calm indifference; he will pay fancy prices for things with a great unconcern . . . he enjoys himself in a very mild way and dribbles out a lot of money under the impression that he is proceeding cheaply.

That clear-eyed view of the world's operation, with an obligatory nod to the efforts of hapless mankind to appear dignified despite the forces arrayed against him, stayed with Crane throughout his writing and culminated in what is universally considered a masterpiece, *The Red Badge of Courage*. Required reading in most American high schools over the past several decades, the novel still resonates today, more than a century after its composition. It was the first American novel to portray the psychological horrors of war. If its grim picture of the battlefield now seems somewhat muted, its indictment of patriotic bluster and flag-waving sentiment as justification for carnage is still potent:

> The youth, in his leapings, saw, as through a mist, a picture of four or five men stretched upon the ground or writhing upon their knees with bowed heads as if they had been stricken by bolts from the sky. Tottering among them was the rival color bearer, whom the youth saw had been bitten vitally by the bullets of the last formidable volley. He perceived this man fighting a last struggle, the struggle of one whose legs are grasped by demons. It was a ghastly battle. Over his face was the bleach of death, but set upon it were the dark and hard lines of desperate purpose. With this terrible grin of resolution he hugged his precious flag to him and was stumbling and staggering in his design to go the way that led to safety for it.

After he read *The Red Badge of Courage*, Ford Maddox Ford said, "The idea of falling like heroes on ceremonial battlefields was gone forever; we knew that we should fall like street-sweepers subsiding ignobly into rivers of mud."

If Crane's work can be reduced to any single summation, then Ford's is probably the most apt. Crane, taking the reader into the mud, left the clear, trout-filled streams to the Romantics who preceded him. His vision of the world was bleak, almost unredeemed, but for the fact that many of his characters *do* endure until their struggles end not by suicide or despair but by time. Crane's struggle ended at the beginning of a century that saw his vision of the horror of war projected on a global scale. He died of tuberculosis in a grimly appropriate place: the Black Forest. His body, taken back to the United States, was buried in Hillside, New Jersey.

FURTHER READING

Books by Crane

Complete Poems of Stephen Crane. Edited by Joseph Katz. Ithaca, N.Y.: Cornell University Press, 1972.

Great Short Works of Stephen Crane. New York: HarperCollins, 1987.

Books about Crane

Robertson, Michael. *Stephen Crane, Journalism, and the Making of Modern American Literature*. New York: Columbia University Press, 1997.

Szumski, Bonnie, ed. *Readings on Stephen Crane*. San Diego: Greenhaven Press, 1998.

Albert Payson Terhune

BORN December 21, 1872, in Newark
DIED February 18, 1942, at his estate at Pompton Lakes
BEST KNOWN FOR His beloved dog stories, especially those dealing with his collie "Lad."
THE JERSEY CONNECTION Immortalized his estate, "Sunnybank," in his writings; created such a vivid impression that visitors from around the world continue to make pilgrimages there.

The name "Terhune" has a rich and storied past in New Jersey. Local historians know it as the adopted name of America's first "Terhune," Albert Albertse, an immigrant who arrived in 1642 from Holland, changed his surname to "Terhune," and settled in the area of Hasbrouck Heights. The family tree boasts a distinguished lineal descent, including a lieutenant in the Continental Army who fought at Valley Forge, important judges, and revered ministers. The family's wealth and notoriety can perhaps be intuited from the countless streets throughout northern New Jersey designated Terhune Avenue, Terhune Place, and Terhune Drive.

It seems likely, however, that the family Terhune would have become a mere geneological curiosity for local history buffs if it weren't for Albert Payson Terhune, whose books and articles about the dogs that he kept at "Sunnybank" were among the most widely read popular literature of the early twentieth century.

Terhune's tales of his tail-wagging companions were mind-bogglingly popular. Although he worked as a journalist for more than twenty years for such papers as the *New York Evening World*—and also wrote mysteries, plays, and serial fiction—it is for his chronicles of Lad and other collies that Terhune was known. And he still is known, among the dog owners, book collectors, and sympathetic readers who still visit the grounds of Terhune's estate. (There is a memorial park, but the house was bulldozed in 1969; much of the adjoining land has been sold to developers.) Terhune's work, whether considered great literature or simplistic formulaic melodrama—and both camps have their proponents—made him rich and famous. He wrote his stories for dog magazines, children's magazines, and general-circulation magazines. By most counts, there are several hundred short stories and more than fifty books. Legend has it that he kept five typewriters in his study and used to go from one to the next while pounding out his works in an almost assembly-line fashion.

Terhune's popularity, however, can be traced to his affectionate portrayal of dogs, not his productivity. His readers sent him hundreds of letters per week— thanks for his warm and wonderful stories, congratulations on his ability to articulate what they had always felt: dogs and people *do* connect with each other, and the bond of friendship between humans and animals can be powerful. Much of Terhune's work was aimed at children. Its appeal to adults is obvious, however; consider both the brisk traffic to his estate and the brisk demand among collectors for his works, many of which are long out of print.

Here's a sample of Terhune's simple, affecting—some say "cloying"—style, taken from 1921's *The Heart of a Dog*. He details the rather cruel behavior of a boy Cyril toward the affectionate, beloved collie Lad:

> Cyril, from the hour of his arrival, found acute bliss in making Lad's life a horror.
>
> His initial step was to respond effusively to the Collie's welcoming advances; so long as the mistress and master chanced to be in the room. As they passed out, the mistress chanced to look back.
>
> She saw Cyril pull a bit of cake from his pocket and, with his left hand, proffer it to Lad. The tawny dog stepped courteously forward to accept the gift. As his teeth were about to close daintily on the cake, Cyril whipped it back out of reach; and with his other hand rapped Lad smartly across the nose.
>
> Had any grown man ventured a humiliating and painful trick of that sort on Lad, the Collie would have been at the tormentor's throat, on the instant. But it was not in the great dog's nature to attack a child. Shrinking back, in amaze, his abnormally sensitive feelings jarred, the Collie retreated majestically to his beloved "cave" under the music-room piano.

Although guided by animal instinct, Terhune's dogs are always shaming humanity through their decency and unconditional affection; observers in the books and stories thus wonder at or salute the dignity of the canine race. But if his biographers are to be believed, the lessons of the animal kingdom were often lost on Terhune, who could be fierce and short-tempered. Physically robust, he had a temperament to match. At 6'2" and 220 pounds, Terhune had an appetite for adventure that took him across Syria on horseback and into the boxing rings of New York City. Accounts chronicle Terhune brusquely handling domestic servants at his Sunnybank estate, insulting visitors who had come to meet the famous writer at his home, and even virtually ignoring his only daughter Lorraine (the girl's mother, Lorraine Marguerite Bryson, died of infection four days after Terhune's daughter was born and only ten months after Terhune and Bryson had married).

There are also accounts of Terhune exhibiting great tenderness toward his animals—and even the occasional human visitor—though most anecdotes from Sunnybank pilgrims focus on Terhune's affection for his canine brood, often at the exclusion of the people who milled about. The picture, therefore, one gets of Terhune is puzzling: notoriously hot-tempered one moment, playful and

childlike the next. Perhaps the only consistent behavior he exhibited throughout his adult life was a tireless passion for writing. And he did write.

During his newspaper days he'd write all day at his desk; then he spent all
night writing travel stories, essays, short stories, even poetry. Reportedly he
pounded away at his typewriter at least five hours a night. His annual output was
formidable: dozens of short stories and travel pieces and a handful of serial
adventures; each was about 60,000 words in length. Still, recognition was slow
in coming until he focused on his dogs. In 1915, *Redbook* published his first dog
story, "His Mate," which captured a wide and adoring readership. Following that
tale, he wrote dozens more dog stories, and in 1919 he published his book *Lad:
A Dog*, a phenomenon that sold more than 50,000 copies and appeared in thirty-
eight printings during the next decade. Amid this success, he and his second wife
Anice Morris Stockton, also a novelist, moved to Sunnybank in Pompton Lakes,
which became known, simply, as "The Place" in his future canine chronicles.

At Sunnybank, he fished, hunted, fenced, played poker, smoked cigars,
tromped through the woods with packs of his four-footed friends, and wrote
hundreds of stories and dozens of books. Throughout his first decade there, his

---

PET PROJECT

The collies who so famously populated Albert Payson Terhune's Sunnybank estate
might have been the most well known pets in the history of the Garden State, but
they were by no means the most unusual. In fact, centuries before Terhune set up
his beloved dog sanctuary, New Jersey colonists were turning the state's natural
wildlife into domestic companions.

Early eighteenth-century records indicate that many colonists—perhaps out of
boredom or curiosity—attempted to domesticate the local critter population,
including squirrels, deer, and even raccoons. This tendency was noticed by no less
an authority than Peter Kalm, a Swedish professor and member of the Royal
Academy of Sciences. In his multivolume work, *Travels in North America*, published
in 1748, Kalm details how early Jerseyans had turned their forest friends into
faithful companions, though often for mercenary reasons:

> A farmer in New Jersey had [a deer] in his possession, which he caught
> when it was very young; at present, it is so tame that in the daytime it runs
> into the woods for its food and towards night returns home, frequently
> bringing a wild deer out of the woods, giving its master an opportunity to
> shoot it at his very door.

Kalm's other observations include: "The raccoon can in time be made so tame
as to run about the streets like a domestic animal," and "Beavers have been tamed
to such an extent that they have brought home what they caught fishing to their
masters." Even wild partridges, under patient guidance, can be taught to return
home "when they are called."

annual income regularly reached $100,000, and his work was circulated internationally. He received hundreds of letters every week and when Terhune's collie Wolf (about whom he had written extensively) died, the *New York Times* published the obituary. He was reluctant to receive visitors at his estate, but he could not stop them from coming. He also received accolades and awards from all sorts of canine organizations, and in 1925 he was named Park Commissioner of New Jersey, a position he held until his death from throat cancer in 1942.

The last decade of his life was, given his fame and fortune, surprisingly disappointing for Terhune, who saw the already-distant relationship with his daughter worsen, his "serious" attempts at literature summarily ignored, and his health decline. He nevertheless poured forth a steady stream of writing: some to satisfy his longtime fans (*A Dog Named Chip*, *The Way of a Dog*), some to "break through" as a writer with a capital "W" (*The Son of God,* a biography of Christ), and some to preserve and polish his reputation (*Now that I'm Fifty*, *To the Best of My Memory*, and *The Book of Sunnybank*, all autobiographies). Terhune's conduct during his last decade reminds readers of his much more renowned contemporary Ernest Hemingway: irascible, hard-drinking, tough, somewhat reclusive. But on the printed page, his bark dissolved into a gentle yelp of recognition and unbridled affection.

Terhune's work not only reached across the generations, but some claim it transcended death. In 1945 his widow, Anice, published *Across the Line*, a book she claims was dictated by Terhune from the great beyond. The book, containing Terhune's vision of heaven, was, according to Anice, only the first in a series of extrasensory communiqués delivered by the departed Albert; however, no other works attributed to or channeled through him ever emerged.

There is certainly enough Terhune to satisfy those readers who simply seek reassurance that someone understands the special bond between pets and owners. Terhune understood and articulated that reassurance, and if it's true that he was much more humane to his dogs than to the people in his life, then it's likely his devoted readers won't hold that against him.

FURTHER READING

Books by Terhune

Best Loved Dog Stories of Albert Payson Terhune. Mattituck, N.Y.: Amereon, Ltd., 1923.
A Book of Famous Dogs. New York: Doubleday, 1937.
Lochinvar Luck. New York: Grosset & Dunlap, 1923.

Books about Terhune

Litvag, Irving. *The Master of Sunnybank: A Biography of Albert Payson Terhune*. New York: Harper and Row, 1977.
Rais, Kathleen. *Albert Payson Terhune: A Bibliography of Primary Works*. Privately Published by Kathleen Rais & Co., 1997.

William Carlos Williams

BORN September 17, 1883, in Rutherford
DIED March 4, 1963, also in Rutherford
BEST KNOWN FOR Probably his five-volume poem, *Paterson,* as well as dozens of small, memorable poems.
THE JERSEY CONNECTION Lived almost his whole life in Rutherford and immortalized many people and places of Bergen County in his work.

In the preface to the two-volume *Collected Poems of William Carlos Williams*, the editors note that Williams tended to mentally group his poems not according to periods or subject matter, but rather "modes of attack." This militaristic metaphor, though perhaps at odds with what one expects from the gentle country doctor and humanist poet, is a perfectly apt way to think of Williams's work. He *does* attack his subjects, isolating them, pinning them down, surrounding them, interrogating them. The things he places in his poetic crosshairs—hard, earthy things, as opposed to abstract ideas—are assaulted and beseiged by Williams's drive to discover their essence. Williams's oft-quoted aphorism, "No ideas but in things," remains a helpful map, and perhaps the only constant, for readers who wish to pursue this native Jerseyan through a half century of literary achievement. As critic Anthony Libby once noted:

> Williams seeks a reality of essences, not surfaces . . . he conveys an exultation close to mystical, but grounded in immediate fact, a mysticism of particulars. This is the power that defines Williams' greatest poetry, his ability to describe a simple word in simple language, and through the logic and purity of his vision to create such genuine flowering.

One of Williams's most famous poems typifies his belief in the power of objects to bear scrutiny, often revealing a depth and significance beyond their mere form:

So much depends
upon
a red wheel barrow
glazed with rain
water
beside the white
chickens

That poem, from the 1923 collection *Spring and All*, has been widely anthologized, but its brevity may mislead some readers into thinking that Williams favored the short lyric. Most of his critical reputation today rests upon his sprawling epic *Paterson,* a five-volume poem with generous samples of prose, history, geography, and historical allusion. He also wrote novels, critical essays, autobiographical fiction, plays, and memoirs. Yet he strove in all his work, large and small, to keep the spotlight on the objects in his world, to wed his insights to a physical source. The "things" in *Paterson* pile up on every page, volume after volume. Williams was the great sifter of American poetry, rummaging through the mental closets of the national body politic, cataloguing the treasures and trash discarded in twentieth-century New Jersey. *Paterson* is filtered through the mind of a doctor-poet named Paterson, who also lives in Paterson, and it relates, among other things, the history and development of Paterson. The work expands on his earlier experimentation with "imagism," as well as his absorption of the modernist literary practices of Eliot, Pound, Joyce, and H.D. In its appropriation of vernacular speech, it looks back to Whitman; in its free-form style and linguistic experimentation, it anticipates the Beats.

Impossible to label, except intermittently, Williams's approach to writing changed regularly, even radically. He moved comfortably in the course of his career through a series of stylistic innovations and genres. His peripatetic literary journey stands in stark contrast to his life. Except for a brief period abroad and a stint in medical school in Pennsylvania, he remained firmly rooted in New Jersey. To his patients, he was the picture of constancy, the rock-solid country doctor, living on his small farm, still making house calls. But Williams didn't simply practice medicine: as with his poetry, he *inhabited* the discipline, always trying to get inside his patients' heads and hearts, diagnosing them like a wheelbarrow in the rain or a Paterson street at dusk, searching for that telling marker of significance. He explained in his autobiography:

> It's the humdrum, day in, day out, everyday work that is the real satisfaction of the practice of medicine; the million and a half patients a man has seen on his daily visits over a forty-year period of weekdays and Sundays that make up his life. I have never had a money practice; it would have been impossible for me. But that actual calling on people, at all times and under all conditions, the coming to grips with the intimate conditions of their lives, when they were being born, when they were dying, watching them die, watching them get well when they were ill, has always absorbed me.

> I lost myself in the very properties of their minds: for the moment at least I actually became *them,* whoever they should be, so that when I detached myself from them at the end of a half-hour of intense concentration over some illness which was affecting them, it was as though I were reawakening from a sleep. For the moment I myself did not exist, nothing of myself affected me. As a consequence I came back to myself, as from any other sleep, rested.

Almost equal to Williams's passion for medicine was his love of America. In 1912 Williams was comfortably established in Rutherford with his wife, Flossie, and later, two sons. He began an earnest study of the great patriotic writers of the American past: Jefferson, Franklin, Freneau, Whitman. Williams's work began to shift in the 1920s and early 1930s from a European-bred modernism to a more "home-grown" American expression. This shift in tone and diction can be seen in his 1930s trilogy *White Mule* (about the immigration experience in America), through *Paterson* in 1946 (succeeding volumes would be published in the next ten years) and in his short stories, which explored American culture and values in collections such as *The Farmer's Daughters* (1961). In his emphasis on character—he was often criticized for neglecting plot in the interest of writing character studies—he helped revitalize a strain of American fiction that stretches from Cooper's Natty Bumppo to Melville's Ishmael to Hemingway's Nick Adams. His celebration of American idealism, the nobility of the individual, and an inescapable connection to the land echo throughout the pages of such Williams-inspired masterworks as Allen Ginsberg's *Howl*.

Williams has been claimed by the symbolists, imagists, objectivists, modernists, postmodernists, and minimalists. His reputation has remained high since his death in 1963—the same year he won the Pulitzer Prize for his poetry collection *Pictures from Brueghel*. His poems, stories, and novels still testify to the magic hidden behind the mundane. He remains a potent watcher; his work records a writer who never lost his power to see the world around him clearly. Whether gazing at Brueghel's painting or a fisherman on the Passaic River,

THE SILK PICKET LINE

The city of Paterson can boast an impressive number of significant contributions to American culture, including being the country's first "planned city"—designed by no less an urban planner than Alexander Hamilton.

Yet Paterson's best claim to enduring notoriety remains the famous Silk Strike of 1913, a five-month labor dispute that gained international attention and marked a new era in the development of the modern union movement. Bloomfield College history professor Steve Golin argues in his book *The Fragile Bridge* (Temple University Press, 1988) that the strikers' defeat represented a turning point for the American intellectual left.

New York 1913 (Scribner's, 1988) links the strike (actually, a rally in support of the strikers at Madison Square Garden) to the ground-breaking Armory show, with its modern avant-garde art works, a revelation to most viewers. Author Martin Green sees both events as "the last manifestations of pre–World War I radicalism," and he shows how the two events shared a roster of participants, such as John Reed, Margaret Sanger, Isadora Duncan, and Lincoln Steffens.

Williams wrestled the physical world into submission, forced it to surrender its secrets, and always scanned for more clues. As he once wrote to his publisher James Laughlin after a day trip to Manhattan from his beloved Paterson in June 1948,

> I weary, Jim, but only in the flesh of this world. Never, I believe, have I been so moved or more moved than I was yesterday on my way to and from your office by the world I beheld (so different from the one I knew in the same locale 50 years ago) on the train, the ferry, the subway and the street—the playground across the street from your office . . . and the nice gang you have assembled to do your work—with their gastric ulcers and strange eyes—looking out of the corners of their eyes at me as if I were a curio. It is childlike and wonderful.

> But Jim, I ain't no religioner. What I saw, however, shows me that there's a whole batter of new men and women—and children—making up what used to be called America (as least as far as New York represents it—and I'm sure it does) who have a yeast in them will show us something pretty soon that we don't expect. It's very simple and very much alive and, I must confess, I love it.

FURTHER READING

Books by Williams

Coles, Robert, ed. *The Doctor Stories*. New York: Norton, 1985.
Litz, A. Walton, ed. *The Collected Poems of William Carlos Williams*. 2 vols. New York: New Directions, 1991.

Books about Williams

Jones, Anne Hudson, ed. *Literature in Medicine: Images of Healers*. Baltimore: Johns Hopkins University Press, 1985.
Markos, Donald. *Ideas in Things: The Poems of William Carlos Williams*. Rutherford, N.J.: Fairleigh Dickinson University Press, 1994.

Joyce Kilmer

> **BORN** December 6, 1886, in New Brunswick
> **DIED** July 30, 1918, in the woods near the French village of Seringes et Nesles in Champagne
> **BEST KNOWN FOR** The poem "Trees."
> **THE JERSEY CONNECTION** Born, raised, educated, and spent his life in the Garden State, which he immortalized in poetry.

Everyone knows "Trees," of course. Its first two lines are as familiar to some Americans as the melody of "Happy Birthday" or the opening question of Hamlet's famous soliloquy. There's a spellbindingly simple appeal in Kilmer's signature

poem—and in his wider, though almost completely unknown other works—
which gives even poetry haters something to recite when asked to name their
favorite lines of verse.

For those who've somehow bypassed its glories, here's the poem that made
Joyce Kilmer a household word. (In this case, it's not merely a hyperbolic expression of speech. "Trees" really did make Kilmer a household word. Almost inex-
plicably, the poem, according to accounts of the times, was being recited by
people coast to coast; its words were embroidered into tapestries or recited at
official gatherings.) After this, nature poetry would never be the same, much to
the chagrin of some critics and readers who prefer their nature odes packaged
more sublimely:

Trees

I think that I shall never see
A poem as lovely as a tree.
A tree whose hungry mouth is prest
Against the earth's sweet flowing breast;
A tree that looks at God all day,
And lifts her leafy arms to pray;
A tree that may in Summer wear
A nest of robins in her hair;
Upon whose bosom snow has lain;
Who intimately lives with rain.
Poems are made by fools like me,
But only God can make a tree.

Whatever tree precisely inspired Kilmer to write his famous homage was most
certainly a Jersey tree. Kilmer had a love for the Garden State as deeply rooted as
his subject. Theodore Jamison noted this fondness in an article on Kilmer published in *New Jersey History* to mark the centenary of the poet's birth:

Despite his affection for New York City pleasures, Kilmer loved his home
in New Jersey more. He was a dedicated family man and an exemplary father
and husband. He could be seen pacing the floors at night singing lullabys to
his children while they screamed in his arms. Once they quieted down,
Kilmer would dictate to his wife until she fell asleep at the typewriter, often
at 2 a.m. After tucking his children into bed, Kilmer would return to his
study, light up his pipe, and begin planning for the next. His feelings for his
home ran deep:

This man has home and child and wife
And battle set for every day.
This man has God and love and life;
Those stand, all else shall pass away.

Kilmer's son, Kenton, provides an additional key detail regarding the poem's provenance in his book, *Memories of My Father, Joyce Kilmer*:

It was in an upstairs bedroom of this house, which served as Mother and Dad's bedroom and also as Dad's office, that Dad wrote "Trees" on Feb. 2, 1913. I have his notebook with that title and date written down. The window looked out down a hill on our well-wooded lawn—trees of many kinds, from mature trees to thin saplings: oaks, maples, black and white birches, and I don't know what else.

Kilmer's New Jersey roots were just as strong. Born in New Brunswick, he attended Rutgers Preparatory School and graduated in 1904. He began his undergraduate career at Rutgers College but completed his degree at Columbia University, where he earned a bachelor's degree in journalism in 1908. Less than a month after graduating, he married Aline Murray, whose stepfather, Henry Alden, was the editor of *Harper's Magazine*.

His first full-time job was teaching Latin in the Morristown Public Schools, but after just one year he tired of the teaching life and set out on a career in letters. Cobbling together a living from his disparate literary pursuits—poetry, editing, dictionary writing—Kilmer survived in the literary world long enough to latch on to the *New York Times* as a contributor to the *Sunday Magazine*. He relocated his family to Mahwah in 1913, where he continued writing magazine articles and poetry.

Contemporary accounts by his neighbors and his increasing circle of friends and admirers paint a picture of a perpetually cheerful, optimistic, and deeply

POETIC TIMBER

When Joyce Kilmer was tragically killed during World War I, America lost a beloved poetic voice. But it was shortly to gain a lasting legacy befitting the poet, a patch of national forest preserved in his name.

The Joyce Kilmer Memorial Forest and National Recreation Trail in North Carolina is one of the largest old-growth preserves in the eastern United States. The forest, known originally as the Little Santeelah, boasts an abundance of mature yellow poplars and chestnut trees.

Among speculators and logging companies the land changed hands several times between 1900 and 1930. When it appeared to be headed for devastation, the forest was temporarily spared by the economic hardship brought on by the Great Depression.

The Forest Service, seizing the opportunity to buy the land in 1935, chose to honor the fallen war hero whose poem "Trees" had forever connected him to such natural settings. The preserve boasts a pristine two-mile recreation trail and a permanent old-growth sanctuary that surely would have delighted the arbor-loving poet.

committed family man, who glorified in verse the seemingly mundane aspects of life. Even his daily commute to New York City inspired the highly impressionable Kilmer to poetic exhortations. Here's an excerpt from the last section of his ode to riding the rails on "The Twelve Forty-Five":

> The Glen Rock welcomes us to her
> And silent Ridgewood seems to stir
> And smile, because she knows the train
> Has brought her children back again.
> We carry people home—and so
> God speeds us, wheresoe'er we go.
> Hohokus, Waldwick, Allendale
> Lift sleepy heads to give us hail.
> In Ramsey, Mahwah, Suffern stand
> Houses that wistfully demand
> A father—son—some human thing
> That this, the midnight train, may bring.
> The trains that travel in the day
> They hurry folks to work or play.
> The midnight train is slow and old
> But of it let this thing be told,
> To its high honor be it said
> It carries people home to bed.
> My cottage lamp shines white and clear.
> God bless the train that brought me here.

The temptation to roll one's eyes at such dewy-eyed treatment of public transportation is offset by the sincerity of expression and zeal for the simple joys in life. That kind of deep-seated affection for home and hearth, one suspects, cannot be faked. Kilmer's orderly life of street lamps, leisurely Sunday strolls, chasing his children around Mahwah, and composing poems in repose ended in 1917 when he entered the U.S. Army.

He first enlisted in the Officers Training Corps but quickly left the unit; Kilmer then joined the 7th Regiment of the New York National Guard and finally the famous 69th Regiment, known popularly as "The Fighting Sixty-ninth." Kilmer the poet found unexpected joy and fulfillment as a member of a corps of soldiers celebrated for being tough, colorful, even brutal. When, for a time, he was assigned to the regimental chaplain's office, Kilmer was deeply frustrated to be shuffling papers rather than slogging through battles with his fellow infantrymen.

Despite the war, Kilmer continued writing poems. Before he shipped out to Europe and while undergoing rigorous training at Camp Mills, Kilmer rushed to finish editing *The Anthology of Catholic Poets*. He was sent to France on October

29, 1917. His letters to his mother, as well as the poems and essays he was writing, suggest a temperament of unusual good cheer. Kilmer's compatriots reported that his boyish enthusiasm and personal sense of moral crusade never dampened. The conviviality of soldiering apparently tapped something deep within the psyche of the vibrant, buoyant Kilmer.

In a letter Kilmer sent to his mother, written a month before he was killed, the poet sounds more like a kid at summer camp than a soldier at war. The innocence and bouyancy are striking:

> All the rest of the fellows in the Intelligence Section have pictures of their mothers, but none of them so good looking as mine. You would be amused at some of the scenes when your picture is exhibited. Tired from a long hike from a stay in the trenches, I am having an omelet and some fried potatoes and some vin rouge beaucoup in a French peasant's little kitchen. . . . After such a repast as I have described I take out my wallet to pay my bill, and the sharp eyes of little Marie or Pierre intently watching this strange soldat Amercain, spy the picture. At once an inquisitive but delighted infant is on my knee, demanding a closer inspection of the picture.
>
> Then mama must see it, and grandpere (the man of the house can't see it; he is away from home on the errand that brought me across the sea). Well. They all say, "elle est jolie ma foi et jeune aussi." These comments have been made on your picture many times, in many towns, which I will one day show you on a map of France.

On July 30, 1918, on surveillance maneuvers in the village of Seringes et Nesles, Sgt. Joyce Kilmer was shot dead by a German sniper. His death was remarked upon in all major newspapers, prominent national magazines, and influential literary journals. The *New York Times* even offered its own poem on his passing, beginning "The singers of a nation / weep as one soul this day." Kilmer himself unwittingly captured the pathos of his own passing in a poem written after discovering two dead blackbirds at his home in Mahwah one spring day. It stands as a fitting epitaph for his short but vibrant life:

> An iron hand has stilled the throats
> That throbbed with loud and rhythmic glee
> And dammed the flood of silver notes
> That drenched the world in melody.

FURTHER READING

Books by Kilmer

The Circus and Other Essays and Fugitive Pieces. New York: Doubleday, 1929.
Dreams and Other Images: An Anthology of Catholic Poets. Edited by Kilmer. New York: Boni and Liveright, 1917.
Trees and Other Poems. Atlanta: Cherokee Publishing, 1989.

Books about Kilmer

Cargas, Harry J. *I Lay Down My Life: Biography of Joyce Kilmer*. Boston: St. Paul, 1964.
Swinnerton, Frank. *The Georgian Scene: A Literary Panorama*. New York: Farrar and Rinehart, 1934.

Allen Ginsberg

BORN June 3, 1926, in Newark
DIED April 5, 1997, in New York City
BEST KNOWN FOR Being one of the founders of the Beat movement and authoring its greatest poetic statement, "Howl."
THE JERSEY CONNECTION Grew up in Paterson, where he developed a student-mentor relationship with William Carlos Williams.

Ginsberg was a flame thrower, poetically speaking. His sexual explicitness, anti-authoritarianism, linguistic innovation, and political activism put him on the front lines of a radical literary movement and kept him there for four decades as its most eminent exemplar. He was literary provocateur, political gadfly, Buddhist icon. A bundle of contradictions, Ginsberg played the role of put-upon prophet, alternating between shrill town-crier and massage therapist for the body politic. Like his poetic father Walt Whitman, Ginsberg contained multitudes. No single frame of reference can contain his poetics, as the following exchange during an interview with the *American Poetry Review* (granted a year before he died) reveals:

Interviewer: So you're a Jewish poet.
Ginsberg: I'm also a gay poet.
Interviewer: I know that.
Ginsberg: I'm also a New Jersey poet.
Interviewer: You're a Buddhist poet.
Ginsberg: And I'm a Buddhist poet. And also I'm an academic poet, and I'm also a beatnik poet, I'm an international poet—

Or, as critic James Mersmann once put it, "Ginsberg is not a great poet, but he is a great figure in the history of poetry."

Regardless of the fluctuating state of Ginsberg's critical stock, his work is seminal. There might have been a Beat movement in literature without Allen Ginsberg, but it would have lacked its most vociferous—and populist—apostle. His poem "Howl," an indictment of post–World War II moral decline and spiritual stasis, put the Beat movement on the map. As his cohorts, like Jack Kerouac and William Burroughs, either burned out or vacated center stage for the fringe, Ginsberg remained the heart of the movement, dedicated to an idealism and activism aimed at improving, not simply assailing, the world.

His works and his public recitations were at times closer to ravings than readings, but what comes through now, less than a decade after his death, are the humanity of his writings and his preoccupation with freedom and self-determination. His playfulness with words is regarded as less ad hoc and more the product of a disciplined craftsman. "Howl," for instance, has sometimes been derided in the critical literature as nothing more than a fractured word puzzle written in a peyote-induced mental fog, but as early as 1958 Ginsberg was vociferously defending his use of form and his highly detailed structural plan undergirding the poem. In a letter to John Hollander, reprinted in Jane Kramer's *Allen Ginsberg in America*, he lashes out at critics who see him simply as an experimenter ("I've read 50 reviews of Howl and not one of them written by anyone with enough technical interests to notice the fucking obvious construction of the poem") and he discusses in a treatiselike manner his technique:

> Back to Howl: Construction. After sick & tired of shortline free verse as not expressionistic enough, not swinging enough, can't develop a powerful enough rhythm. . . . I changed my mind about "measure" while writing it. Part one uses repeated base who, as a sort of a Kithera Blang, Homeric (in my imagination) to mark off each statement, with rhythmic unit. So that's experiment with longer & shorter variations on a fixed base—the principle being that each line has to be continued within the elastic of one breath—with suitable punctuatory expressions where the rhythm has built up enough so that I have to let off steam by building a longer climactic line in which there is a jazzy ride. All the ear I've developed goes into the balancing of those lines.

Allen Ginsberg was born in Newark and grew up in Paterson. His father was a high school teacher and poet. His mother, whose death was the subject of his classic elegy poem "Kaddish," was a radical Marxist with a history of mental illness. The young poet himself grew up somewhat withdrawn and conflicted as he wrestled with the knowledge of his homosexuality. A shy, bookish student, Ginsberg began writing in high school, usually in the more structured verse forms of the time (though he had developed something of a mentor-acolyte relationship with Paterson's William Carlos Williams in the late 1940s and 1950s, his verse became more colloquial, less indebted to stanzaic form).

At Columbia University he first began expressing himself in print—as well as sexually—among a bohemian group of students who formed the core of the Beat movement. His circle included Kerouac, Burroughs, and Neal Cassady, the main character in *On the Road*. Ginsberg embraced the counter-culture lifestyle, conversant with heavy drug use, Eastern religions, political radicalism, and bisexuality. "Howl," which the unknown Ginsberg premiered at a reading at San Francisco's Six Gallery in 1955, made his name, but he continued to produce provocative and experimental streams of verse throughout the next several decades. Traveling around the world with his lover Peter Orlovsky, Ginsberg became the unofficial spokesperson for an "enlightened" radicalism founded upon an amalgam of Buddhist thought, political activism, literary theatricality, and the embrace of alternative lifestyles. He agitated for gay rights, the end of "capitalist oppression," and the legalization of marijuana, among many other causes.

Although his readings in the 1960s and early 1970s were wildly animated, raucous, and often uproarious, Ginsberg was more than a mere "performing poet." In his writings he also addressed the most serious issues of his time: racism, war, discrimination, and human rights abuses. His essays, as well as his poetry, reveal a deep commitment to social justice. Far from being the naïve political clown of which his critics sometimes accused him, Ginsberg was a shrewd observer of his time; however, his beliefs that such generally useful concepts as "time," "space," and "existence" were illusory and irrelevant didn't aid his quest to be considered a serious thinker. And he *was* prone to find conspiracies just about everywhere he looked:

> Because systems of mass communication can communicate only officially acceptable levels of reality, no one can know the extent of the secret unconscious life. No one in America can know what will happen. No one is in real control. America is having a nervous breakdown. . . .
>
> Those of the general populace whose individual perception is sufficiently weak to be formed by stereotypes of mass communication disapprove and deny the insight. The police and newspapers have moved in, mad movie manufacturers from Hollywood are at this moment preparing bestial stereotypes of the scene.

As that excerpt from a 1959 essay in the *San Francisco Chronicle* reveals, Ginsberg saw a lot—including, later in life, ghosts, angels, and the resurrected spirits of long-dead poets. The same jaundiced eye that detected the pull-strings of governmental authority lurking above human institutions also keenly perceived the evils of mass conformity. Ginsberg was egalitarian to the core, a pacifist who urged everyone to meditate to find common areas of psychic convergence. Monotheisms are dangerous; meditation should be "preferably non-theistic," he told *High Times* magazine in 1992. "So you don't get trippy on Hindu Gods, or Christian Gods, or Jewish Jehovahs, or monotheistic monsters in the sky, or devils."

Such esoteric explorations didn't keep Ginsberg from being feted by "respectable" society. Indeed, he became the subject of serious critical scrutiny as his career progressed, and he was profiled in documentary films and scholarly biographies in his later years. He even became a "distinguished professor" at Brooklyn College. He continued to write poetry and essays and keep a journal until his death in 1997. And he remained a beloved, even awe-inspiring figure on the poetry circuit, where he was generally accorded the status of reigning poetic patriarch—an ironic turn of events for someone whose career was built largely on assailing hierarchies and deflating the idea of idol worship. Yet Ginsberg took the bows, the applause, and the money. In 1994, after shopping his archives around, he agreed to sell his papers to Stanford University for a million dollars—quite a coup for a man who the FBI once labeled a "subversive." Throughout his life, Ginsberg championed the idea that the only dangerously subversive social act is censorship. In an online interview in 1996 sponsored by George Washington University, he explained the Beat movement was aimed at

---

SUBVERSIVE VERSES

Ginsberg's writing gained him fans the world over, but the critical opinion of one reader is now the stuff of official historical record. FBI Director J. Edgar Hoover, labeling Ginsberg a "subversive," called the poet "potentially dangerous" in a 1965 memorandum.

According to Herbert Mitgang's *Dangerous Dossiers: Exposing the Secret War Against America's Greatest Authors* (Donald Fine, 1988), the FBI, concerned over what Hoover called his "expressions of strong or violent anti-U.S. sentiment" as well as his "propensity for violence and antipathy toward good order and government," tracked Ginsberg both here and abroad.

Two decades later, Ginsberg was still an irritant to the Washington establishment. During the Reagan administration, Ginsberg's name was placed on a U.S. Information Agency list of people deemed "unsuitable" to serve as government-paid speakers abroad.

---

breaking the bonds of censorship, which we did, and being able to speak freely. There was an exuberance in art rather than any sort of wet blanket, some sense of exuberance that, as Blake said, "Exuberance is beauty," and even some visionary element.

Translating that "visionary element" into poetry became the lifelong obsession of the writer from Paterson who, in the words of biographer Michael Schumacher, "has evolved into a sort of living symbol of kindness and generosity, and an artist who dared to make his own life a form of literature."

FURTHER READING

Books by Ginsberg

Fall of America: Poems of These States,1965–1971. San Francisco: City Lights Books, 1984.
Collected Poems: 1947–1980. New York: HarperCollins, 1988.

Books about Ginsberg

Hyde, Lewis. On the Poetry of Allen Ginsberg. New York: St. Martin's Press, 1994.
Schumacher, Michael. Dharma Lion: A Critical Biography of Allen Ginsberg. New York: St.
    Martin's Press, 1994.

Mary Higgins Clark

There is perhaps an irony in the title of Mary Higgins Clark's first book, *Aspire to the Heavens* (1969). The book was a colossal failure ("remaindered right off the press," Clark has said). Clark's own lofty aspirations must have seemed wildly unrealistic at the time. After all, Clark had begun her writing career trying to sell a short story; after six years and forty rejections, she finally sold it for $100.

Aspire to the heavens? In 1964, when her husband Warren F. Clark died, she was a widow with five children. Thirty-five years old, she was trying to manage a household on an income generated by churning out radio scripts. She liked writing but realized that short stories, even if she could sell them, wouldn't bring in much additional income. She started writing novels—more than twenty by the last count—at five a.m. at the kitchen table "to help fill the gaps" in her life.

Instead, she filled bookshelves and became one of contemporary fiction's most bankable authors; her works have been filmed as major motion pictures and made-for-television movies, and her name has become a brand (*Family Circle* publishes *Mary Higgins Clark Mystery Magazine*). What's the secret of her success? Clark has said her appeal derives from adhering to a simple, consistent formula: "I write about very nice people whose lives are invaded," she once told Bookreporter, a literary website.

Sometimes those lives belong to New Jersey residents. For a sampling of Clark's metier, take a look at this excerpt from *On the Street Where You Live* (2001), which displays her trademark mix of a sense of normalcy while restless phantoms hover just beyond the page:

> He enjoyed Spring Lake best once autumn set in. By then, the summer people had closed their houses, not appearing even for weekends. . . .
>
> Spring Lake, with its Victorian houses that appeared unchanged from the way they had been in the 1890s, was worth the inconvenience of the trip, they explained.
>
> Spring Lake, with the fresh bracing scent of the ocean always present, revived the soul, they agreed.
>
> Spring Lake, with its two-mile boardwalk, where one could revel in the silvery magnificence of the Atlantic, was a treasure, they pointed out.

All of these people shared so much—the summer visitors, the permanent dwellers, but none of them shared his secrets.

That's Clark's method: take a Norman Rockwell painting and start scratching the canvas to reveal a darker portrait underneath. She portrays an idyllic life and then interrupts it, sometimes subtly, sometimes with extreme prejudice. Her sense of irony and her grim foreshadowing have introduced many of her best works, including *Stillwatch* (1984), a thriller about a TV producer and a U.S. senator. The book's opening paragraph almost buckles under ironic expectations:

> Pat drove slowly, her eyes scanning the narrow Georgetown streets. The cloud-filled sky was dark; streetlights blended with the carriage lamps that flanked doorways; Christmas decorations gleamed against ice-crusted snow. The effect was one of early American tranquility. She turned onto N Street, drove one more block, still searching for house numbers, and crossed the intersection. That must be it, she thought—the corner house. Home Sweet Home.

Those last three words telegraph Clark's underlying themes. In her suspense fiction, "Home Sweet Home" becomes a mocking epitaph.

Clark once told *Cosmopolitan* magazine that she likes "nice, strong people confronting the forces of evil and vanquishing them." Her consistent (detractors would say "formulaic" or even "redundant") use of that mode of story generation has put her frequently on the *New York Times* bestseller list. Her devoted fans have pounced upon each year's new production, set up countless adulatory websites dedicated to her works, mobbed her at book signings, and helped spawn

---

THE PLAINS OF SOUTH ORANGE

As a suspense writer, Mary Higgins Clark is in the top commercial ranks. But New Jersey can also boast of being home to one of the best-selling authors in the genre of women's fiction: South Orange's Belva Plain.

The author of twenty novels—loosely classified as romance, women's fiction, or contemporary literature (depending on which bookstore or library you happen to search), Plain has earned critical kudos for her taut plots, realistic characterizations, and her refusal to embellish her books with gratuitous sex. She explains her approach on her website, "Unfortunately, much of women's fiction contains far more graphic and sexual content, as if it be adult one has to leave nothing to the imagination. I do prefer a more subtle approach."

It seems to satisfy her readers, who turned *Random Winds* (1980, Delacorte) and *After the Fire* (2000, Delacorte) into near-instant bestsellers. Like her fellow New Jerseyan Clark, Plain is also an honorary member of the Board of Trustees of the New Jersey Literary Hall of Fame. And, like Clark, she is a morning person.

"I can scarcely think after ten o'clock," she says.

ancillary enterprises like the *MHC Library of Suspense*—a special "collector's edition" of her novels—and the *Mary Higgins Clark Mystery Magazine,* which features the work of such estimable suspense writers as Elmore Leonard and P. D. James. One could spend the better part of a day scrolling through the author's official website, sponsored by her publisher (at *www.simonsays.com/mhclark*). The site includes biographical facts, interviews, fan reviews, synopses of all her works, links to information about the movies made from her books, fans' postings, trivia, previews of forthcoming books, and links to the booksellers who have profited handsomely from the insatiable appetite for works by the "Queen of Suspense."

Clark's novels represent the pinnacle of "popular fiction," beach reading year-round for people seeking a writer who delivers by-the-numbers fiction. There's little literary pretense in Clark's body of fiction, but within the covers of any of her books one finds a solid command of the storyteller's art. She might never be canonized in the pantheon of "important" writers, although she is an honorary trustee and an inductee of the New Jersey Literary Hall of Fame, but her ability to weave a page-turning tale should ensure her continued cult of worship. She is as bankable as she is predictable. As the *Washington Post* once noted, "Buying a Mary Higgins Clark book is like buying a ticket to ride on the roller coaster. We strap ourselves in and once on the track, we're there until the ride is over."

It wouldn't take a novelist's imagination to apply the roller coaster image to Clark's own life. After her father's death when she was ten, the family struggled. Mary went from high school to secretarial school; then she spent a year as a stewardess flying to Africa and Europe. In 1949 she married Warren Clark, who died in 1964. She was still ten years away from her first real writing success, *Where Are the Children?* (1975). In 1978, she married attorney Raymond C. Ploetz; six years later, the marriage was annulled. In 1996, she married retired Merrill Lynch executive John Conheeney. Amid the career shifts and personal upheaval, a love of writing has been an anchor in her life. She says on her website that she wanted to be a writer since she was a child:

> The first thing I wrote was a poem, when I was seven. I still have it. It's pretty bad, but my mother thought it was beautiful and made me recite it for everyone who came in. I am sure the captive audience was ready to shoot me but that kind of encouragement nurtures a budding talent. From the time I was seven, I also kept diaries. I can read them now and look back at what I was like at different ages. I still keep diaries; they are a great help to my novels. No one has seen them—they are locked in a trunk.

Secret diaries locked in a trunk? A famous novelist who just bought an old mansion? A career path that wound from a mundane secretary's job to flying to exotic lands to international literary fame? Marriage to a former high-powered executive at a blue-chip firm? Sounds like the seeds of a plot for one of America's most celebrated suspense writers, a woman *The New Yorker* aptly named the "mistress of high tension."

FURTHER READING

Books by Clark

Daddy's Little Girl. New York: Simon and Schuster, 2002.

He Sees You When You're Sleeping (coauthored with daughter Carol Higgins Clark). New York: Simon and Schuster, 2001.

Books about Clark

Pelzer, Linda Claycomb. *Mary Higgins Clark: A Critical Companion*. Westport, Conn.: Greenwood Publishing, 1995.

Toni Morrison

BORN February 18, 1931, in Lorain, Ohio
BEST KNOWN FOR A handful of highly acclaimed novels, especially *Beloved*.
THE JERSEY CONNECTION Since 1988, she's been a professor at Princeton.

Few readers would identify Toni Morrison, first and foremost, as a writer of ghost stories. Her fame and critical success would surely bring other designations to mind: Pulitzer Prize winner, literary critic, Ivy League professor, Nobel laureate. Spirits, however, linger among and behind and flit through her fictional worlds. Morrison's work is informed by an urgent awareness of the past and its inhabitants—how they suffered, how they triumphed in the face of evil or disregard, how they animate the present. Her books embody the plaintive wail of ghosts from African tribal communities, ghosts who first enchanted the writer as a youth in Middle America.

Her novels, though rich in naturalistic detail, dissolve into kaleidoscopic views of the unseen and the surreal. Her characters draw strength from the legends and lore of a distant, sometimes mutilated, legacy. Indeed, images, impressions, dreams, memory are all more important than reality. Morrison explained in her essay *Memory, Creation, and Writing*: "I depend heavily on the muse of memory . . . I cannot trust the literature and sociology of other people to help me know the truth of my cultural sources." As a writer she claims one of her primary missions is to "centralize and animate . . . information described as 'lore,' or 'gossip,' or 'magic,' or 'sentiment.'" Like the Romantic poets to whom she is sometimes compared by critics, Morrison aims to recreate the feelings of the dreamer, the terror of the unknown, the beauty of the transcendent. Memory is the key to understanding, and to surrender it is to participate in the annihilation of one's own culture. Critic Carolyn Denard noted in *Modern American Women Writers*:

Toni Morrison.

She is able to cull what she believes is the shared, cultural, ancestral memory of experiences not specifically her own and make them ring true to her readers. It is important, Morrison believes, to begin this kind of memory-based retrieval because that part of black life which is not sensational, statistical, or extraordinary has so often been discredited. But it is that life, that remembered part of past experience, informed by a recessed code of values, practiced daily and involuntarily, which reveals the cultural essence.

Toni Morrison was born Chloe Anthony Wofford, the second of four children of George Wofford, a welder, and Ramah Willis Wofford. The family lived in the industrial town of Lorain, Ohio, after Morrison's parents had relocated from the South to escape racism. Lorain was integrated, and Chloe grow up hearing the stories many Black southerners brought with them to Lorain. She learned to read early—reportedly, she was the only student in her first grade class who could read—and widely. Morrison has said her earliest favorite writers were Tolstoy, Flaubert, and Jane Austen.

She graduated from Lorain High School in 1949 and then attended Howard University in Washington, where she majored in English and minored in the classics. In 1955, she received an M.A. degree from Cornell University; she then taught English at Texas Southern University from 1955 to 1957 and at Howard from 1957 to 1964. At Howard, she met Harold Morrison, an architect from Jamaica. They married and had two sons, Harold and Slade.

The couple divorced, and she left Howard University to return to Lorain, where she lived for a year and a half. She then began a career in publishing, first as a textbook editor with Random House in Syracuse, New York, and later as senior editor at Random House in New York City. While working in publishing, she resumed writing a story she had begun after her second child was born; the story grew into the novel *The Bluest Eye* (1970).

From the late 1960s, Morrison taught at a number of colleges and universities, including Yale, the State University of New York at Albany, and Rutgers. In 1988, she assumed the Robert F. Gohen Professorship of the Humanities at Princeton University, becoming the first Black woman writer to hold a named chair at an Ivy League university. She remains at Princeton, where she teaches creative writing, African-American studies, and women's studies.

Her books include *Sula* (1973), *Song of Solomon* (a National Book Critics Circle Award Winner, 1977), *Tar Baby* (1981), *Beloved* (1987), *Jazz* (1992), a collection of essays called *Playing in the Dark: Whiteness and the Literary Imagination* (1992), and *Paradise* (1998). She has also written several articles and essays for publications such as *Mademoiselle*, *Michigan Quarterly Review*, and the *New York Times Magazine*.

Critical reaction to Morrison's work has always been passionate—and on occasion bitterly divided. The aspects of her work that have generated the most

discussion are probably her tendency toward the melodramatic, overly sentimental theme and her use of rhythmic, rich language: the former engenders
much debate, the latter almost universal acclaim. The novel *Beloved* is a good
place to explore both.

Beloved is based loosely on the real story of a slave named Margaret Garner
who escaped to the North but, when recaptured, tried to kill one of her daughters rather than allow the girl to be brought up in slavery. The book's stark
presentation of the evils of enslavement—including graphic scenes of hanging,
human incineration, rape, and other degrading exercises in racism—shocked
and deeply moved most readers and critics. Margaret Atwood breathlessly hailed
the arrival of *Beloved* in the *New York Times Book Review* as "another triumph," for
Morrison:

> Indeed Ms. Morrison's versatility and technical and emotional range
> appear to know no bounds. If there were any doubts about her stature as a
> pre-eminent American novelist, of her own or any other generation, *Beloved*
> will put them to rest. In three words or less, it's a hair-raiser.

It also raised hackles. In terms of its portrayal of human suffering under slavery, some critics found the book reductive, excessively sentimental, and morally
simplistic. In a now-famous review panning the book, critic Stanley Crouch
assailed Morrison's "pulp style":

> *Beloved* explains black behavior in terms of social conditioning as if
> listing atrocities solves the mystery of human motive and behavior. It is
> designed to placate sentimental feminist ideology, and to make sure that the
> vision of black woman as the most scorned and rebuked of the victims
> doesn't weaken. . . . As in all protest pulp fiction, everything is locked into
> its own time, and is ever the result of external social forces. We learn little
> about the souls of human beings. We are only told what will happen if they
> are treated very badly. The world exists in a purple haze of overstatement, of
> false voices, of strained homilies; nothing very subtle is ever really tried.
> *Beloved* reads largely like a melodrama lashed to the structural conceits of the
> mini-series. [The novel, incidentally, was made into a movie starring Oprah
> Winfrey.]

The book caused quite a stir in international literary circles as well. After
Beloved failed to win either the 1987 National Book Award or the National Book
Critics Circle Award, forty-eight prominent black writers and literary critics
launched a salvo in support of Morrison. In protest of her being shut out of the
major awards, they signed a lengthy, adulatory statement that recorded "our
pride, our respect, and our appreciation for the treasury of your [Morrison's]
findings," and then they published the page-long declaration in the *New York
Times Book Review* in early 1988.

But some critics and writers who admired Morrison were put off by the gesture, which seemed to some to smack of coercion, an effort to portray Morrison as the victim of racial politics. Critic Jonathan Yardley stated at the time that "however much we may sympathize with their feelings and their desire for recognition, we must not let this blind us to the rather less attractive implications of their protest." Later that year, *Beloved* was awarded the Pulitzer Prize. The secretary of the Pulitzer Board, Robert Christopher, said "Obviously, the board was aware of the statement, but no, it didn't affect their decision."

Morrison's use of language in her novels,

PRESSING ITS CLAIM

Princeton University has not only been home to many of the nation's most important writers, such as Toni Morrison, but it also boasts another, albeit more obscure, literary distinction. The University is home to one of the first daily college newspapers: *The Daily Princetonian*.

The paper, which was first published every two weeks in 1876 and then weekly in the 1880s, became a daily paper on April 11, 1892—a decade before Woodrow Wilson would become the institution's president, but only a decade after that same Woodrow Wilson served as managing editor of the paper. In the course of its prestigious press run, the paper has printed articles and commentary by and about figures such as Albert Einstein, Bill Bradley, and Joyce Carol Oates. Staff writers at the paper have included Adlai Stevenson (class of 1922) and the *New York Times*'s R. W. Apple (class of 1957).

The very first issue of *The Princetonian* on June 14, 1876, appeared with little fanfare and even fewer inklings of the storied heritage it would spawn. A front-page story noted that the paper "shall, therefore, go quietly to work with no flash of rhetorical show, no genuflections nor airs, and no noise of horn-blowing. To the college-world, we give greeting. We are among you, and mean in all our dealings to carry fair."

however, has inspired much more of a critical consensus. Ann Snitow, writing in the *Village Voice Literary Supplement*, called Morrison's work "full of beautiful prose, dialogue as rhythmically satisfying as music." Atwood calls her writing "rich, graceful, eccentric, rough, lyrical, sinuous . . . and very much to the point." Indeed, a comprehensive critique of Morrison's writing style is difficult to deliver because of her multiplicity of narrative voices and shifts in diction, tone, and perspective. Just the first few pages of *Song of Solomon* offer a stunning array of prose styles. There is the richly descriptive:

Solid, rumbling, likely to erupt without prior notice, Macon kept each member of his family awkward with fear. His hatred of his wife glittered and sparkled in every word he spoke to her. The disappointment he felt in his daughters sifted down on them like ash, dulling their buttery complexions and choking the lilt out of what should have been girlish voices.

Then there is the colloquial:

I knew it. Soon's I get two dimes back to back, here you come. More regular than the reaper. Do Hoover know about you?

One finds the mock-journalistic:

The North Carolina Mutual Life Insurance agent promised to fly from Mercy to the other side of Lake Superior at three o'clock. Two days before the event was to take place, he tacked a note on the door of his little yellow house.

Morrison can be dryly humorous:

She did not try to make her meals nauseating; she simply did not know how not to.

She can also be epigrammatic:

But there was nothing you could do with a mooring except acknowledge it, use it for the verification of some idea you wanted to keep alive. Something else is needed to get from sunup to sundown: a balm, a gentle touch or nuzzling of some sort.

Morrison's work, with its themes of timelessness and triumph, provides just such a balm for her legion of fans.

FURTHER READING

Books by Morrison

The Nobel Acceptance Speech. New York: Knopf, 1994.
Paradise. New York: Knopf, 1998.
Playing in the Dark: Whiteness and Literary Imagination. Cambridge: Harvard University Press, 1992.

Books about Morrison

Gates, Henry Louis, Jr., and K. Anthony Appiah, eds. *Toni Morrison: Critical Perspectives Past and Present.* New York: Amistad, 1993.
Middleton, David, ed. *Toni Morrison's Fiction: Contemporary Criticism.* New York: Garland, 1997.
Peterson, Nancy J., ed. *Toni Morrison: Critical and Theoretical Approaches.* Baltimore: Johns Hopkins University Press, 1997.

Amiri Baraka (LeRoi Jones)

BORN October 7, 1934, in Newark

BEST KNOWN FOR Some would say his radical, even violent, writings, while others might say his social activism; also, a famous midlife name change.

THE JERSEY CONNECTION Grew up in Newark, attended Rutgers University, and helped found Newark's Black Community Development and Defense Organization. He was also named the official "Poet Laureate" of the state in 2002.

An important figure, Baraka's presence on the literary landscape is as hard to classify as it is to avoid. He's been involved in a number of major artistic movements during his highly productive—and provocative—career. Attempts to classify his oeuvre must take into account a multiplicity of styles, themes, genres, and political postures.

His early work came out of the Beat movement. He became, briefly, the unofficial "Father of the Black Arts" movement, moved through Islam, helped found the Pan-African Congress, and then became a committed Marxist—all the while creating avant-garde plays, essays, poems, and position papers for Leftist organizations and forging a whole new identity along the way.

Born LeRoi Jones (some literary anthologies still include him under his birth name, although he changed it in 1965), he grew up in Newark and studied at Rutgers and Howard universities. After serving in the U.S. Air Force, he moved to Greenwich Village in the late 1950s and joined a loosely allied group of writers, artists and musicians, through whom he initiated his immersion in the Beat movement. He married Hettie Cohen in 1958, and together they edited the avant-garde literary journals *Yugen* and *Floating Bear*. His social circle included writers such as Allen Ginsberg and Frank O'Hara. In 1960, he took a trip to Cuba (chronicled in his essay, "Cuba Libre"); this travel precipitated a movement away from Beat experimentation and toward Marxism and Black cultural nationalism.

Baraka's first big literary score, *Preface to a Twenty-Volume Suicide Note* (1961), established his reputation as a poet of keen insight, garnering critical kudos for its mix of bohemian desperation and infusion of Black culture and experience. At the same time, his plays began receiving attention for their unflinching presentation of race and sexuality. Dramatic works such as *Dante* (1961) and *Dutchman* (1964), which won the *Village Voice*'s Obie Award, cemented his place as artistic spokesman for the dispossessed. *Dutchman* is considered by some Baraka critics to be not only his best work but one of the best plays ever to come out of the African American theater. The play presents a highly stylized though stark and disturbing look at the oppressive, murderous white power structure (embodied by the character Lula). Norman Mailer called *Dutchman* the best play in America.

After the 1965 assassination of Malcom X and the breakup of his own marriage, Baraka left Greenwich Village, moved to Harlem, and established the Black Arts Repertory Theater. A year later, he maried Amina (Sylvia Robinson), moved to Newark, changed his name (Amiri Baraka comes from the phrase "Ameer Baraka," which means "blessed prince" in the Kawaida faith), and rededicated himself to the promotion of Black cultural nationalism through his fiction and essays. In Newark (where he continues to live—writing and editing, lecturing, reading, and serving as the hub of a nascent Black Arts community), he founded the Spirit House Players, a theater group that presented his works, such as *Arm Yourself or Harm Yourself* (1967) and *Home on the Range* (1968), originally staged as a benefit for the Black Panthers. During this period, he also wrote much criticism—social, literary, and musical, all aimed at elevating the level of awareness of Black artistry. For example, in an essay called "African Slaves/American Slaves—Their Music," he writes,

Poet Amiri Baraka (right) autographs a book
for fellow New Jersey poet Allen Ginsberg.
Courtesy of Star-Ledger Photographs. Copyright *The Star-Ledger*.
All rights reserved.

Jazz is commonly thought to have begun around the turn of the century, but the musics jazz derived from are much older. Blues is the parent of all legitimate jazz, and it is impossible to say exactly how old blues is—certainly no older than the presence of Negroes in the United States. It is a native American music, the product of the black man in this country; or to put it more exactly the way I have come to think about it, blues could not exist if the African captives had not become American captives.

Throughout the next three decades, he continued to write poems, plays, novels, criticism, and essays; edit anthologies and newspapers aimed at raising Black consciousness; and at the university level teach, lecture, and give readings.

Baraka is seen by some critics as a latter-day Walt Whitman, a full-throated spokesman for the culturally dispossessed. Others find his militant posture frequently overwhelming his artistic expression—more *provocateur* than *auteur*. His infamous reading at the 2002 Dodge Poetry Festival of a poem written about the September 11 tragedy—in which he alluded to the possibility that certain Jewish leaders had foreknowledge of the attack—caused a firestorm of controversy. Many of the state's political leaders, including Governor Jim McGreevy, called for Baraka to step down from his post of Poet Laureate of New Jersey. Perhaps not unexpectedly, Baraka refused to do so.

Whether he's comparing Newark's depressed neighborhoods to Dante's *Inferno* (it's pretty much a tie, according to *The System of Dante's Hell*, published in 1965) or calling for the formation of a separate Black Nation (in *Raise Race Rays Race*, 1971), Baraka deals candidly (some would say violently) with the status quo. Here's a small sampling across the decades:

> Nations are races. (In America, white people have become a nation, an identity, a race.) Political integration in America will not work because the Black Man is played on by special forces. His life, from his organs, i.e., the life of the body, what it needs, what it wants, to become, is different—and for this reason racial is biological, finally. We are a different species. A species that is evolving to world power and philosophical domination of the world. The world will move the way Black People move!
>
> —From *The Legacy of Malcolm X and the Coming of the Black Nation* (1966)

> The Afro-American nation is an oppressed nation, and its people, whether in the black-belt land base of that nation or as an oppressed nationality spread out around the rest of the nation-state, still face a revolutionary struggle. That nation is still oppressed by imperialism, and its liberation and self determination can only be gained through revolution.
>
> —From *Daggers and Javelins: Essays, 1974–1979*

Finally, I understood that to characterize my ideology as hate whitey is accurate since the only whitey is system and ideology, that whitey is a class and the devil what do d evil. Though, for sure "white" peepas (and what is that "white" when everybody's mama is black?) has been socialized to be hierarchical monsters.

—From "Preface," *The LeRoi Jones/Amiri Baraka Reader* (1991)

Despite these essay-excerpted pronouncements, Baraka is probably best known for his poetry. Like all his writing, his poems are intense, passionate, even fuming. But the artistry is unmistakable, derivative of the Beats and such modernist masters as Ezra Pound. Baraka's control of rhythm, his playful, complex syntactical schemes, and his unorthodox typography elevate his poetry on the page, and the stage. Those who have heard him read his poetry live report an incomparable aural experience, an incantory explosion, every line massaged into meaning by his intonation. For some readers, the biggest barrier to getting into his work may be simply getting past such militant-sounding titles as "BLACK DADA NIHILISMUS" and "Poem for HalfWhite College Student."

There's little critical consensus on the quality of Baraka's work, with critics sharply divided over his merit or importance. *The Cambridge Guide to American Literature* accords him a single paragraph, labeling him a "revolutionary" who "lashes out at whites." *The Encyclopedia of African-American Literature*, in four full pages, calls him "influential and prolific" and "a key facilitator in the maturation of a good number of innovative young artists."

A MANIFESTO

Amiri Baraka was a powerful spokesman for the Black Nationalism movement, a political revolution aimed in part at raising the consciousness and profile of African American artists. In the early 1960s, when the movement was being forged, Baraka and his fellow Black artists articulated their artistic goals:

1. An art that is recognizably Afro-American.
2. An art that is mass-oriented, that will come out of the libraries and stomp.
3. An art that is revolutionary, that will be with Malcolm X and Rob Williams, that will conk Klansmen and erase racists.

Baraka's life work has been aimed at promulgating these goals. In the preface for his *Baraka Reader* he wrote:

I joined and helped create organizations, political and cultural, to work at the social transformation I sought. I wrote poetry and essays and plays and stories towards this end as well. It was, and I am still certain of this, part of the same work.

There seems little doubt that his reputation as an innovator, cultural revolutionary, and consciousness-raiser in the Black community is secure. But the debate about his ultimate place in the pantheon of American literature shows few signs of being stifled. What he once said while eulogizing the writer James Baldwin may be no less true of Baraka himself:

> What he gave us, we perceived instantly and grew enormous inside because of it. That black warm truth. That invincible gesture of sacred human concern, clearly projected—we absorbed with what gives life in this world contrasted as it is against the dangerous powers of death.

In the final analysis, Baraka's work seems fated to remain largely on the margin of literary culture, essentially because from there Baraka has always fired his salvos. It's also where he seems most comfortable and inspired. Like Ezra Pound (a less and less unlikely artistic model the more one thinks about their similarities), Baraka may become one of those writers that everybody's heard of but few have ever actually read. His artistic maturity has done nothing to attenuate his rage, but the pool of readers interested in his stark and bitter portrayal of race in America may be limited: "The African American people roll the huge stone of slavery up off them through consistent struggle but also with continuous revolutionary outbursts. Then at another point the villains conspire to push it back down upon us." In the massive canon of his published works, he's remained true to the struggle. Hence, there's very little "light reading" from Baraka. He seems uninterested in either broadening his popular appeal or addressing topics that don't bear directly on race. Those who look to him as a sage on this country's most enduring problem would have it no other way.

FURTHER READING

Books by Baraka

The Autobiography of Leroi Jones/Amiri Baraka. Chicago: Lawrence Hill & Co., 1997.
Blues People: Negro Music in White America. New York: William Morrow & Co., 1983.
Four Black Revolutionary Plays. London: Marion Boyars, 1998.
Vangelisti, Paul, ed. *Transbluesency: The Selected Poems of Amiri Baraka*. New York: Marsilio Publishing, 1995.

Books about Baraka

Reilly, Charley, ed. *Conversations with Amiri Baraka*. Oxford: University Press of Mississippi, 1994.
Woodward, Komozi. *A Nation Within a Nation: Amiri Baraka and Black Power Politics*. Chapel Hill: University of North Carolina Press, 1999.

Joyce Carol Oates

BORN June 16, 1938, in Lockport, New York
BEST KNOWN FOR Probably her productivity. She's the author of more than thirty-five novels, countless essays and reviews, several collections of short stories—and she publishes the *Ontario Review* with her husband.
THE JERSEY CONNECTION She's lived in Princeton for the past twenty-five years, where she's a professor in the creative writing program.

Joyce Carol Oates inspires equal amounts of searching, deep-thinking critical commentary and simple, jaw-dropping awe. Efforts to characterize her body of work are usually hampered by the forebidding menu of possibilities. This includes her novels, which appear under both her own name and the pseudonym Rosamond Smith (a tribute to her husband, Raymond J. Smith); her short stories, which have been anthologized, dramatized, and bound in various collections; and her essays, from the acutely perceptive and literary to more pop-cultural productions for *TV Guide*. She's written several collections of poetry, and she's even worked as a television commentator for a sports network during a heavyweight prizefight. In between these disparate stints, she edits and publishes a highly respected literary review.

Hence, critics are as likely to spend as much time wondering *how* she does it all as looking closely at *what* she does. Even those critics who dismiss her from the first rank of American writers feel compelled to qualify their critiques with a salute to her industry (though the critic James Wolcott once berated Oates's prolific tendencies in a review entitled "Stop Me Before I Write Again: Six Hundred More Pages by Joyce Carol Oates"). In a 1999 essay, Oates said, "I can't recall a time when I wasn't writing." She traces this impulse to its very preliterate roots:

> Before I could write what might be called human words in the English language, I eagerly emulated grownups' handwriting in pencil scribbles. My first "novels"— which I'm afraid my loving parents still have in a trunk or a drawer on our old farm property in Millersport, New York—were tablets of inspired scribbles illustrated by line drawings of chickens, horses, and upright cats. For I had not yet mastered the trickier human form, as I was years from mastering human psychology.

The urge to chug along, to produce even if the tools were inadequate or the understanding imperfect, may help explain the diorama of subjects in Oates's literary fun house: Marilyn Monroe, boxing, suburban ennui, serial killers, sexual violence, the symbolism of *Moby-Dick*, and Ted Kennedy's plunge off the Chappaquiddick bridge have all been dissected in book-length studies. As an English major at Syracuse University, she reportedly wrote one novel *per* semester. Fellow novelist John Barth once remarked, "Joyce Carol Oates writes all over the aesthetical map."

For someone who engages in such a wide range of literary explorations, she often surprises with just how right she gets it. Her eye for the telling detail is unerring, expert. Anyone who has driven along Route 1 through Hudson County after nightfall can vouch for the veracity of the scene that unfolds before a shadowy figure, a photographer called Nighthawk, in Oates's latest book, *The Barrens*:

> Those hours of Nighthawk "sitting watch" as he came to call it along the Turnpike, in the parking lots of 24-hour gas stations and restaurants, outside bus stations, train depots. Close-ups of waitresses he'd gotten to know, who'd liked and trusted him. Truckers. The graveyard shift of the Hoboken bakery. . . . There were lots of cheap hotels along this strip. Budget Inn, Days End. One of those anonymous two-storey stucco places with VACANCY signs in bright neon.
>
> Years ago, Nighthawk had photographed motels like these and their patrons along Route 1 outside Jersey City. He'd photographed the rooms. And the women who came with the rooms. Hookers who'd been happy to pose for Nighthawk, as long as he paid them, and he'd always paid them generously.

In *The Barrens*, Oates (writing as Rosamond Smith), has arguably produced her most Jersey-centered work. Other well-known Jersey writers, such as John McPhee, have portrayed the naturalistic wonders of the Pine Barrens. But in Oates's latest—as in much of her best-known work—the pastoral world is a thin curtain hiding the sinister and the macabre. Oates always sees the cloud lurking behind the silver lining. Terror and inhumanity are the signposts in Oates's fictional landscape. The urge for revenge is as potent a part of nature as the renewal of the seasons. She seems to revel in the intertwined images of natural beauty and manmade destruction by weaving a tapestry of glory and gore. Consider this passage from the opening page of *The Barrens*:

> A coastal marsh near the south Jersey shore, at the edge of the Pine Barrens. Where the incoming tide lifts the body, buoys it up then surrenders it by degrees back to the marsh. To the dead girl. This slow rhythmic rising and ebbing, rising and ebbing of the tide. Like breathing a stinging north-east wind off the Atlantic, pushing through the cattails, seagrass . . . long tangled hair rippling like seaweed when the coastal water returns. The sun burns through the mist, the body is exposed. A dead body is a broken thing. Stumps of dead trees, dead vines. The naked, broken body is stirred by the incoming tide as if waking, returning to life. But scummy with coagulated blood.

Regular readers of Oates's fiction are used to seeing such squirm-inducing prose. Graphic scenes of violence—rape, murder, arson, suicide, or a lethal pummeling in a boxing ring—are commonplace. Critics find much irony in all of this unflinching horror coming form the pen of the genteel-seeming Princeton professor, a writer *Newsweek* once called "a tall, pale woman with enormous eyes and a timid, little-girl voice" and *Salon* magazine called "The Dark Lady of American letters."

Oates's career began in earnest after she won a fiction contest sponsored by *Mademoiselle* magazine while still an undergraduate at Syracuse. Two collections of short stories, *By the North Gate* (1963) and *Upon the Sweeping Flood* (1966), received positive reviews and helped build the buzz for a forthcoming slew of novels, including *Them* (1969), the National Book Award winner and the third in a trilogy of novels that began with *A Garden of Earthly Delights* (1967) and *Expensive People* (1968). This handful of works helped establish Oates as a writer who exposed the violence and ugliness lurking beneath the veneer of the American Dream. Often, her characters are forced to survive in brutalizing families or relationships.

Yet, she ranges so far beyond any single genre that labels such as "violent" or "dark" seem inadequate to convey the depth and complexity of her output. She has written piercing literary analyses of Herman Melville and D. H. Lawrence, mused on the country's fascination with Marilyn Monroe, and offered trenchant technical commentary on Mike Tyson's fighting style. All the while, she's maintained a distinguished academic career,

POUNDING THE PAVEMENT BEFORE POUNDING THE KEYS

Readers who marvel at Joyce Carol Oates's productivity—and who wouldn't find two to three novels a year, plus essays and reviews, an Ivy League professorship, and overseeing the operation of an active private press something to marvel at—might be surprised to discover her inspiration isn't mental. It's physical. "In running, the mind flies with the body; the mysterious efflorescence of language seems to pulse in the brain, in rhythm with our feet and the swinging of our arms. Ideally, the runner who's a writer is running through the land—and cityscapes—of her fiction, like a ghost in a real setting," she wrote in an essay explaining how she charges her creative battery.

Oates is in good company. Some of literature's greatest luminaries were also rather locomotive. Whitman, Keats, even Henry James all logged some serious miles each day. Henry David Thoreau reported spending at least four hours a day hiking around Walden Pond. As Oates says, in true Thoreau-like spirit, "I never saw a 'No Trespassing' sign that wasn't a summons to my rebellious blood. Such signs, dutifully posted on trees and fence railings, might as well say 'Come Right In!'"

first at the University of Windsor in Canada and for the past twenty years at Princeton University, where she was writer-in-residence and is now the Roger S. Berkind Distinguished Professor of Humanities. She continues to turn out two to three books per year, but it would be wrong to characterize her work as hastily produced. Oates is a careful craftsperson, a writer with technical mastery over her material, capable of producing passages of searing beauty. Even while she's putting new words on the page, she is obsessively editing her previous output. As she once explained in an article discussing her approach to writing,

> My method is one of continuous revision. While writing a long novel, every day I loop back to earlier sections to rewrite, in order to maintain a consistent, fluid voice. When I write the final two or three chapters of a novel, I write them simultaneously with the rewriting of the opening, so that, ideally at least, the novel is like a river uniformly flowing, each passage concurrent with the others.

And since that flow shows no signs of abating, there will be much more work to enjoy, marvel over, argue about, and plunge into from New Jersey's resident expert in (according to the *Oxford Companion to American Literature*) "dwellers in a dark and destructive society."

FURTHER READING

Books by Oates

Bellefleur. New York: Dutton, 1980.
Upon the Sweeping Flood and Other Stories. New York: Fawcett Crest, 1966.
We Were the Mulvaneys. New York: Penguin USA, 1996.

Books about Oates

Bloom Harold, ed. *Joyce Carol Oates: Modern Critical Views*. Broomall, Pa.: Chelsea House Publishers, 1987.
Johnson, Greg. *Invisible Writer: A Biography of Joyce Carol Oates*. New York: Plume, 1999.
Wesley, Marilyn C. *Refusual and Transgression in Joyce Carol Oates' Fiction*. Westport, Conn.: Greenwood Publishing Group, 1993.

Peter Benchley

BORN May 8, 1940, in New York
BEST KNOWN FOR His novel (and worldwide phenomenon) *Jaws*.
THE JERSEY CONNECTION Longtime resident of Princeton.

Among all the noted writers who have called New Jersey home, the biggest mouth belongs to Peter Benchley:

The fish thrust again, and Hooper saw with the terror of doom that the mouth was going to reach him. The jaws closed around his torso. Hooper felt a terrible pressure, as if his guts were being compacted. He jabbed his fist into the black eye. The fish bit down, and the last thing that Hooper saw before he died was the eye gazing at him through a cloud of his own blood.

"He's got him!" called Brody. "Do something!"

"The man is dead," Quint said.

"How do you know? We may be able to save him."

"He is dead."

Holding Hooper in its mouth, the fish backed out of the cage. It sank a few feet, chewing, swallowing the viscera that were squeezed in its gullet.

It's impossible to read that excerpt without thinking of the movie that put Benchley's *Jaws* in the minds of the American public. It's perhaps no slight at Benchley's literary abilities to say most beach-goers would have been blissfully unaware of the menace lurking just offshore if it hadn't been for the movie, Stephen Spielberg's inaugural big-screen masterpiece. Would *Jaws*—Benchley's first novel—have made waves without a major motion picture? Unlikely, given the reviews of the book, which mostly ranged from merely respectful to excoriating. Here's how the *Village Voice* assessed the nation's newest literary sensation:

> *Jaws* is awful.
>
> *Jaws* has rubber teeth for a plot.
>
> *Jaws* is stunningly bad, a . . . fish opera featuring cardboard people and an overblown shark. *Jaws* is a failure in almost every way possible for a novel to fail. It's boring, pointless, listless, bewitched by banality; if there's a trite turn to make, "*Jaws*" will make that turn. It seeks new reaches of tedium. It packs more padding than a pound box of surgical cotton. It is weary, vacant, and tasteless.

Though some other reviewers found *Jaws* a compelling page-turner, Benchley's literary stock has never traded at a premium. The former Harvard English major has, however, carved out a niche as contemporary fiction's most celebrated ichthyologist. His body of work, though including serious dramatic fiction, journalism, and nature writing, is distinguished largely by his novels of undersea adventure, starting with *Jaws* and continuing through his most recent work, *Shark Trouble: True Stories about Sharks and the Sea* (2002).

Writing fish stories was not really an unexpected endeavor for this Ivy Leaguer. He came by his nautical knowledge through many summers spent in Nantucket as a youth, and he came by his literary disposition through inheritance as grandson of the celebrated humorist Robert Benchley and son of the successful novelist Nathaniel Benchley.

Peter Benchley's first foray into writing had nothing to do with the sea, but it did hint at some of his future favorite themes: travel in an unfamiliar landscape, the clash of cultures, and the emotional fallout when one's identity is challenged—also, how a landscape shapes the creatures who live there. The book was a travelogue of sorts, part gazetteer, part memoir, based on his own postcollegiate wanderings. Titled *Time and a Ticket*, it was published in 1964 to brief, polite reviews. Turning his writer's eye on alien cultures has given Benchley a career's worth of material, but his interest in life beneath the sea has morphed from a useful motif to an urgent calling, as he once explained in an online interview sponsored by *Time*:

> As far back as *Jaws*, which was my first novel, the voice of Hooper the scientist was my voice urging the populace not to embark on some vendetta against an animal that was just doing what nature programmed it to do. If there's an underlying theme in the books I've written about marine creatures, it's that man has a responsibility to co-exist with his environment, not to try to dominate it.
>
> If man doesn't learn to treat the oceans and rain forest with respect, man will become extinct. I don't know about you, but I don't feel like being extinct.

There is an undeniable reverence for the sea in many of Benchley's works, an attempt to see beneath the surface of not only the ocean but also reality, to dissect what's really going on in the deepest levels of the animal kingdom. When

---

REALITY BITES

Think shark attacks along the shore are just the stuff of fiction? One of the influences on Peter Benchley's *Jaws* was the series of real shark attacks just off the Jersey Shore in July 1916. In a period of less than two weeks, four swimmers were fatally attacked, and a fifth was seriously hurt, a series that prompted breathless headlines in newspapers from Beach Haven to Matawan. New York City newspapers played up the attacks, with the *New York Evening Mail* of July 13 announcing "Hundreds Seek to Slay Shark; Think Monster Trapped in Creek." Though dozens of sharks were in fact caught, no definitive resolution of the mass maulings was ever achieved. Experts remain divided on whether it was a rogue shark, a school of predators, a coincidence, or, it has even been suggested, a possible German terrorist plot to unleash man-eating sharks in waters along America's resorts. Two recently published books explore these attacks: *Twelve Days of Terror: A Definitive Investigation of the 1916 New Jersey Shark Attacks* by Richard Fernincola (Lyons Press, 2001), and *Close to Shore: The Terrifying Shark Attacks of 1916* by Michael Capuzzo (Broadway Books, 2001). Fernincola notes in his study, "In reality, many or most of the elements which gave *Jaws* its punch have a correlate in a real-life horror that unfolded eighty-five years ago."

Benchley is at his best, the creatures who squirm and slither and slash through the darkest regions of life assume a dignity all their own. Benchley's great contribution to the horror/suspense genre is his veneration of beings generally considered monstrous. His sharks, his squids, his menacing undersea legions act not so much out of malignancy but out of indignation. *Their* world has been invaded by humanity, and they react in ways that are, upon reflection, wholly logical. *They* are creatures of eternal night—what else should day fishers expect? In *White Shark*, for instance, the reader gets a tour of the environs that breed these subterranean beasts. One emerges with some understanding of these inhuman creatures' erratic behavior:

> Absolute darkness is rare on earth. Even on a moonless night, with clouds hiding the stars, the loom of civilization glows against the sky.
> In the deep oceans, absolute darkness is commonplace. Rays of the sun, thought for millennia to be the sole source of life on earth, can penetrate less than half a mile of seawater. Nearly three quarters of the planet—vast plains, great canyons, mountain ranges that rival the Himalayas—are shrouded in perpetual black, broken occasionally by bioluminescent organisms that sparkle with predatory or reproductive intent.

But not just the marine world engages Benchley's scientific gaze. In his novel *"Q" Clearance*, a story about White House intrigue, Benchley employs his focus on naturalistic detail to reveal the habits (predatory and otherwise) of the human kingdom. Here, for example, a speechwriter works on a presidential address:

> Burnham loved the E.O.B. He had an enormous office, twenty by thirty feet, on a ground-floor corner of the building, with a pleasant view of the South Lawn and the Ellipse. The windows were tall and the ceilings were high, and there were easy chairs and a great conference table (for gin rummy) and a massive oak desk and a typing table and a word processor that he hated and an electric typewriter that he loved and a phone console with sixteen buttons and three television sets (one of his early assignments had been to monitor the evening news on all three networks and to analyze each for anti-Administration bias) and a huge leather couch which came in very handy when the quest for *le mot just* became exhausting.

That's Benchley's method: a catalog of physical objects and a suggestive link between environment and behavior. Sharks devour because they are eating machines; writers recline because the muse is coy. Benchley becomes the learned tour guide to the world he creates. This tendency has sometimes led to pages that buckle under the weight of research. His readers emerge from his books informed, if not always enthralled. As the *New York Times* noted in its review of *The Deep*, Benchley's follow-up to *Jaws,* "Many readers will feel improved by the constant flow of sheer information the book contains on such pertinent topics as the history, sociology, and climate of Bermuda, the flora and fauna of the sea, skin diving, treasure hunting, and underwater salvage."

One critical knock on Benchley is that he's become redundant by seeking new and clever ways to simply recast his success with *Jaws*. If that is the case, one can hardly blame him for trading on one of the most successful novels published in the last thirty years. Although it's true that he's taken a stab at other genres—and even other media (he hosted the syndicated television show *Peter Benchley's Amazon* and contributed a regular feature called "The Ocean Report" on public radio)—he'll likely never swim out of the shadow of his great white shark. His more serious work, such as a visiting professorship at Princeton and his authorship of a number of impressive pieces for *National Geographic*, may never adequately compensate, in some critics' minds, for the pure schlock appeal of his beast-driven narratives. Benchley would perhaps protest the judgment that his novels don't reveal human truths, but, as a reviewer for *Rolling Stone* once noted about *Jaws,* "None of the humans are particularly likeable or interesting; the shark was easily my favorite character—and, one suspects, Benchley's also."

And certainly his best remembered. Although critics have received Benchley's subsequent novels with occasional praise, *Jaws* is the book that keeps his reputation afloat. It remains, ironically, one of the greatest beach-reading books of all time, a chilling modern-day *Moby-Dick*, starring the great fish itself, its primal nature coldly captured in the book's classic opening paragraph:

> The great fish moved silently through the night water, propelled by short sweeps of its crescent tail. The mouth was open just enough to permit a rush of water over the gills. There was little other motion: an occasional correction of the apparently aimless course by the slight raising or lowering of a pectoral fin—as a bird changes direction by dipping one wing and lifting the other. The eyes were sightless in the black, and the other senses transmitted nothing extraordinary to the small, primitive brain. The fish might have been asleep, save for the movement dictated by the countless millions of years of instinctive continuity.

FURTHER READING

Books by Benchley

Beast. New York: Random House, 1991.

Girl of the Sea of Cortez. New York: Doubleday, 1982.

Ocean Planet: Writings and Images of the Sea (essays by Benchley et al.). New York: Harry N. Abrams, 1995.

Books about Benchley

Gottlieb, Carl. *The Jaws Log: Twenty-fifth Anniversary Edition*. New York: Newmarket Press: 2001.

Anna Quindlen

BORN July 8, 1953, in Philadelphia
BEST KNOWN FOR Her *New York Times* columns and a midcareer shift from journalist to novelist.
THE JERSEY CONNECTION Resident of Hoboken for many years.

Many interesting dichotomies can be explored to help one understand the life and work of Anna Quindlen.

First, there is the public/private split, which provided the title of her *New York Times* column, for which she won a Pulitzer in 1992. Publicly, she has weighed in on most "hot button" divisive social issues of our time. Yet her opinions are always filtered through her own feminist, Roman Catholic, working-mother sensibility. She has likened writing the column to "standing in the spotlight naked." She may be the most private writer working publicly today.

Then there is the fiction/nonfiction divide. Is she a journalist who writes novels or, at heart, a novelist who practiced journalism because it allowed her to find her voice? Was her departure from the *Times* an abandonment of her loyal readers or the starting point of a great novelist's career?

There are other intriguing dichotomies in the biography of Hoboken's Anna Quindlen, but many singularities are worth noting: a profound belief in the importance of literature; an unapologetic embrace of home and hearth; and a commitment to be honest in her writing, to honor her reader with the candor due a close friend. As she noted after receiving the Pulitzer Prize, "I think of a column as having a conversation with a person that it just so happens I can't see. . . . It's nice to know that my end of the conversation was heard."

Her frankness, her direct appeal to the reader as secret ally, allowed Quindlen to carve out a devoted readership when she was sandwiched among the rather staid political analysts of the *Times* Op/Ed page. Her whisper-in-your-ear style has informed her fiction as well—stories marked by not only a heartfelt urgency, but also her characters' despair, sacrifice, and brutal honesty in the face of tragedy. Here's a typical example from her novel *Black and Blue*, in which Fran Benedetto considered her position as an abused spouse:

> On the outside, I looked fine. The job, the house, the kid, the husband, the smile. Nobody got to see the hitting, which was really the humiliation, which turned into the hatred. Not just hating Bobby but hating myself, too. I stayed because I thought things would get better, or at least not worse. I stayed because I wanted my son to have a father and I wanted a home. For a long time I stayed because I loved Bobby Benedetto, because no one had ever gotten to me the way he did. I think he knew that. He made me his accomplice in what he did.

Such turbulent and distressing situations in her fiction offer another dichotomy to chew over: how can someone as successful, famous, critically praised, and commercially viable (and, one suspects, genuinely happy) as Quindlen write such somber and depressing novels? In his review of *One True Thing*, the story of a mother dying while her daughter cares for her in her last days, Frederick Busch noted: "Ms. Quindlen knows how to batter our hearts."

ELYSIAN FIELD OF DREAMS

Although fans of Anna Quindlen might think of Hoboken as former home to their favorite scribe, knowledgeable sports fans know Hoboken to be the home of the first recorded modern game of baseball.

Abner Doubleday was once accorded the honor of being the "father of American baseball," and his hometown of Cooperstown, New York, was once thought to be the site where baseball's rules were established; but sports historians have dismissed this legend as fanciful and almost certainly untrue. Anyone who remains unconvinced of baseball's abiding debt to Hoboken need look no further than *The Jersey Game: The History of Modern Baseball from its Birth to the Big Leagues in the Garden State* (1991, Rutgers University Press). Authors James DiClerico and Barney Pavelec, both lifelong baseball fans and residents of New Jersey, solve the mystery of just where the American pastime was born. "What is known," they state in their first chapter, "is that at 2:00 p.m. on Tuesday,

Hoboken's two most enduring contributions to popular culture.
Copyright 2002 Reena Rose Sibayan.

October 21, 1845, the first match game of modern baseball began on Elysian Fields in Hoboken, New Jersey, fully eight months before the game between New York and the Knickerbockers that has until today erroneously borne that monumental designation."

A small monument marks the spot today where the game was played, and a sign welcoming drivers to Hoboken trumpets the city's *two* most famous contributions to pop culture. It reads: "Welcome to Hoboken—Birth Place of Baseball and Frank Sinatra."

She began her career as a reporter at the *New York Post* in 1974 after graduating from Barnard College. In 1977, she became a general assignment and city hall reporter for the *New York Times*, and from 1981 to 1983 she wrote a bi-weekly column, "About New York." After a couple of years as deputy metropolitan editor Quindlen began writing a syndicated weekly column called "Life in the 30s," which really launched her career as a commentator. In 1990, she moved to the Op/Ed page with her column "Public & Private." Her columns have been collected in the books *Living Out Loud* (1988) and *Thinking Out Loud* (1994). Her novels include *Object Lessons* (1991), *One True Thing* (1994), *Black and Blue* (1998), and *Blessings* (2002). She wrote the children's books *The Tree That Came To Stay* (1992) and *Happily Ever After* (1997). Quindlen has published book-length essays espousing both her personal philosophy and the joy of reading and commentary to accompany the photo collections *Naked Babies* (1996) and *Siblings* (1998).

Though she traipses through genres with disarming ease, critics have identified a consistent Quindlen style—clear, elegant in its simplicity, epigrammatic. Her reporter's eye is always roving for the overlooked detail. Quindlen's fans have come to expect her writer's gaze to fall upon the "little things." As the reviewer/critic Sybil Steinberg once noted, Quindlen "has a gift for turning the quotidian into the existential, the mundane into the meaningful."

Her essays in *Naked Babies*, a book that celebrates "the beauty of the human form and character in its most nascent and perfect state," provide perhaps the clearest distillation of her vision. Though it lacks the heft of opinion-shaping prose, its buoyancy and gently observed truths make this meditation on human beginnings a real smile-inducer:

> That is how babies come to look, at their ripest, somewhere between four and nine months, like balloons full to the brim with promise. It is why most people seem drawn to them like ants to a pool of spilled syrup, because of an unconscious feeling that they can bask for a moment in what we love and know we will lose: pure, unadulterated life. And maybe even something before, or after. I remember my amazement when I first took our eight-month-old daughter into the pool and watched her drop like a submarine beneath the surface, her lips pursed, her eyes open, two black stones and a circle of rose quartz beneath the glistening sheen of blue. She surfaced and went down again, surfaced and went down, and I saw in her sure movements a kind of prememory of a life lived underwater, her lungs useless, her hair waving wet around her melon head. I wished that I could crawl inside her to know what she was thinking and feeling as she went up and down, up and down, as she struggled and screamed when she was taken from the clear water, dried, diapered, clothed, forced back to land, to earth.

Such engagement in the quest to know, to understand a thing, a person, or the genesis of an idea makes Quindlen the columnist such a rewarding read. She eschews abstract rationalizations or utopic theories. She's lived in the real world and reports on both its wonders and its perils. In a column reprinted in *Living Out Loud* on the topic of childhood fears of monsters under the bed, she wrote:

> That's why I can't deny the monster, tell him that nothing is under the bed.
>
> Because I believe in monsters, and someday my kid will believe in them even more surely than he does now. My mother lied. When you grow up, you realize that there isn't really any Santa but the monsters are still around. If only they were big and hairy; now, they're just dark and amorphous, and they're no longer afraid of the light.

So then, a final Quindlen dichotomy: a clear-eyed realist who believes in monsters, an ambassador of childlike wonder issuing bulletins in the adult world.

FURTHER READING

Books by Quindlen

Blessings. New York: Random House, 2002.
How Reading Changed My Life. New York: Ballantine, 1998.
A Short Guide to a Happy Life. New York: Random House, 2000.

Part Two   The Books

Cheaper by the Dozen (1949)

Of all the New Jersey–based books that have won a wide audience, *Cheaper by the Dozen* is perhaps the most difficult to classify. The publisher calls it a "biography"—defensible, yet there is really little traditional biographical information within its pages. No effort is made to provide specific information about the many odd events, the dozens of characters or places that flit through the book, appear briefly, and then disappear. Many bookstores stock it in their children's section. Although the book exudes a childlike charm—and is, in fact, a story about growing up—its poignancy requires an adult perspective. It is considered by critics to be a novel, although it can sometimes be found on library shelves among collections of short stories. It could also be considered a scientific book (its principal subject was the originator of motion study) or even science fiction, with its early predictions of such future developments as ergonomics and same-day surgery. Finally, and perhaps most appropriately, it could be thought of as a "how to" book for anyone daring enough to attempt to raise twelve children. Should one choose to do so, he or she will find the Frank Gilbreth method of child rearing helpful, if perhaps overly systematized:

> Our house at Montclair, New Jersey, was a sort of school for scientific management and the elimination of wasted motion—or "motion study," as Dad and Mother named it.
>
> Dad took moving pictures of us children washing dishes so that he could figure out how we could reduce our motions and thus hurry through the task. Irregular jobs, such as painting the back porch or removing a stump from the front lawn, were awarded on a low-bid basis. Each child who wanted extra pocket money submitted a sealed bid saying what he would do the job for. The lowest bidder got the contract.
>
> Dad installed process and work charts in the bathrooms. Every child old enough to write—and Dad expected his offspring to start writing at a tender age—was required to initial the charts in the morning after he had brushed his teeth, taken a bath, combed his hair, and made his bed. At night, each child had to weigh himself, plot the figure on a graph, and initial the process charts again after he had done his homework, washed his

hands and face, and brushed his teeth. Mother wanted to have a place on the charts for saying prayers, but Dad said as far as he was concerned prayers were voluntary.

That early passage in the book sets the stage for the next two hundred pages and contains most of the ingredients that give the book its delightful flavor: a stern but loving father, efficient to the point of absurd; a willing but often confused household of kids from infant to eighteen, who see their father's stratagems as games to be played rather than procedures to be followed; a mother who serves as buffer between the two camps, blessed with an intuition that maintains the household's equilibrium; and an infusion of zeal into the performance of even the most mundane tasks. The book's focus on Depression-era household thrift and its embrace of the concept of large families also make the book something of a historical artifact. Even in 1949, the year it was published, reviewers were citing the book as a marker of a fading era. The *Saturday Review of Literature* noted, "The big family is on the way out, if it isn't already—a fact which makes *Cheaper by the Dozen*, among other things, the case history of an anachronism. Which, of course, is no fault of the brother-sister authors."

The brother-sister authors are Frank Gilbreth, Jr., and Ernestine Gilbreth Carey. In collaboration through the mail, they reflected on their childhood from

Montclair's Frank Gilbreth with some of his famous "dozen" children.
Courtesy of the Newark Public Library.

the time the family moved from Providence, Rhode Island, to Montclair in 1915 until their father's death in 1924. (The subsequent story of how the family coped after his death is told in the sequel *Belles on Their Toes,* written by the same authors and published a year later.) Both *Cheaper* and *Belles* were turned into popular movies and both books remain in print today. The secret of the books' success lies in the authors' warmed-over reminiscences and heart-tugging vignettes that present their father as both tyrant and teddy bear and—especially in *Belles*—celebrate their mother's steely determination through a boundless capacity to love and comfort. The prose style is perfectly pitched to convey the scenes of controlled chaos in the Gilbreth household: slightly detached, just a touch ironic, playful, yet charged with genuine sentiment. The authors can churn out memorable phrases: "Dad had enough gall to be divided into three parts, and the ability and poise to backstop the front he placed before the world." And they can address the reader with disarming clarity and directness when defending their father's systems: "It was regimentation, all right. But bear in mind the trouble most parents have in getting just one child off to school, and multiply by twelve."

That "regimentation" came to be known far beyond the confines of the family's Montclair home, an imposing Victorian abutting fruit trees and garden paths at 68 Eagle Rock Way. Gilbreth's fame as an innovating engineer was firmly established long before his children trumpeted his organizational fixations. Both he and his wife, Lillian Moller Gilbreth, were pioneers in the

---

FOOD FOR THOUGHT

Lillian Gilbreth's expertise in efficiency not only helped her sustain her bustling household after her husband Frank's death in 1924, but it also helped a nation.

Lillian, serving on the President's Emergency Committee during the Depression as an expert, instructed household managers to stretch their food dollars. She regularly issued advice to Depression-strapped families on how to shop with maximum efficiency. In an article distributed nationally—and reprinted in the January 21, 1931, *Montclair Times*—she prescribed a weekly food budget of $15.50 for a family of seven (though she conceded this cost may vary somewhat in different localities). Here are some items from that frugal food basket:

—Flour and Cereal (1½ pounds bread equals 1 pound cereal), 25–30 pounds; cost in terms of bread at $0.84 a pound, $3.78.

—Whole fresh milk, 30 to 40 quarts, or canned unsweetened milk, 15 to 20 tall cans, at $0.15 a quart, $5.20.

—Fats, such as lard, salt pork, bacon, margarine, butter, etc., four pounds, $0.84.

—Sugar and Molasses, five to seven pounds, $0.35.

field of motion study, a discipline aimed at decreasing wasted motion among assembly workers and increasing productivity and time savings. Lillie and Frank spent most of the two decades after they married in 1904 engaged in further refinement of the "Gilbreth System" by using their children as guinea pigs and taking their findings onto the floors of manufacturing plants throughout the world. Frank pioneered the use of cinematographic motion study, which involved taking movies of workers performing various duties and subjecting each movement to chronometer analysis. After filming dozens of people doing the same job, Gilbreth could thus determine within one one-thousandth of a second if an act contained any wasted motion. One of the most amusing scenes in the book involves Frank's determination to apply his techniques to surgery; he convinces his family doctor to remove all of his children's tonsils at their home, on the same day, while being filmed throughout each operation:

> He explained [to Lillie] that he needed to take moving pictures of five or six operations, all of the same type, so that he could sort out the good motions from the wasted motions. The trouble was that most patients refused to be photographed, and hospitals were afraid of lawsuits.
>
> "Never mind, dear," Mother told him. "I'm sure the opportunity will come along eventually for you to get all the pictures that you want."
>
> Dad said that he didn't like to wait; that when he started a project, he hated to put it aside and pick it up again piecemeal whenever he found a patient, hospital, and doctor who didn't object to photographs. Then an idea hit him, and he snapped his fingers.
>
> "I know," he said. "I've got it. Dr. Burton has been after me to have the kids' tonsils out. He says they really have to come out. We'll rig up an operating room in the laboratory here, and take pictures of Burton."

Lillie reluctantly agrees, as does Dr. Burton. The day arrives, and all goes as planned. The children are etherized, one by one, and on cue from Mr. Coggin, the beleaguered photographer hired by Frank to shoot his motion studies, Dr. Burton begins. The tonsils are removed, the children recover, but the father comes down with a postoperative infection after his tonsillectomy, and he takes to his bed. Finally, after two weeks, his voice comes back—a discovery made by the family as the father reads his morning mail:

> There was a card from Mr. Coggin, the photographer.
>
> "Hate to tell you, Mr. Gilbreth, but none of the moving pictures came out. I forgot to take off the inside lens cap. I'm terribly sorry. Coggin. P.S. I quit."
>
> Dad threw off the covers and reached for his bathrobe. For the first time in two weeks, he spoke:
>
> "I'll track him down to the ends of the earth," he croaked. "I'll take a blunt buttonhook and pull his tonsils out by the jingoed roots, just like I promised him. He doesn't quit. He's fired."

Cheaper by the Dozen isn't literature with a capital "L." It's sweet rather than sublime. Tales such as the one above fill each of its nineteen chapters. But most readers, surely responding to the simple charm of the book, are won over finally by the affectionate portrait of a man who, although he took his work ultra-seriously, seems not to have taken himself too seriously. Humanizing glimpses of the over-orderly father abound. For example, in one scene Frank, with exaggerated patriarchal bearing, summoned all the children to "fall out" in fire-drill style of rapid decampment in the living room. As they stood there, expecting to be scolded for their sloth, he told them to put their hands out for a nail trim inspection. As he walked up and down the line, he surprised them by placing in their hands a trinket from some toy factory he had just visited. The father was always doing something to engage the children: whether pitting them against each other in spelling contests or piling the whole clan into the family Pierce Arrow for a Sunday drive through Essex County. The mother is bathed in a similarly affectionate light, but she remains mostly offstage, a mediating influence against her husband's eccentric schemes. As a Ph.D. and eventually a professor on the engineering faculty of several universities, Lillie became every bit as distinguished as her husband; *Belles on Their Toes* is her book, and *Cheaper by the Dozen* is his.

Frank and Ernestine Gilbreth once wrote that "we children used to suspect, though, that one reason he had wanted a large family was to assure himself of an appreciative audience." In *Cheaper by the Dozen*, their father's wish has been granted.

FURTHER READING

Books by the Gilbreths

Gilbreth, Frank. *Applied Motion Study.* Reprint. Easton, Pa.: Hive Publishing, 1989.
Gilbreth, Lillian. *The Quest of the One Best Way.* Easton, Pa.: Hive Publishing, 1973.

Books about the Gilbreths

Gilbreth, Frank, Jr. *Time Out for Happiness.* New York: Ty Crowell Co., 1971.

Goodbye, Columbus (1959)

Many readers have found things to praise, criticize, or debate in Philip Roth's first big literary splash, *Goodbye, Columbus*. This modern-day coming-of-age story critiques postwar culture and quests for religious identity, but if read a certain way, the book is really a love letter to Newark:

Down Washington Street, behind me, was the Newark Museum—I could see it without looking; two oriental vases in front like spittoons for a rajah, and next to it the little annex to which we had traveled on special buses as schoolchildren. The annex was a brick building, old and vine covered, and always reminded me of New Jersey's link with the beginning of the country, with George Washington, who had trained his scrappy army . . . in the very park where I now sat. At the far end of the park, beyond the Museum, was the bank building where I had gone to college. It had been converted some years before into an extension of Rutgers University. . . . And then I looked out to Broad Street again. Jammed between a grimy-windowed bookstore and a cheesy luncheonette was the marquee of a tiny art theater—how many years had passed since I stood beneath that marquee, lying about the year of my birth so as to see Hedy Lamarr swim naked in *Ecstasy*; and then, having slipped the ticket taker an extra quarter, what disappointment I had felt at the frugality of her Slavic charm. Sitting there in the park, I felt a deep knowledge of Newark, an attachment so rooted that it could not help but branch out into affection.

The Newark Public Library, when *Goodbye, Columbus* was written.
From the Collections of the New Jersey Historical Society.

The plot of *Goodbye, Columbus* isn't complex, though a broad-brush outline of the action doesn't really convey the degree to which the book is steeped in the dichotomies of New Jersey. The story commutes back and forth between the rarified suburb of Short Hills and the gritty, gruff cityscape of Newark. Neil Klugman, the protagonist and narrator of the book, both despises and aspires to life in the loftier verdant hills of west-of-Newark:

> Once I'd driven out of Newark, past Irvington and the packed-in tangle of railroad crossings, switchmen's shacks, lumberyards, Dairy Queens, and used-car lots, the night grew cooler. It was, in fact, as though the hundred and eighty feet that the suburbs rose in altitude above Newark brought one closer to heaven, for the sun itself became bigger, lower and rounder, and soon I was driving past long lawns which seemed to be twirling water on themselves, and past houses where no one sat on stoops, where lights were on but no windows open, for those inside, refusing to share the very texture of life with those of us outside. . . .

Roth, who lived in Newark for decades, exploded onto the literary scene with *Goodbye, Columbus*, which was published as a novella bundled with five short stories. The reviewers hailed the arrival of a new and important literary voice. No less a writer/critic than Saul Bellow celebrated this fictional annunciation in the July 1959 issue of *Commentary*:

> *Goodbye, Columbus* is a first book, but it is not the book of a beginner. Unlike those of us who come howling into the world, blind and bare, Mr. Roth appears with nails, hair, and teeth, speaking coherently. At twenty-six, he is skillful, witty, energetic, and performs like a virtuoso.

Goodbye, Columbus was the first shot in a decades-long barrage of top-tier fiction. The book won the 1960 National Book Award. (One of the book's short stories, "Defender of the Faith," won second prize in the O. Henry Story Contest of 1960.) His work has continued to garner critical kudos. Perhaps his best-known book is the stream-of-consciousness masterpiece, *Portnoy's Complaint* (1969), a work that has been called pornographic, tragic, farcical, and transcendent. He won the National Book Critics Circle Award in 1987 for *Counterlife*, and again in 1992 for *Patrimony*. *Operation Shylock* was named "Best American Novel" by *Time* magazine in 1993. He won the National Book Award again in 1995 for *Sabbath's Theater*. In *American Pastoral* (1998), Roth's fictional alter ego Nathan Zuckerman attends his high school reunion in Newark; Roth attended Newark's Weequalic High School. Roth remains a prolific influence on the literary landscape.

Attempts to link all of Roth's work usually fail, but some themes do emerge from his overall corpus: the struggle to maintain an individual identity in an increasingly ego-shattering world; the tension between the desire for success and the desire to assist one's fellow human beings; the falseness and hypocrisy of much of American religious life; and the inescapable vulgarity and grossness of much of human life.

He hints at many of those themes in *Goodbye, Columbus*, which also began Roth's career-long penchant for unresolved or unhappy endings. The book is often discussed in terms of its presentation of American Jewishness, but readers of *Goodbye, Columbus* should take a look at an op-ed piece Roth wrote for the

> ### IMPRESSIONISM OR REALISM?
>
> A recurring plot point in *Goodbye, Columbus* involves a young, inner-city boy's fascination with a book of Gauguin's exotic paintings, which is on the shelf in the Newark Public Library. Neil Klugman, the protagonist who works at the library, arranges for the book to always be available to the boy by hiding it from other patrons. One persistent, elderly customer continues angrily demanding the book each day, but Neil keeps telling him it's been checked out.
>
> Perhaps in 1959, when *Goodbye, Columbus* was written, only one book of Gauguin's paintings was available to patrons of the library, but the situation has changed. A recent review of the current online catalog of the Newark Public Library revealed more than sixty books that contain works by Gauguin.

New York Times in 1969. Although a decade removed from Neil Klugman's awakening, it clarifies important aspects of the work. For example, some readers have found Neil's attachment to the Newark Public Library as representative of the flaws impeding his growth. Like the library, Neil, they argue, is cloistered, bookish, overly orderly, withdrawn from the real world, even archaic. But others take Roth's library-centered narrative as an encomium to the pacific world of books and the joy and the liberation books provide. Roth wrote the 1969 essay, affirming that view, to generate support for the library in the face of proposed government cutbacks in funding; he celebrates the good things that come from the communal enterprise of public libraries:

> When I was growing up in Newark in the forties, we assumed that the books in the public library belonged to the public. Since my family did not own many books, or have the money for a child to buy them, it was good to know that solely by virtue of my municipal citizenship I had access to any book I wanted from that grandly austere building downtown on Washington Street, or from the branch library I could walk to in my neighborhood. No less satisfying was the idea of a communal ownership, property held in common for the common good. Why I had to care for the books I borrowed, return them unscarred and on time, was because they weren't mine alone, they were everybody's. That idea has as much to do with civilizing me as any I was ever to come upon in the books themselves.

If the idea of a *public* library was civilizing, so was the place, with its comforting quiet, its tidy shelves, its knowledgeable, dutiful employees who weren't teachers. The library wasn't simply where one had to go to get the books, it was a kind of exacting haven to which a city youngster willingly went for his lesson in restraint and his training in self-control.

Could the real hero of *Goodbye, Columbus* be the Newark Public Library? At the end of the book, Neil Klugman rushes back to the library after a love affair is finally and completely shattered by the tremors rumbling along the fault lines of suburban class consciousness. Does he return there in defeat or relief? At the enigmatic conclusion, Klugman turns from the blurred image of his former lover (he's looking at her through a series of distorting glass panels) back to his job at the library:

> I did not look very much longer, but took a train that got me into Newark just as the sun was rising on the first day of the Jewish New Year. I was back in plenty of time for work.

FURTHER READING

Books by Roth

The Dying Animal. New York: Houghton Mifflin, 2001.
The Facts: A Novelist's Autobiography. New York: Vintage Books, 1997.
The Great American Novel. New York: Vintage, 1995.

Books about Roth

Bloom, Harold, ed. *Philip Roth*. New York: Chelsea House, 1986.
Milowetz, Steven. *Philip Roth Considered: The Concentrationary Universe of the American Writer*. New York: Garland Publishing, 2000.
Rodgers, Bernard. *Philip Roth*. Boston: Twayne Publishers, 1978.

The Pine Barrens (1969)

John McPhee's remarkable travelogue through New Jersey's million-acre enigma would be worth reading even if its impact had not been so shatteringly profound. But someone coming to the book for the first time today has the added thrill of knowing that amid those pages lie the embers that sparked a firestorm of interest in the Pine Barrens and fueled a struggle to preserve this pristine tract of dwarf pines, rust-colored streams, and not a few threatened species—animal and human.

The Pine Barrens, which began as so many of McPhee's books have—as a series of essays in *The New Yorker*—illuminates a massive, and massively misunder-stood, New Jersey region that is almost identical in size to Grand Canyon National Park. Even to many native-born Jerseyans, the Pine Barrens have always seemed to be this odd, weirdly-removed place, populated by clans of backwoods retrogrades, birthplace of devils, forge of brushfires. McPhee inhabits the Pinelands, as the region is also called, both personally and vicariously by attach-ing himself to an old-time piney named Fred Brown and chronicling the life cycle of the land and its people in a piecemeal narrative that reveals this award-winning writer in pre-Pulitzer mode (he won the prize for nonfiction in 1999).

McPhee, employing a prose style that is economical yet colorful, delineates character traits and provides naturalistic details while keeping the narrative mov-ing briskly:

> When he is not working in the bogs, he goes roaming, as he puts it, set-ting out cross-country on long, loping journeys, hiking about thirty miles in a typical day, in search of what he calls "events"—surprising a buck, a gray fox, perhaps a poacher, or a man with a still. Almost no one who is not native to the pines could do this, for the woods have an undulating sameness, and the understory—huckleberries, sheep laurel, sweet fern, high-bush blue-berry—is often so dense that a wanderer can walk in a fairly tight circle and think that he is moving in a straight line. State forest rangers spend a good part of their time finding hikers and hunters, some of whom have vanished for days.

One of the many cranberry bogs in the Pine Barrens.
Courtesy of the Newark Public Library.

McPhee's gift for understatement allows him to slip in interesting details with little literary fanfare. For instance, buried within a lengthy paragraph about the geographic location of the pinelands is this fascinating tidbit: "The Pine Barrens are so close to New York that on a very clear night a bright light in the pines would be visible from the Empire State Building."

There's a lot of that in this book. McPhee never misses a chance to introduce an odd fact or take a narrative detour. One minute you're learning about how to layer a cranberry bog, the next you're in the eighteenth century, trudging along with the workmen as they make their way from the iron forge to the public house. His particularly good discussion on the subject of forest fires, which merits an entire chapter in the book, describes the ecology and behavior of this frequent pinelands intruder:

> One of the first lessons in forest fire survival is: get onto burned ground. But this is not always easy.

McPhee maintains this matter-of-fact tone throughout the chapter. Few writers would show such restraint when faced with the opportunity to embellish on such a dramatic topic. He reins in the impulse to expound breathlessly on these terrible phenomena. Only occasionally does he assume an above-it-all "writerly" tone, and then his attempts fall rather flat. For instance, when describing the interior of Fred Brown's cabin, McPhee wryly notes, "There were seven calendars on the walls, all current, and none with pictures of nudes"—a rather awkward, and uncharacteristic, attempt at humor at his subject's expense.

But for all of McPhee's writerly aplomb, what makes *The Pine Barrens* a significant book is its impact on its subject, the land itself. At the time of the book's composition, the Pine Barrens had been the focus of a number of far-flung development schemes, including a proposal for a self-contained quarter-of-a-million-resident city-of-the-future (complete with international jetport). This proposal intrudes into McPhee's narrative at several points, almost as a character itself, a villainous modern foil to the primitive simplicity and backwoods naiveté of the woodlands. Looking back thirty years later, it seems unthinkable—highly comic, in fact—that such a wholesale annihilation of the Pine Barrens was ever pondered seriously. McPhee can barely maintain his mantle of objective observer as he describes the proposal:

> Of all the schemes that have ever been created for the development of the Pine Barrens, the most exhaustive and expensive one is the proposal for a jetport and a new city. Under this plan, a spur of the Garden State Parkway would take off into the woods from Toms River, soon passing beneath the central business district of a city of two-hundred-fifty thousand people. Beyond the city, the road would go through a green belt, then through an industrial park, and then under the runways and past the terminal building

of the largest airport on earth—four times as large as Newark Airport, La Guardia, and Kennedy put together. As a supersonic jetport, it would serve a third of the United States and supersonic jets would land there ninety minutes after leaving Paris.

First-edition readers were left wondering if this plan, or any of the various other development proposals, would decimate the Pine Barrens. But in a welcome example of the pen being mightier than the bulldozer, McPhee's work did more than simply illuminate a potential crisis. It helped prevent one. *The Pine Barrens* became "Exhibit A" in the conservationists' struggle to preserve the pinelands. McPhee put the mystery and majesty of this unheralded tract of land on reading desks throughout the country. He also put the issue on the desks of state and national lawmakers, who responded with unusual passion and speed, resulting in landmark legislation to preserve the acreage. Parisians would have to find someplace else to land.

But would the Save-The-Pine-Barrens movement have triumphed in the end without McPhee? Hard to say. Some state officials credit McPhee with salvaging the Pine Barrens from widespread misunderstanding, longstanding legislative neglect, and starry-eyed developers. Of course, McPhee was writing about nature just as the environmental movement was gaining some muscle. And even the most devout concrete-and-steel proponent must have shuddered at the prospect

---

FROM SEA TO SHINING SEA

What do hikers in California, junior forest rangers in North Carolina, and cranberry bog men in New Jersey have in common? They all found refuge—and breathed a sigh of relief—after the passage of the "National Parks and Recreation Act of 1978." The federal law extended the boundaries of Sequoia National Forest, established a "cradle of forestry education center" in the Pisgah National Forest of North Carolina, and protected the Pine Barrens from development.

This wide-ranging act also established protected forest reserves in New Mexico and Arizona. The law provides a model for both government-backed preservation efforts and bureaucratic-legalistic jargon. Here's just one of the law's many labyrinthine passages dealing with federal acquisition of tracts within the Pinelands:

The grants authorized by subsection (h)(1)(A) of this section together with the grants made under paragraph (4) of this subsection, shall (i) be made in a manner consistent with the requirement of the Land and Water Conservation Fund Act [16 U.S.C. 4601-4 et seq.]: (ii) not exceed 75 percent of the total cost of all property acquired by the State pursuant to this subsection; (iii) be supplemental to any other Federal financial assistance for any other program; and (iv) be subject to such additional terms and conditions as the Secretary may deem necessary to effectuate the purposes of this section.

of another quarter of a million people summarily being deposited in the Atlantic City–Philadelphia–New York corridor.

In an otherwise prescient study, McPhee, assuming the worst, leaps to a conclusion that posterity has shown to be greatly mistaken. As he steps uneasily into the role of social commentator, McPhee critiques the coming battle between conservationists and developers:

> Given the futilities of that debate, given the sort of attention that is ordinarily paid to plans put forward by conservationists, and given the great numbers and the crossed purposes of all the big and little powers that would have to work together to accomplish *anything* on a major scale in the pines, it would appear that the Pine Barrens are not very likely to be the subject of dramatic decrees or acts of legislation. They seem to be headed slowly toward extinction.

Was McPhee being disingenuous? Provocative? Or did he genuinely believe the Pine Barrens were doomed? Those questions became academic a decade later, when in 1978 the unthinkable happened: Big and little powers *did* work together to save the Pinelands.

"The Congress finds that the Pinelands area in New Jersey, containing approximately 1,000,000 acres of pine-oak forest, extensive surface and groundwater resources of high quality, and a wide diversity of rare plant and animal species, provides significant ecological, natural, cultural, recreational, educational, agricultural, and public health benefits." So begins Section 471i of the National Parks and Recreation Act of 1978, the legislative firewall that now stands between the Pine Barrens and development. The act established something called the "Pinelands National Reserve," a governmental network of national, regional, and local bodies, all helping to shape the Pinelands' future. The lion's share of responsibility was given to New Jersey's newly established Pinelands Commission.

A year after Congress acted, the state supplemented the federal law by passing the Pinelands Protection Act, which implemented the requirement that county and municipal land use proposals within the Pinelands "be brought into conformance with the Comprehensive Management Plan" developed by the Pinelands Commission.

In addition to putting clear and stringent limits on development within the Pine Barrens, the commission embarked on an ambitious cataloging of those natural assets that make the area worth protecting. The commission's corps of geologists, botanists, and biologists documented "a potable water supply estimated at over 17 trillion gallons . . . 580 native plant species, including 54 classified as threatened or endangered, and 299 kinds of birds, 91 fish, 59 reptiles and amphibians, and 39 mammals found in the Pinelands."

Whether the Pine Barrens will endure in their present configuration seems at least slightly more sure now than at the time McPhee's book was first published.

FURTHER READING

Books by McPhee

Encounters with the Archdruid. New York: Noonday Press, 1990.

In Suspect Terrain. New York: Noonday Press, 1991.

A Sense of Where You Are: A Profile of William Warren Bradley. New York: Farrar Straus & Giroux, 1999.

Books about the Pine Barrens

Boyd, Howard P. *A Field Guide to the Pine Barrens of New Jersey*. Medford: Plexus Publishing, 1991.

McMahon, William. *Pine Barrens Legends, Lore and Lies*. Wilmington, Del.: The Middle Atlantic Press, 1980.

Moonsammy, Rita Zorn, et al. *Pinelands Folklife*. New Brunswick: Rutgers University Press, 1987.

Eddie and the Cruisers (1980)

If rock and roll is a sort of religion, then New Jerseyans are among the most devout worshippers. The temples—jammed, dimly-lit clubs strung along the Shore—testify to the enduring power of music to transform the ordinary into the profound. A real revelation can emerge from under the smoke and clangor of a boardwalk barroom:

> "Every night I'm up there working, three, four sets a night, and I look down at people dancing and drinking, which is fine by me. But what I want is . . ."
>
> He stopped. He stared down at the floor.
>
> ". . . is songs that echo. We play and sing all right, but that's just the beginning of it. I want more. Most of the stuff we're singing now, they're like the sheets in somebody's bed. Spread 'em, soil 'em, ship 'em out to the laundry. You know? But our songs—I want us to be able to fold ourselves up in them forever."

That's the calling of Eddie Wilson, the fictional rocker at the center of P. F. Kluge's *Eddie and the Cruisers*, the 1980 novel that poignantly captures the spirit of Jersey rock. Much more familiar in its movie incarnation (the 1983 film starred Tom

Berenger and Ellen Barkin), *Cruisers* remains a touchstone text for the Jersey music scene, with some nice digressions on the state's psychic geography:

> That summer was our time. And that stretch of shoreline—humid, tar-blistery streets, rotted wood, salt air, deep-fried foods—that was our un-challenged territory. We were lords of the plywood jungle, those miles of jerry-built beach homes with barely enough of a yard between them to hang out a wet bathing suit or toss an empty beer can.

Eddie and the Cruisers tells the story of the rise of a rock-and-roll band, called the Parkway Cruisers in the novel (changed for the film). The title char-acter fronts a rock band and achieves some notoriety playing around Atlantic City, but he wants to achieve something more than a local following. The band releases a moderately successful record, but Eddie's musical ambitions go beyond simple two-part harmony. In preparation for a follow-up album, he rents a Quonset hut–style recording studio in Lakehurst. For a month, he works in seclusion with only Wendell, the band's sax player. Whatever music they create remains unclear, although tapes are said to exist of the sessions, and the sax man—a junkie who eventually loses his mind—hints that the music was mind-blowingly deep, a modern "Leaves of Grass, man." (There's a nicely rendered scene at the historic Camden home of the poet Walt Whitman, where Eddie has gone to make a pilgrimage.) The month in the studio ends, Eddie rejoins the band, the sessions are never spoken of again, but Eddie seems changed, dejected and distant. A week later, Eddie's car plunges off the Raritan Bridge (the movie hinges on the "Is Eddie Dead?" mystery, whereas the book includes it only as an incidental plot point near the end, when a mysterious Eddie impersonator begins menacing the band members). The rest of the book is a quest to find the tapes of that Lakehurst session, twenty years later, prompted by media interest in Eddie Wilson's life after the Parkway Cruisers have been "rediscovered."

That's the plot. But *Eddie and the Cruisers* is really a book about New Jersey. Even if the well-worn clichés flit thickly through its 240 pages, the characters always embrace their origins:

> I remember that westward drive in springtime. I remember it so clearly that if I drove the same route today, I'd associate certain conversations with landmarks, a whole soundtrack of memories all along the road. I remember how dawn found us crossing the Pulaski Skyway, with Jersey's polluted marshes turning gold below, and warehouses, factories, and railroad yards stretched out forever, and a convoy of early garbage trucks stirring up hun-dreds of birds that had been nesting on a mountain range of landfill refuse. "Good-bye, Garden State," Eddie said, waving at the three-ring sign over the Ballantine brewery in Newark.

"This is where we're from, Wordman," Eddie said. I'd never seen him higher. "People drive through here, they roll up their windows so they don't have to breathe none of the air. Not me!"

He rolled down the windows and took a deep gulp of New Jersey.

"Ain't that ripe! Man, I thrive on it. I make music outa it. It knocks me out! You got miles of swamp and mountains of dumps and all different colored rivers. You got automobile graveyards and radio transmitters and ball parks and breweries all mixed up, birds and rats and people making garbage and using garbage and pilin' it up to the damn sky. Holee shit, man! No wonder the Statue of Liberty faces the other way."

Perhaps only those people who've found themselves grinding along the Pulaski Skyway at daybreak can fully appreciate Eddie's intoxication with that part of the state. Kluge certainly knows his local geography. He grew up in Berkeley Heights and worked as an intern at the *Vineland Times-Journal* newspaper during the summer of 1962. He has said that the characters and atmosphere of the novel were drawn from that experience. Certainly, one of the more pivotal scenes in the book (and movie) can be traced to local knowledge: the late night visit to the ruins of the Palace Depression. "Part Hooverville, part Disneyland, Palace Depression was an amalgam of discarded appliances, hammered-out cans, empty bottles, junked automobiles." Most readers have probably attributed such a bizarre locale to a novelist's imagination. The Palace Depression was, of course, real; it was also real strange.

DOUBLE TAKE

In the first *Eddie and the Cruisers* film, one scene—perhaps the best in the movie—takes place on a beach along the Jersey Shore and involves a conversation between rocker Eddie Wilson and newly sanctioned group member Frank Ridgeway. Eddie tells Ridgeway—known as "the Wordman"—that he wants to achieve more than just fame. He wants "greatness." His vision is to produce music that goes beyond simple barroom harmonies and dance hall rhythms. It's a touching piece of cinema, a poignant imparting of wisdom from the usually stoic, inscrutable Eddie Wilson, while a plaintive saxophone plays gingerly in the background and the camera moves tentatively toward the principals.

The scene is so critical to the idea of *Eddie and the Cruisers* that it was spliced into *Eddie and the Cruisers II: Eddie Lives!* But, unforgivably, the character of the Wordman is spliced out in the reedited scene, and Eddie is shown talking to his bass player, Sal Amato. As drama, it loses all of its punch to have Eddie confess this desire to a bit player in the first and second film.

The book's author, P. F. Kluge, who had no involvement in the second film, said *Eddie Lives!* "was an excuse to release another album. It makes me wince."

The Palace Depression was the mangled brainchild of one George Daynor, who was reportedly guided to Vineland by angels. Little is known of Daynor's biographical background, but his "home" was well documented. The Palace Depression was a sort of inverted castle fashioned from junk: old car chassis for the floor beams, doors made of bed frames, rocks and garbage molded into its eighteen spires (and painted throughout with a mixture of pulverized red bricks and discarded motor oil). The castle featured revolving doors made from wagon wheels and several hidden passageways and secret rooms. Daynor guided tourists through his junkyard labyrinth for twenty-five cents. His eccentric homestead was featured in newspapers and magazines of the 1930s and 1940s.

Jailed for fraud in the late 1950s after claiming to have information about a federal kidnapping case, Daynor (and the Palace Depression) began to crumble. Unsupervised by its aged, wild-eyed superintendent, the property became the playground of vandals. Before Daynor died in 1964 at the age of 104, he requested burial on the then-thoroughly looted and decrepit grounds of the Palace Depression. Authorities denied the request; he's buried in a pauper's grave in Oak Hill Cemetery. The few remaining recognizable remnants of the Palace were demolished in 1969 by order of the City of Vineland.

Eddie Wilson's girlfriend Joann Carlino offers this critique of Daynor's magnificent monstrosity:

> "The whole place gave me the creeps," Joann said. "You could still see that it had been nice once. A kid could find it fascinating and ingenious. A terrific place to play. I mean, there were bathtubs set into the ground for fishponds, and birdbaths made from toilets, and sidewalks lined with upside-down bottles, beer and soda, so when the sun hit them you thought you were walking on stained glass. And the house—the castle I should call it—was three stories of hubcaps and car hoods and refrigerator doors and I don't know what all. You could see the old man who built the place had something. I don't know what you'd call it, a joke, or a goof, or a piece of art."

Variously in and out of print over the past twenty years, the 1999 Kenyon College Bookstore edition of *Eddie and the Cruisers* (Kluge is the writer-in-residence at Kenyon) contains an "Afterword," which gives the author's take on the book, the movie, and the state of New Jersey. Kluge, continuing to churn out both fiction and nonfiction, turned his attention toward the decidedly un-Jersey landscapes of Micronesia and the Philippines (though he's not forsaken his rock-and-roll passions because his most recent work is about a trio of Elvis Presley impersonators in the Philippines).

Cruisers, Kluge's second novel, failed to make much of an impression when it was first published. Selling only about ten thousand hardcover copies, the book wasn't reprinted in a paperback edition until almost twenty years later. What kept the memory of Eddie Wilson alive wasn't Kluge's book so much as the movie—and a soundtrack that brought some brief AM-radio attention to John Cafferty and the Beaver Brown Band (the soundtrack's hit, "On the Dark Side," spent seven weeks on the pop charts, and the album sold three million copies—astounding for a soundtrack to an unsuccessful theatrical release). A 1989 sequel to the movie, *Eddie and the Cruisers II: Eddie Lives!*, fared poorly at the box office and quickly disappeared. Kluge's critique: "The less said about it, the better."

Eddie and the Cruisers, while not a masterpiece of modern fiction, remains a highly readable, even occasionally moving, work. Translating the fevered energy of a Jersey rock dream into a biography-cum-mystery is an ambitious goal. By appropriating several genres *Cruisers* doesn't fit snugly into any single literary classification: mystery, pot-boiler, literary fiction, even bildungsroman, as Kluge traces the arc of the band's rise and fall. The book could also be considered something of a modern tragedy, hinging as it does on the death of a visionary leader and the collapse of his musical empire. Perhaps the most tragic figure, though, is the band's manager, "Doc" Robins (played in the movie for all he is worth, and more, by veteran character actor and Hoboken resident Joe Pantoliano). In the book, Doc is hustler, friend, fiend—heartless, pathetic, even murderous: "Everybody knows at least one person like Doc Robins. One's usually all you can take."

That's the book's signature style. *Cruisers* is loaded with such short, snappy lines, the literary equivalent of pop song catchphrases: a memorable couplet, rhythmic cadences, deep-seeming while the music is playing (or the pages are turning). *Cruisers* aims directly at the impulse that leads you to crank up the radio when a favorite song intersects with a favorite stretch of road. Read the book while listening to some classic rock-and-roll album. Kluge's words will give you something to ponder, at least while the music is playing.

FURTHER READING

Books by Kluge
Alma Mater. Reading, Mass.: Addison-Wesley Publishing, 1993.
Biggest Elvis. New York: Viking, 1996.
The Edge of Paradise. Honolulu: University of Hawaii Press, 1993.

Books on the Jersey Rock-and-Roll Scene
Bon Jovi, Jon. *Blaze of Glory*. Milwaukee: Hal Leonard Publishing, 1991.
Horn, Jeff. *Hungry Heart: The Music of Bruce Springsteen*. Bloomington, Ind.: 1st Books Library, 2000.
Perotta, Tom. *The Wishbones*. New York: Berkeley Publishing Group, 1997.

Jersey Luck (1980)

Only a few literary productions have earned the label "timeless." Most literature resides comfortably somewhere between the transience of the nightly news broadcast and the relative permanence of historical record. There is a class of writing, however, that demands to be read in its time. Its themes, ideas, and narrative flotsam depend on the reader catching the same wave before it crashes onto the evanescent shore of pop culture. Future readers, therefore, can only guess at what must have given it its particular resonance. This is not to say that the work is neither worth admiring nor well-wrought. But something—usually much—of the book's charm fades like last summer's tan. Such a work is Tom De Haven's *Jersey Luck*, a novel that lacks only a reason to read it now that twenty years have passed since its publication.

Fans of De Haven's considerably well received body of work may wince at such a characterization. And chroniclers of life in the Garden State at the end of the 1970s certainly could not ask for a more thorough dissection of life among the urban underclass. De Haven doesn't just dip his characters into New Jersey currents to provide them a shabby urban charm; these are real Jersey guys and girls. Only someone with De Haven's geographic pedigree, his surgical precision in choosing details, and his obvious affection for the down-and-outers of Hudson County, circa 1979, could imbue his novel with such Jersey-flavored verismo.

ALONG THE JERSEY STRIP

At one point in the novel *Jersey Luck*, the principal characters all meet at a nude beach along the Jersey Shore somewhere off the Garden State Parkway. De Haven spends several pages describing the clothing-optional beach and picnic area, with characters exhibiting various degrees of comfort as they stroll about the sands sans clothes. Readers of the novel may be unaware that New Jersey does, in fact, boast the largest nude beach in the entire Northeast: Gunnison Beach, located at Sandy Hook's Gateway National Recreation Area. Almost two full miles of the beach is reserved for naked bathers and the designated no-clothes area is well marked, fully policed, and thoroughly supervised by lifeguards. A number of websites offer information about the beach. For people who'd like to experience Gunnison for themselves, take the Parkway to exit 117, then take Route 36 east to Sandy Hook and follow the signs to "North Beach" until you come to the Old Gun Battery on the right, about five miles past the park entrance. Parking is available for $10 per day, although fees are waived after 4 p.m. Serious "naturists" can purchase a season pass for $50.

De Haven, who has found a way to sneak Jersey into many of his novels, was born in Bayonne and lived in Jersey City for a number of years, presumably associating with many of the same characters who populate his book: *Jersey Journal* reporters, unreconstructed hippies living in squalid, one-room apartments, Bayonne secretaries who live at home with their mothers, and low-life thugs who play at being big-time mobsters but fold when the pressure is on. So De Haven knows the place. And he also knows the time: the book reminds anyone old enough to remember Watergate of the following trends of the late seventies: customized vans, cricket lighters, bumper pool, Bowie knives, "My Sharona," closed-circuit porno movies in hotels, "YES" stadium concerts, and a typical roster of *Tonight* show guests that includes Carl Reiner and Jerzy Kozinski. Future readers of this book may conclude that the reason his characters smoked dope constantly was because of the bland television programs and the lack of visually compelling video games. Here's a typical scene from *Jersey Luck*: the protagonist Jacky Peek is channel surfing (manually, of course) when his upstairs neighbor, who fences stolen goods, pops in with a hot new toy:

> I stopped at the Mike Douglas show. It was just starting. Ben Vereen was the cohost, and Lucie Arnaz, James Earl Jones, and the Zolpe Chimps were the scheduled guests.
>
> I left it, and threw six little frozen pizzas in the oven, opened a beer. Then Malcolm from upstairs knocked once and walked in. "I said maybe next week," I told him. "You just walk in? I don't need anything now."
>
> "No, I know that," he said. "You see what I got?" What he had was an electronic television game, it came in a box like a board game, called "Tank Death." "Doing anything? You got a color set? See you do." He went over to the TV and squatted and started hooking the game to the antenna terminals. "You don't mind, do you? It's raining. I'm bored."
>
> "Want a beer? Some pizza?"
>
> "Sure. Beer's good. Pizza's good."
>
> Malcolm showed me how to play—see this toggle? see that button?—then we played for a while and I asked him, "You get this at Radio Shack?"

De Haven is so observant that he may have catalogued himself right out of a perpetual readership for this book. Toggle switches and Mike Douglas, while perhaps seminal once upon a time in the daily life of the average Jerseyan, may leave a new generation of fiction readers mystified. Can the Mike Douglas show's appeal *ever* be adequately explained? Still, these characters who spend all day getting high, spinning original Broadway cast albums of rock musicals, reading *Penthouse* letters, and purifying stagnant workspaces with Airwick deodorizers do generate a mercenary sympathy. One finds oneself wondering how they'll all continue to afford their scratch-off lottery tickets and Chewbacca action figures, and so we follow them: to Journal Square, to the Miss America Diner in Jersey City, to the cheap souvenir stands along the boardwalk.

Yet, De Haven carries it all forward with such energy that the book holds together until the last, rather pathetic turn of events on the final page. His subsequent work has revealed him to be a writer of such range, style, and real insight that one finds oneself mining *Jersey Luck* for clues of the burgeoning craftsman. Many stylish, memorable passages presage the books to come:

> She blew out her cheeks and went into the store. I followed her with my eyes. It's boring after a while to make love in your imagination to every woman, practically every one, you see, but at least it keeps you alert and well groomed. And otherwise you might never leave the house.

And so it proceeds, small-time hoodlums dreaming futile dreams of love and success amid the squalor of Jersey City's urban rot or the oppressive ennui of Bayonne, "where every third lawn is staked with a chiropractor's sign, the gutters are swept, the people are white. Church, tavern, church, tavern. Church, temple, maternity shop, tavern."

De Haven has broadened the scope of his fictional interests well beyond such parochial borders. Admirably prolific, he has written more than a dozen novels since *Jersey Luck*, including *Funny Papers* (1985) and *Derby Dugan's Depression Funnies* (1996)—both of which reflect De Haven's consuming interest in classic newspaper comic strips. In his acknowledgements to *Derby Dugan* De Haven writes, "thanks and praise be to all those great newspaper cartoonists of the Golden Age, especially Harold Gray and Chester Gould, whose work, I'm proud to say, invented me." De Haven, a book critic for the *New York Times* and *Entertainment Weekly*, currently teaches creative writing at Virginia Commonwealth University. One of his hapless characters laments, "Look, my luck isn't ever gonna change. Know how come? 'Cause my luck is Jersey luck, which is the same thing as no luck at all." De Haven himself has been able to avoid the curse of his fictional creations, who must forge ahead despite being the repositories of Jersey-borne karma.

Such a harsh critique seems justified within the world of De Haven's novel, the literary equivalent of one of New Jersey's infamous traffic circles. The characters drift round and round, exchanging joints, insults, girlfriends. De Haven doesn't try to imbue his story with a *faux* significance. Reading *Jersey Luck* is like watching a Samuel Beckett play with a Bruce Springsteen soundtrack. Intimations of escape, phantoms of satisfaction haunt the book. And De Haven teases the reader with a glimmer of hope finally propelling the narrative: Jacky Peek decides at the end of the novel that he's going to make a clean break (actually, go underground and live like his former fugitive bank-robbing girlfriend). But he gets shot. Another casualty of Jersey luck.

FURTHER READING

Books by De Haven

Derby Dugan's Depression Funnies. New York: Henry Holt, 1996.
Dugan Under Ground. New York: Metropolitan Books, 2001.
Freak's Amour. New York: Harper and Row, 1979.
Funny Papers. New York: Viking Penguin, 1985.

Of Related Interest

Kaplan, James. *Two Guys from Verona*. New York: Grove/Atlantic, 1999.
Moody, Rick. *Garden State*. New York: Little Brown, 1995.

Rosamund's Vision (1983)

Any Jersey resident who has ever been put in the uncomfortable position of having to defend the state against its detractors knows the drill. For every mention of the glories of the Shore, one is reminded of landfills and industrial pollution. Bring up important figures like Alexander Hamilton, Albert Einstein, or Thomas Edison, and the nay-sayers counter with Dutch Schultz, Tony Soprano, or some gum-chewing teenaged girl at the Big Hair Mall. Dare to celebrate the state's ethnic diversity—disparate cultural communities yoked together by a single thoroughfare—and prepare to hear the old turnpike canard: "You live in New Jersey? What exit?"

It turns out that one needn't take sides at all. It's possible to embrace both the glorious *and* the grungy, the fertile and the moribund. With the right perspective, one can see the magnificence of the whole picture, a dreamy vision refracted through broken glass, graffiti, and the warm glow of cheap video games. One can look upon the neglected Jersey urban landscape and find the New Jerusalem. Consider the reaction of Rosamund Coleridge, a direct descendent of the great poet Samuel Taylor Coleridge, as she first lays eyes on Planet New Jersey:

> They had left their bags behind them piled among cartons of musty old books in the battered book van whose owner, Jonah Woodstock, was at that moment roller-skating in the Jerseyland Rollerama: a sixty-year old book dealer with shaggy grey hair and the stub of a dead cigar in his mouth, whirling about with crowds of teenagers amid a chaos of fluorescent lights and superamplified rock and roll. Such was New Jersey—or, as Muldane liked to call it, "darkest New Jersey"—where tea could be had at petrol stations and there were floodlit carparks the size of airfields and wheelchairs painted onto parking spaces (reserved for the handicapped) in front of skat-

ing rinks, and supermarkets (open twenty-four hours) that looked as big and busy at ten o'clock as the customs hall at Kennedy where she had stood hours before in the line for "aliens," mentally composing an angry letter to inform the customs authorities that the surest way to alienate visitors from another country was to corral them under a word generally associated with creatures from outer space.

The "Muldane" is C. C. ("Charlie Chaplin") Muldane, an eccentric radio talk show host at the unstable center of *Rosamund's Vision*, Stuart Mitchner's funny, clever, genuinely moving work, which attempts no less a feat than to articulate the sublime qualities of debased New Jersey. In pages that recall the best of Saul Bellow, the author unveils a bizarre but haunting vision of the Garden State, "darkest New Jersey," that is as compelling as it is absurd.

Mitchner, author of the quasi-autobiographical travelogue *Indian Action* (1976), is a longtime resident of Princeton with an obvious passion for all things literary. *Rosamund's Vision* is stuffed with lots of references that find English majors nodding in recognition. Mitchner began his writing career by winning the Thomas Crowell college novel contest at age twenty with *Let Me Be Awake* (1959), which *The New Yorker* called "young, alive, and extremely earnest." That novel was set in the Midwest, New York, and a small college in Pennsylvania. *Rosamund's Vision* takes place in the fictional New Bristol, New Jersey, a town filled with more than its share of quirky characters. Into this burg of idiosyncratic people and geography (a haunted bridge, a huge, illuminated lightbulb, a mysterious nocturnal hum that only some residents can hear) steps Rosamund Coleridge from the English town of Bristol. The book generates much of its narrative thrust by parsing the psychic interplay of the two closely named towns.

The plot involves Rosamund's attempts to reconcile herself to life in Bristol's poorer, demented New Jersey cousin. Of the many oddballs in New Bristol, most are loosely connected to an enchanted fire-trap of a used bookstore called Second Comings. Everyone in the book is distinguished by their weirdness (prompting one critic of the book to label it a "talented fiction with far too many eccentrics per square inch"). The bookstore's owner, Jonah Woodstock, comes into possession of what appears to be the original handwritten manuscript for Melville's *Moby-Dick*. In his attempt to protect the manuscript, C. C. Muldane must remove it from his own apartment above the bookstore and transport it with him while his wife Rosamund goes into labor and is rushed to the hospital in a ramshackle van owned by a Sikh garage mechanic, though the path is blocked outside the bookstore by a crowd cheering the removal of a space-invaders-type video game.

Other points of narrative significance include a shadowy badger introduction ceremony in the forest, a tussle to drag a hand-carved wooden cradle through a

SEEING THE LIGHT IN NEW JERSEY

In *Rosamund's Vision*, a giant lightbulb illuminates the fictional town of New Bristol. Somewhat similar in description to the actual memorial in Edison (though in the book, drunks and derelicts climb inside the bulb to hide from the world as they indulge in their vices), the unavoidable monument seems fitting, for the great inventor did most of his work in New Jersey—first in Newark, then Menlo Park, and finally West Orange, where his laboratory has been preserved and is open to the public.

At Menlo Park in 1881 Edison finally perfected his electric light. He did not invent incandescent light, but he was the first to demonstrate that its large-scale use in public lighting systems—as a replacement for traditional gas lamps along city streets—was possible. His practical improvements in existing electric light designs, such as the use of filament instead of wires or rods, added to the average life of a bulb and paved the way for relatively cheap mass production of bulbs.

The story of Edison's quest to develop an incandescent bulb has been told in count-

The Edison Memorial in Menlo Park.
Copyright 2002 Reena Rose Sibayan.

less scientific encyclopedias and book-length biographical studies. Readers interested in the full story should consult *Edison's Electric Light: A Biography of an Idea*, by Robert Friedel, Paul Israel, and Bernard S. Finn (Rutgers University Press, 1986). For a quick and user-friendly overview of Edison's career and his work in Menlo Park, take a look at the chapter "Edison's Electric Bulb" in *The Seven Wonders of New Jersey—and Then Some*, by Thomas C. Murray and Valeria Barnes (Enslow Publishers, 1981).

cemetery, a tyrannical Greek landlord who has a habit of throwing wrenches at a black kid who calls himself "Bad News," and a group of derelicts who hover about the giant light bulb (modeled after the real, and real big, light bulb monument in Edison, New Jersey), basking in its warmth. Oh, and there's that business about the reincarnation of George Washington's vision of a celestial city in the sky, which Muldane has been prophesying for months to his night-owl radio show listeners.

For all that, the book really illuminates just a handful of simply stated themes: literature as one of the few reliable signposts in our hapless quest for contentment; the sustaining power of faith—in anything (including an abiding faith that the composer Franz Schubert is still alive); and the timelessness of great art. In what must be one of the most spirited defenses in modern literature of the value of books—the physical, musty, inky objects themselves—Jonah, the bookstore owner, launches a tirade after being told his old books are "junk":

> "Junk, that's the word, right? To me junk is something you throw away, something that don't last, all the stuff that goes down the drain we been talking about. Here. Look. I'll close my eyes." Jonah closed his eyes and plucked out a book at random from the Poetry section. "Here, good, let's look at the date." He opened the book to the copyright page. "There, see: eighteen fifty-one, by God! Think about how much dirty clothes and cough syrup and other little human things, and how many broken hearts and broken heads and just plain people been washed away and down the spout and into who knows where since eighteen fifty-one! You know anybody still alive from eighteen fifty-one? Or any thing? . . . Here, feel it, take hold of it! You can still feel the little bulges where the press hit the paper! You can feel the rag in it, sure, maybe it's a mishmosh of old rags and dead trees, but here it is in the nineteen eighties with us, by God, and no junk about it!"

Rosamund's Vision also celebrates New Jersey, from its occasional pungency ("It's an odor of magnitude the British could never have approached; only in the cities of Hindustan and New Jersey could one find such a stench.") to the genteel streets of Princeton ("That intellectual wasteland! That Ivy League rest home!"). It's not a blind love but one all too aware, for New Bristol is besotted with

> Soggy prophylactica. Whore's spittle. Mugger's knifewort. Roach sedge. Hairy Day-Glo wall moss schlepped from the hanging garden of graffiti growing along the insides of the Prospect Avenue underpass. Blood-red slimebright mopped up from the blood-red banks of the river near the Poe Bridge. Fallen leaves of broken glass scattered along Jersey Avenue.

Mitchner's New Jersey dares you to embrace it, but, like the book itself, it is ultimately irresistible.

FURTHER READING

Books by Mitchner

Indian Action: An American Journey to the Great Fair of the East. Boston: Little, Brown, 1976.
Let Me Be Awake. New York: Thomas Crowell: 1959.

Laying Down the Law (1989)

It's unlikely that Joe Clark's name would appear on most readers' list of important New Jersey authors. *Laying Down the Law* is Clark's only book. Yet Clark himself is one of the state's most notable (notorious?) public figures—a brash iconoclast who, for a time, found himself at the fulcrum of a national debate about education reform in the inner city. Clark's philosophy, articulated through his ubiquitous bullhorn, ignited raucous protests both supporting and strongly condemning his methods. The controversy has cooled, and the debate has shifted, but for those curious about all the commotion, *Laying Down the Law* shatters any ignorance. It also reminds readers how distressing the situation was in many urban school districts in the 1970s and 1980s—and how draconian the methods to corral those out-of-control schools were.

Just like his philosopher-pugilist persona in the corridor, Joe Clark the author pulls no punches. For nearly two hundred pages, Clark—the former principal of Paterson's Eastside High School, made famous in the movie *Lean on Me*—diagnoses a plague-infected educational system and proposes uncompromising, unorthodox measures. He wastes no time; the first few pages establish his thesis with his typical hyperbole and messianic zeal:

> How long can mainstream America turn its back on the crisis of the inner cities, like the foolish characters in Poe's "Masque of the Red Death" who fancied themselves safe from the raging plague? Will we wait until there's a bludgeoning robber behind each bush, until no garbage can goes unsearched for food scraps, until every fourth grader has tried crack? Will we let matters go until one of every two Americans cannot read, until the population is so uninformed and stupid that we vote to destroy the constitution? Will we say it can't happen here until it does, until the drug gangs use suburban parks and shopping malls and neighborhoods for battlefields, until suburban youths join the skinheads in resurrecting nazism, until there is an American version of the Final Solution, and no street is safe?

Once he diagnoses the symptoms, he starts to enumerate the causes, repeating some entrenched stereotypes and creating a few of his own:

Do not underestimate the danger. The world teaches the middle-class and affluent youths to amass wealth by any means possible, and to hell with ethics and your fellow man. The world teaches the inner-city youth to amass wealth by the fastest, most evident means available—that usually means drugs and crime—and to hell with decency, family, and future.

Such a world view makes an oddly compelling narrative. Even the most resistant reader finds himself or herself eventually seduced by Clark's "It's me against the modern forces of evil" mantra. *Laying Down the Law* (subtitled *Joe Clark's Strategy for Saving Our Schools*) reads like an amalgam of *The Adventures of Superman* and *When Bad Things Happen to Good People*.

The book, written with the assistance of Bayonne freelance writer Joe Picard, follows the traditional David-versus-Goliath template. Clark discusses his career as an educator who worked his way up from a disadvantaged Newark rearing, through the struggles of high school, college, and the beginnings of a career that led him first to a troubled elementary school that he turned around single-handedly ("'The Miracle on Carroll Street'—the name parents gave the sweeping reforms and massive improvements I engineered at PS 6") and then to the infamous, formerly unmanageable Eastside High. Before Clark arrived at Eastside, the school's problems were critiqued in an investigative panel's forty-page report, initiated after a math teacher was assaulted by students while serving as cafeteria monitor. Among its many findings, the report noted:

—A chain of command is virtually nonexistent.

—Drugs are brought into the school not only by individual students and nonstudents but also by gangs who both use and sell.

—Assaults of students and teachers take place for a variety of reasons which run the gamut from robbery to revenge to outright viciousness.

And on and on. The stage is set for the new sheriff to ride into town. Clark's book really gets going when he finally accedes to the repeated pleas of the district superintendent to take over Eastside. Before he formally assumes the principalship, he drops by his new home:

When my appointment had not yet been officially announced but was being bruited about, I paid a number of informal visits to Eastside, looked around, and talked to some teachers.

"Welcome to east hell, Mr. Clark," said one gym teacher.

An English teacher, attempting to keep things humorous, added, "What does the portal sign in Dante say? 'Abandon every hope, ye that enter'."

"No offense to the great poet," I said. "But I'm having that sign removed."

Most of the book is then dedicated to chronicling the measures Clark adopted to bring order to Eastside. The most "extreme" actions were portrayed dramatically in *Lean on Me*, with Clark (played by Morgan Freeman) patrolling the halls every day with a bullhorn, berating tardy students or dressing down kids who wear gang colors, browbeating recalcitrant teachers who look the other way at drug deals or weapon-toting, or expelling on sight hundreds of students who Clark deems as "troublemakers." Watching Clark take control of the situation as the book progresses provides certain undeniable pleasures, not unlike watching Arnold Schwarzenegger dispatch a network of terrorists. Clark's top-down style has him taking charge of every aspect of the school's operation, from personal counseling to building maintenance. Clark enumerates each success in an oddly-wrought, pseudoliterary style, as in the following excerpt, where some longstanding graffiti gets sandblasted: "The grinding and booming whir was a symphony to my ears. I often stepped outside in the bright day and watched the vile scribblings get blasted to oblivion. The sober strength of the old building began to shine through with the beauty of renewal."

   That sense of splendor seems genuine. A great part of the appeal of reading *Laying Down the Law* is being able to participate in the uncompromising, almost obsessively forceful vision of a guy like Clark. As the book proceeds, one discards any hope of subtlety, nuance, or complexity clouding the narrative. Because Clark writes about what actually happened, the book moves from mere self-serving rhetoric to modern-day revenge fantasy. Clark is the hero of the book, hero to both those he feels he has saved from annihilation and our society

---

LEAN ON ME—BUT NOT TOO HARD

Joe Clark's record of disdain for the status quo and his defiance of institutional bureaucracy continued to engulf him in controversy a decade after he left Paterson's Eastside High School. In 1995, Clark became the director of the Essex County, New Jersey, Juvenile Detention Center. Mimicking the pattern of Eastside's reformation, Clark took control of the facility, which had become, in the estimation of county officials, overcrowded, undisciplined, and unhealthy. Clark won praise, mostly, for turning the institution around, although he continued his unique application of tough love—including the use of shackles and, in one instance, a straitjacket.

   Some employees of the facility complained to county officials or the media about Clark's methods and later charged that Clark retaliated against them through harassment, demotions, and firing. Seven of them filed suit and claimed their right to free speech was violated. Clark, who according to press accounts called his accusers "a batch of blundering, blathering idiots," was ultimately found guilty in May 2002 of violating the rights of two of the seven plaintiffs. After the case, in the *Newark Star-Ledger* Clark called the group "a bunch of extortionists." He resigned the next month.

in general—even if society hasn't properly recognized or rewarded him for his bravado.

Therein lies the book's principal shortcoming: in the absence of a counterweight to Clark's deluge of self-aggrandizement, the reader is unable to fully appreciate Clark's accomplishment. There is no perspective, no context in which to place Clark's achievements or evaluate his methods. Clark's critics—including many parents, teachers, newspaper columnists, and administrators—can't *all* be part of a conspiracy of mediocrity. Yet that is Clark's spin. He dismisses the frequent criticism of the Paterson Board of Education as bureaucratic hand-wringing and he claims he—and often, he alone—knows best. Let them criticize, he intones. Joe Clark will prevail:

> I had the Board of Education on my back, the media in my face, and the
> Fire Department and the mayor at my throat. The rumor mill was working
> overtime. My enemies were counting me out.

Never count out Joe Clark, he would be the first to say. In fact, he does say it, many times. He's willing to be unloved but not unheeded. As he prepared for his first day as principal, he mused about the stakes of getting off to a good start:

> I had no illusions. There would be no honeymoon period. A first day
> coup d'etat, from which there would be no turning back, was essential. And
> it would, indeed, be a coup d'état, a toppling from power.

Most readers will be swept up by the back-from-the-brink saga of Eastside High. Clark's success with the institution speaks for itself, if only he would let it. Where change was slow to come Clark blames institutional inertia or media misrepresentation. There's no doubt he left the place in much better shape than he found it. But great work, both at Eastside and in the broader world, still waits to be done, he reminds us at the end of the book. In fact, he offers a prophetic exhortation to follow his example—or else:

> I give you the example of myself. I have shown you what one man, a
> black man born into abject poverty, can accomplish against the odds. Now
> it is your turn to act and effect change. Help save our schools, our children,
> and the future of our civilization.

FURTHER READING

Of Related Interest

Evans, Robert. *The Human Side of School Change: Reform, Resistance, and the Real-Life Problems of Innovation.* San Francisco: Jossey-Bass, 2001.

Golin, Steve. *The Newark Teacher Strikes.* New Brunswick: Rutgers University Press, 2002.

One for the Money (1994)

(The first Stephanie Plum novel)

You can often tell a lot about an author by the kinds of people who attend a book signing. There is the sedate, tweed-and-tea crowd, waiting politely to meet an author and thank him or her for the book's impact on the reader's life. There's the how-to crowd, eager to engage the author about the fine points of the book (tax preparation, home repair, holistic medicine, parenting) and offer some personal tips. There's the celebrity-watching set, more interested in meeting a famous person than in actually reading the book.

Then there's the Janet Evanovich crowd. What are they like? Here's an excerpt from the author's official website about a recent signing:

> Last June, we had the kick-off signing for the *Seven Up* book tour in New York City, and it was our first (but not last!) stage show, complete with band, drag queen, and half-naked biker guy. Jersey Janet did a reading with Sally Sweet (remember Sally from *Four to Score*?) that was beyond description, and we got the gorgeous biker guy to take his shirt off. All this was very tastefully done, of course, because Jersey Janet is nothing if not tasteful. Yeah, right. Jersey Janet also discovered that bands are LOUD. So probably it's best not to put the author signing table directly in front of the amps. Think I still have some hearing loss.

In other words, fans of Janet Evanovich's wildly popular Stephanie Plum series of novels exhibit a rowdy-but-respectful posture, tough, fun, loud, devoted, quirky, but deadly serious when necessary. Just like the bounty-hunting Trenton-based Plum, who is equal parts Wonder Woman, Inspector Clouseau, and Peppermint Patty.

For the uninitiated, Evanovich's once-a-year fictional forays into the seedy world of the bounty-hunting Plum have catapulted the former South River resident to the top of the best-seller lists. After a decade of writing garden-variety romance novels, Evanovich (who graduated from South River High School and attended Douglass College, Rutgers University) decided to turn up the heat on her writing career. Trenton's bail-jumping FTAs (failure to appear) haven't been safe since Evanovich's segue from genteel bodice-rippers to brash, ballsy Stephanie Plum novels freed Evanovich to be more herself. In an online interview she explained, "I have more freedom of language with mystery. Okay, so I have a trash mouth. I'm from Jersey. What can I say?"

One for the Money, the inaugural Stephanie Plum novel, is also very much a Jersey book. Evanovich paints a picture of Trenton, and the Garden State in general, that is dead-on accurate, if a bit unflattering. Writing about "the Burg,"—

the Trenton neighborhood where Plum lives—Evanovich provides a psychic snapshot of the territory:

> Morelli and I were both born and raised in a blue-collar chunk of Trenton called the Burg. Houses were attached and narrow. Yards were small. Cars were American. The people were mostly of Italian descent, with enough Hungarians and Germans thrown in to offset inbreeding. It was a good place to buy calzone or play the numbers. And, if you had to live in Trenton anyway, it was an okay place to raise a family. . . .
>
> During winter months, wind ripped up Hamilton Avenue, whining past plate-glass windows, banking trash against curbs and storefronts. During summer months, the air sat still and gauzy, leaden with humidity, saturated with hydrocarbons. It shimmered over hot cement and melted road tar. Cicadas buzzed, dumpsters reeked, and a dusty haze hung in perpetuity over softball fields statewide. I figured it was all part of the great adventure of living in New Jersey.

Life in the Burg is not without its enticements. But almost:

> Food is important in the Burg. The moon revolves around the earth, the earth revolves around the sun, and the Burg revolves around pot roast. For as long as I can remember, my parents' lives have been controlled by five-pound pieces of rolled rump, done to perfection at six o'clock.

One could fill dozens of pages with the sly, knowing, and often cutting references to Jersey life that fill the eight Stephanie Plum books, but one gets the distinct impression neither Plum nor her creator would think of busting small-time bail skippers anywhere else.

One for the Money, despite its clear debt to crime fiction conventions, is a surprisingly original and fun read, filled with characters who transcend genre-template development and snappy writing that engages the ear. Evanovich is perhaps underestimated as a writer because of her popularity in such a well-worn groove as page-turning crime fiction. Her scenes unfold in a spectacularly satisfying way, unpredictable but exactly right. Her protagonist is more aware of her liabilities and more vulnerable than the stock detectives and PI's who generally prowl through these trigger-pullers. Evanovich seems to have stumbled upon the perfect mix of can-do egomania and middling ability in the conception of her heroine. It's hard to imagine any reader not registering a sympathetic smile as Plum boldly buys a gun but then remains too frightened to take it out of her handbag. As she says later, during another of the endless humiliations that plague her efforts to learn the bounty-hunting trade (for instance, she can't figure out how to discharge a self-defense spray until the clerk tells her, patronizingly, to just "put your finger on the button"): "I didn't feel like a professional. I felt like an idiot."

The basic outline for the series was established in *One for the Money*: quick-witted Plum (who fell into the job after being downsized from a stint as a lingerie buyer), assisted by a veteran bounty hunter, the sarcastic but highly professional Ranger, and an ex-cop and sometime love interest Joe Morelli, seeks bail-jumping felons, occasionally returning for comfort to her mother's cooking and her grandmother's idiosyncratic enthusiasms (she attends funerals in bright blue spandex shorts and stockings rolled down to her knees). On the streets of Trenton, Plum patrols for deadbeats; the reader is treated to lots of naturalistic details about the cityscape:

> The Trenton police department houses itself in a cubelike three-story brick building representing the Practical Pig approach to municipal architecture. Clearly low on the funding food chain, Police Headquarters has been afforded few frills, which is just as well considering it is surrounded by ghetto, and the location almost certainly ensures annihilation should a riot of major proportions ever occur.

Stephanie Plum spends a lot of time hauling uncooperative criminals to that police headquarters building. Often, they resist, but that just goes with the territory; she reasons: "The way I see it, living in New Jersey is a challenge, what with the toxic waste and the eighteen wheelers and the armed schizophrenics. I mean, what's one more lunatic shooting at you?"

The *New York Times* called Stephanie Plum "a Jersey girl with Bette Midler's mouth and Cher's fashion sense." Evanovich displays a similar gift for bold fash-

---

CAPITOL IMPROVEMENTS

Janet Evanovich's series of Stephanie Plum novels has certainly raised Trenton's profile for a modern generation of readers. But anyone who thinks she put Trenton on the cultural map would be wrong—by more than two hundred years.

In 1776, Trenton was home to only a hundred or so houses, but on Christmas Eve that year, George Washington made his famous crossing of the ice-choked Delaware, stunning the Hessian soldiers quartered in those houses and leading the Continental troops to victory in the "Battle of Trenton," which many historians cite as the turning point of the Revolutionary War.

Aside from the famous painting of Washington's crossing by artist Emanuel Leutze, the battle has been chronicled in a number of books, articles, documentaries, movies, plays, and poems. Among the best books on the battle are *The Day Is Ours! An Inside View of the Battles of Trenton and Princeton, November 1776–January 1777*, by William Dwyer (1998, Rutgers University Press), *The Winter Soldiers: the Battles for Trenton and Princeton*, by Richard Ketchum (1999, Owl Books), and, for younger readers, *Crossing the Delaware: A History in Many Voices*, by Louise Peacock (1998, Athenaeum).

ion statements, posing for book jacket cover photos in motorcycle leather. The author, who now lives in New Hampshire but regularly returns to New Jersey "to work on my slang," is planning to write at least one more Stephanie Plum novel, to bring the total to ten. Beyond that, she's not saying. But in each book in the series, one senses Evanovich's real affection for Stephanie Plum, and as the series has expanded, the relationship between creator and creation has never betrayed any sign of boredom, merely a mutual sense of comfort—though in Plum's world, the comfortable is intertwined with feelings of anxiety. As Stephanie says when she arrives at her parents' house in *One for the Money*, "There was safety here, along with love, and stability, and the comfort of ritual. The clock on the dash told me I was seven minutes late, and the urge to scream told me I was home."

FURTHER READING

Books by Evanovich

Full House. New York: St. Martin's Press, 2002.
Hard Eight (A Stephanie Plum novel). New York: St. Martin's Press, 2002.
Two for the Show (A Stephanie Plum novel). New York: Scribner's 1996.

Of Related Interest

Hyman, Dick. *The Trenton Pickle Ordinance and Other Bonehead Legislation*. Brattleboro, Vt.: Stephen Greene Press, 1976.
Klim, Christopher. *Jesus Lives in Trenton*. Berkeley, Calif.: Creative Arts Book Co., 2002.

Our Guys (1997)

Geographically, Glen Ridge is tiny. Shoehorned between its two heftier neighbors (Bloomfield to the east, Montclair to the west), it appears as a thin, elongated bacon-shaped strip of land—if it appears at all—on maps of New Jersey. But Glen Ridge, for a time, loomed quite large on the American psychic landscape. According to journalist and prize-winning author Bernard Lefkowitz,

> Millions of Americans discovered that Glen Ridge was not a foreign and alien culture, but all too closely resembled their own communities. Glen Ridge's test of character became America's test of character. Glen Ridge ultimately found that it could not insulate itself against the turbulence created by an outrage that in the past would have been hidden and buried. Like Glen Ridge, America has been forced in recent years to define what are fair, just, and principled relations between men and women. That has not been easy for Glen Ridge to do. And it hasn't been easy for America either.

The impetus for this national round of soul searching was ugly—the entice-
ment and brutal violation of a Glen Ridge teenager by her peers. The victim, a
mentally challenged high school girl, was sodomized by a handful of athletes,
who also penetrated her with a baseball bat and broomstick. A group of thirteen
high school boys participated in the assault or heckled the girl with cheers and
catcalls during the incident. The world first became aware of the crime (and the
world, in fact, was part of the audience, with reports of the Glen Ridge case
picked up by several international news agencies) on May 23, 1989, when New
York television stations reported on an investigation into an alleged sexual
assault on a seventeen-year-old girl by some "star" athletes from the affluent suburb of Glen Ridge.

As the case unfolded—first in the New York media and later in book-length
studies and a made-for-television movie—America got a peek behind the hedges
of "the perfect suburb" (to borrow a phrase from Lefkowitz's subtitle). What was
uncovered was a frightening value system that countenanced the regular
(mis)behavior of Glen Ridge's jock elites.

But even this story had two sides, and from press accounts, court testimony,
and local newspaper op-ed pages, many residents of the gas-lamp-lit suburb
about ten miles west of Manhattan felt their town was being unfairly singled out
for the behavior of a few spoiled teens. Others, including the attorney who
defended the accused boys against charges of gang rape, relied on the often-
discredited but always bruising "she-was-asking-for-it" defense.

Though much has been written about the case, Lefkowitz's book, *Our Guys:
The Glen Ridge Rape and the Secret Life of the Perfect Suburb,* stands as the bench-
mark analysis of the circumstances that contributed to the incident—before,
during, and after. Throughout the book, Lefkowitz burns with indignation about
the culture of privilege that led to casual acts of irresponsibility, criminality, and
inhumanity. In the end, he fingers everybody who was around town, watching,
tolerating, doing nothing to stop the erosion of morality that encouraged the
teenaged misogynists:

> Glen Ridge placed the elite kids—the kids with masculine good looks,
> the kids who stood out on the playing field—on a pedestal. But there
> wasn't much room there for those who didn't fit the Glen Ridge model of
> achievement. It was doubtful whether there was any space at all on that
> pedestal for young women or whether it was strictly reserved for boys.
>
> Adults might have forestalled the unfolding tragedy in their town if they
> had questioned their own values, if they had challenged the assumptions of
> the culture that defined how people treated one another in Glen Ridge. They
> could have provided an alternative model of behavior to youngsters, one that
> emphasized fairness, compassion, humanity, and decency. But that required
> too much self-examination, too many embarrassing admissions of failure.

They weren't up to it. They decided to hope for the best. And they got the worst.

He also goes after the justice system, suggesting that the judge who sentenced the boys to a "young adult offenders' institution" was more interested in preserving the reputation of the "elite" offenders and their families than in promoting justice:

> When he [Judge Benjamin Cohen] recalled how they had appeared in court and the distress on the faces of their families and friends, he also thought about how he had acted when he was a teenager. He asked himself, how much sense and discretion did I have? He told himself that there was no excuse for what they did, but then, he thought, if it hadn't been for that one horrible day, they would have been someone's All-American boys. You didn't want to lock up All-American boys and throw the key away. That's the way Judge Cohen thought.

Our Guys has the urgency of a compelling thriller, but Lefkowitz also imbues the book with sociological heft. Lefkowitz isn't afraid to grapple with the big issues. In fact, he can't seem to keep from finding universal (or at least postmodern suburban) truths in the small details of the case. He keeps both lines of inquiry—how this came to happen in Glen Ridge; how things like this came to happen all the time in America—moving. His journalistic eye resembles one of those snapshot cameras that move back and forth from zoom to wide angle instantaneously. In the following passage, for example, the perspective lurches between Newark (close enough to be considered a neighboring city, but light years away in the things that matter to many suburbanites) and Glen Ridge:

> The kids in Newark, black and brown, speaking Spanglish, hoods over their heads wheeling their stolen cars over to the local chop shop—they were aliens in America. Strange, forever separate and separated from the American ideal. But these Glen Ridge kids, they were pure gold, every mother's dream, every father's pride. They were not only Glen Ridge's finest, but in their perfection they belonged to all of us. They were Our Guys.

Lyrical, and in its way accurate, yet one can almost feel Lefkowitz straining to sound profound. It's one thing to note the differences between communities divided by class; it's another to suggest that a bunch of spoiled, mannerless jocks "in their perfection" represent the ideal to most mature people (let alone whether anyone would proudly claim them as "Our Guys"). But Lefkowitz's thesis is deflated unless he can sell the idea that the Glen Ridge jock class is everyone's American dream. It's true that Lefkowitz uncovers some painful, piercing truths about American society's reverence for athletic achievement. But throughout

the book, there hovers an uncritical acceptance of the belief that most suburbanites would be proud to have parented children who turn out like "Our
Guys." Long before they showed their true colors in their horrific gang assault,
these teens were famously crude, vain, shallow, and bullying. When Lefkowitz
writes that the accused were "every mother's dream, every father's pride," it's
hard to know if he's being sarcastic or earnest. Such writerly excess, however,

A GRISLY LIST

The Glen Ridge rape case grabbed national attention, at once mesmerizing and
repulsing people with the accounts of the gleeful involvement of the perpetrators.
But for sheer calculated brutality, New Jersey's 1971 "List murders" arguably
holds the distinction as the state's most heinous crime.

John List and his family lived in Westfield. Well known throughout the community for his extreme piety and austere personality (the humorless, businesslike
List used to mow his lawn in a suit and tie), List began experiencing several financial problems. In addition, his teenaged daughter Patty had begun to act, well, like
a teenager. List feared for the salvation of her soul.

To save his children from God's damnation and his family from economic hardship, List took what he saw as a necessary—even protective—step. He murdered
them all: wife, three children, and even his mother who lived with them in their
nineteen-room mansion.

Police discovered the bodies laid out symmetrically on sleeping bags, each having been shot at point blank range. His fifteen-year-old son, John Frederick, was
shot nine times because, as List revealed, "when he fell, his body had some jerk-
ing movements. So I pulled out the .22 and I shot to hit him in the heart. I didn't
want him to suffer." In a lengthy letter to his pastor, List detailed his reasons for
his actions. Through a series of clear, calmly composed letters at the crime scene,
he explained what he had done and why; he added: "After it was all over, I said
some prayers for them all from the hymn book. That was the least I could do."

The postscript to the case took eighteen years to write: List fled New Jersey
after murdering his family and lived under an alias. In Midlothian, Virginia, he
remarried, became a respectable businessman, and resumed his position as a pil-
lar in his church. His fulfilling new life as "Bob P. Clark" came to an end after List's
cold-blooded crime was profiled on the nationally broadcast television show
"America's Most Wanted"; host John Walsh called it "New Jersey's most famous
murder." After police artists created a bust of what List probably looked like
eighteen years after the crime, hundreds of calls came in to the show's hotline.
Several callers suggested the appearance and psychological profile fitted a man
they knew called Bob Clark.

List/Clark was arrested by FBI agents at his place of work, although he initially
denied that he was the fugitive. Fingerprint evidence quickly established that they
were one and the same. List was extradited to New Jersey, where he was tried,
convicted on five counts of first-degree murder, and sentenced to life in prison.

weighs little against his book's overall impact. Critically lauded, the book became a *New York Times* Notable Book of the Year and a finalist for the Edgar Award. *Our Guys* was praised by journalists, sociologists, criminologists, and rape counselors. Lisa Gitelman wrote in her review of the book for *New Jersey History*,

> *Our Guys* is an important book for anyone interested in the sociological origins of criminal behavior. As Lefkowitz points out in his introduction, the sociology of crime too often involves the rehearsal of simplistic connections between bad environments and bad deeds. What about bad deeds in (supposedly) good places? Lefkowitz offers no satisfying answer, but the complexity he adds to questions like this is well worth our consideration.

For all the attention the case brought to Glen Ridge, it's difficult to characterize the attitude of the town itself toward the book. Lefkowitz has commented that Glen Ridge seems little changed and that he still receives letters scolding him for sensationalizing the case. Some evidence supports charges of a lingering bunker mentality in some quarters. When ABC-TV showed the movie version of Lefkowitz's book, the local papers chastised the network for opening old wounds. Most residents acknowledge the heinous nature of the crime and berate the values underlying such behavior; others, however, are simply waiting for the memory of the whole incident to become as dim as the town's vintage Victorian gas lamps.

FURTHER READING

Of Related Interest

Eckert, Penelope. *Jocks and Burnouts: Social Categories and Identity in the High School.* New York: Teachers College Press, 1989.

Laufer, Peter. *A Question of Consent: Innocence and Complicity in the Glen Ridge Rape Case.* San Francisco: Mercury House, 1994.

Miedzian, Myriam. *Boys Will Be Boys: Breaking the Link between Masculinity and Violence.* New York: Doubleday, 1991.

Lost Legends of New Jersey (2000)

Recent visitors to Essex County's Turtle Back Zoo in West Orange might be surprised to find the facility in such good shape. For years—decades, really—the zoo languished as little more than a repository for animals who were rather long in the tooth or had been rescued from the wilds of suburban New Jersey. But the zoo now contains buffalo, deer, llamas, otters, and a "cougarland waterfall" exhibit, as well as all the usual petting-zoo-type farm animals. There are even bald eagles, prairie dogs, and elephant rides (on selected weekends). It's not the Bronx Zoo, to be sure, but it's also not a bad place to kill a couple of hours on a summer afternoon.

Readers of Frederick Reiken's novel *The Lost Legends of New Jersey* get to travel back in time to the early 1980s, to the dingier days of Turtle Back's neglect, when torn fences and boarded-up pens were the norm. In a wonderfully realized scene in the book, a teenaged girl who feels adrift sneaks into the zoo at dusk to ponder the fate of the incarcerated animals—as well as her own:

> And so she drove, very slowly, to the South Mountain Arena in West Orange. West Orange was one town over from Livingston. The rink was next to Turtle Back Zoo. She'd never been inside the zoo. . . . It was dusk when she coasted into the wide lot and parked a little way from the rink's entrance. She saw the zoo across the lot. She started wondering if she could manage to get inside the zoo. [She does get in, hopping a fence and making her way past some maintenance shacks and dingy animal pens. And then—] She started wondering about the animals. What the hell did they do at night? It was so quiet that it was strange to think the animals were in there. By the zoo's entrance, she sat down and tried imagining she'd turned into an animal.

Such nature-induced introspection occurs frequently in Reiken's novel of adolescent longing and suburban ennui. Left to forage in five-hundred-year-old Arthurian tales for true mythic insight, Reiken's characters buy supermarket checkout-line star charts and then use them to identify constellations with mock-epic names like "Miriam the Kvetch" and "Manny the Disappointment." Deprived of ancient burial grounds in which to connect to the past (and largely uninspired by their middling embrace of their Jewishness), the characters of *Lost Legends* sift for meaning in a mysterious graveyard for marching band instruments, discovered wholly by accident when they get lost in the New Jersey swamps on the way home from a Meadowlands rock concert.

As one can easily deduce from the title, this book is tied to the Garden State in both mindset and geography. Reiken clearly knows the terrain, although he gets carried away with local references that don't do much to amplify his theme or carry his meaning beyond a quick nod of recognition, such as "coasting down the hill towards Don's Restaurant," or "He'd just walked over to Nettie Ochs, the extant apple orchard in Livingston." Reiken, though, is a bona fide New Jersey writer: he grew up in Livingston and has lived in South Orange, West Orange, Summit, Short Hills, and Boonton.

Reiken's first novel, *The Odd Sea* (1998), won the Hackney Literary Award for a first novel and was selected as one of the best first novels of 1998 by *Booklist* and *Library Journal*. *The Odd Sea*—like *Legends*, also told from the viewpoint of an adolescent boy—revolves around the disappearance of fifteen-year-old Ethan Shumway and his family's reaction to this tragedy. Several reviewers praised Reiken's restrained tone and journalistic attention to detail, perhaps unsurprising given Reiken's connection to the periodic press. For years, Reiken wrote a weekly column for the *Daily Hampshire Gazette*, a newspaper in Northampton, Massachusetts. His keen eye for naturalistic detail and an equally sharp ear for authentic dialogue are apparent in his journalistic snapshots of the hill towns of western Massachusetts. Consider this excerpt from a piece about ice fishing:

> While I was speaking with LaRochelle, he got a "tip-up," meaning a nibble from a fish had caused the neon-orange flag on the device to release into a vertical position. So I went racing across the ice with him, this being the first tip-up I had ever witnessed. As it turned out, a smart or else lucky fish had managed to steal the bait without being hooked. Seeing that he would have to re-bait the line, Rochelle turned and yelled over fifty yards or so of frozen lake, "Hey Mark, meet me half way with a schmer!" Then he turned to me and said, "Patience, that's the major f——ing strategy."

Reiken, a writing instructor in the graduate program at Boston's Emerson College, knows his way around a frozen pond. In *Lost Legends* protagonist Anthony Rubin lives to play hockey, whether roller skating on his driveway practicing slapshots in the summer or coaching a Pee Wee–style hockey camp. The world of hockey, with its violence, athleticism, and complexity, is the world to Anthony. *The Lost Legends of New Jersey* is filled with bits of his vast information about hockey and ice skating. But Reiken does little to make the sport meaningful to readers who don't already share his enthusiasm; he merely peppers the book with hockey talk. Both the general appeal of the sport and Anthony's specific obsession with the game or his feelings on the ice are absent. Reiken could as well be writing about soccer or baseball as hockey.

Reiken seems, at times, to expect his reader to automatically, and meaningfully, connect to the many pop cultural references he's making; for instance, musicians Bruce Springsteen, the now-forgotten top-40 act Supertramp, and the rock group "Rush" figure in the book; Reiken even alludes to the title of Rush's song "Red Barchetta." Although the song's lyrics tell the story of a wild chase through time in an old, restored race car, the characters' references to this fairly obscure song are wasted on unfamiliar readers.

In many instances Reiken might, for example, suddenly reveal a main character to be an accomplished clarinet player or a late-blooming scuba diver—possibly effective details, if they didn't feel so much like quirky add-ons. Readers expect these particulars to reflect some hidden quality, some telling detail, that brings them closer to understanding what makes these characters tick.

Such criticism, however, places one in the minority of readers, many of whom hailed *The Lost Legends of New Jersey* as a modern masterpiece. On the strength of Reiken's first two books, some critics have already begun comparing him to Philip Roth and John Updike, famed chroniclers of the hidden world of suburban entropy. The *Los Angeles Times* hailed Reiken for creating "a rich, seductive mythology out of the ordinary places and people of the Garden State." The very idea that New Jersey, as designated in the book's title, could conceal such mythic echoes is confronted in a passage where Anthony muses about his mother:

> And always Anthony wanted answers. He wanted some logical story to explain why she was gone. So he invented the explanations. He tried to think of her the way he thought of characters in legends. But he was always doing that, making things up, trying to see how it all might fit into a legend. He didn't understand why he did this, because New Jersey was not a legend. It was the armpit of America, according to most people. Still, he saw everything around him as a legend.

STATE OF ENLIGHTENMENT

Midway through *The Lost Legends of New Jersey*, Frederick Reiken introduces a minor character who becomes fixated with exploring the Kabbalah. Readers who find their spiritual appetites whetted by this episode might want to know a bit more about this fascinating and mysterious practice.

In Talmudic Hebrew, Kabbalah signifies post-Mosaic tradition, such as rabbinical laws not contained in the Pentateuch. In the Middle Ages, Kabbalah came to be associated with mystical doctrines developing in France and Spain. Ever since, Kabbalah is often used synonymously with "Jewish mysticism," although practitioners of Kabbalah distinguish between "esoteric" Kabbalah and "practical" Kabbalah, the magical use of Kabbalistic teaching to further one's own spiritual awareness.

Kabbalah is often portrayed as an archaic, wildly complex religious practice whose secrets are open only to Orthodox rabbis able to decode highly symbolic sacred Hebrew texts. Such a picture may represent one aspect of Kabbalah, but many non-Jews have embraced the Kabbalah as a means of increasing self-awareness and fostering spiritual evolution.

Modern Kabbalahists focus on reaching a state of concentration such that the mind achieves a synthesis between the seen and unseen worlds. The Kabbalah's reputation for complexity resides, in part, in its appropriation of elements of Egyptian magic, Rosicrucian ritual, Christian prayer, and Masonic secret oath swearing. The aim of Kabbalah practice is to introduce the conscious mind to the wonder of the world most people can't see—angels, demons, and the like. Kabbalahists believe such spiritual enlightenment can be drawn from the serious study of the Old Testament, the Tarot deck, and an interconnected symbol called the "Tree of Life."

Reiken gives us much to see and marvel at; he parades characters who may have no more distinction than their ability to do a standing backflip on command or dispense love-life advice while driving a tow truck. The story moves briskly between times (the early 1980s and the present), places (Florida and New Jersey), social status levels (Jewish middle-class suburban and shabby genteel Italian pseudo-mafioso), and narrative postures (first-person to third-person). Reiken does an admirable job of keeping several narrative threads running simultaneously. His "now look over here" approach keeps the pacing brisk and the characters fresh. Reiken packs the text with allusions to institutions up and down the Garden State: diners, hospitals, union halls, concert halls, private schools, bakeries, a kind of fictional gazetteer for the Jersey-ignorant. Yet, for all the local reference, one feels the book could have been set almost anywhere, with a different menu of place names, and the impact would have been about the same. The reader of this book learns the names of lots of New Jersey places, but not much about what makes those places unique.

Yet Reiken has imbued almost every page with some Jersey-based anchor. Creating a sense of place in his work is clearly one of his goals; he explained his geographic creation in an interview:

> A sense of place is where everything starts for me. Before I can even create characters I have to attach imaginatively to a place. I'd even go so far as to say that in some way I have to feel something like love for a place, and that the characters and story I come up with are usually direct extensions of that place.

Many readers and critics, responding passionately to Reiken's fictional world of *Lost Legends*, claim that the book leaves them feeling, if not legendary, at least renewed affection for the state. Reiken's protagonist says it all while landing at Newark Airport: "It's always strange to me that all this is so comforting. And yet it is."

FURTHER READING

Books by Reiken
The Odd Sea. San Diego: Harcourt Brace, 1998.

Of Related Interest
Hankins, Grace Croyle. *True Stories of New Jersey.* Philadelphia: John Winston Co., 1938.
Kaplan, James. *Two Guys from Verona: A Novel of Suburbia.* New York: Grove/Atlantic, 1999.

Part Three **The History**

Searching for Captain Kidd's Treasure

Well, you have heard, of course, the many stories current—the thousand vague rumors afloat about money buried, somewhere upon the Atlantic Coast, by Kidd and his associates. These rumors must have had some foundation in fact. And that the rumors have existed so long and so continuous, could have resulted, it appeared to me, only from the circumstance of the buried treasure still remaining entombed.

— Edgar Allan Poe, "The Gold Bug" (1843)

Every August, a number of hotels and tourist-fueled businesses in the Cape May area sponsor the "Annual Captain Kidd Treasure Hunt." The event, designed for children but attracting the occasional mature scavenger, has been held for the past thirty-five years. To date, no real pirate treasure has been found (though some savvy merchants have taken to burying tin boxes filled with gift certificates).

In Cliffwood Beach, beginning in the spring, handfuls of treasure seekers can be found at dawn earnestly digging for buried booty said to be worth untold millions, after its dispatch more than three hundred years ago. The same scene is repeated, with varying degrees of seriousness, in Sandy Hook and along the mouth of the Toms River. Local beach combers, curious tourists, and even international scholars have all picked up shovels, metal detectors, and aged maps; they set out in search of hidden tracts and natural formations that mark the exact spot where the famous outlaw buried his considerable cache of ill-gotten goods.

Who was this infamous pirate? And just why would England's most reviled—and, in some quarters, celebrated—seventeenth-century brigand bury his plunder in the soil of the Garden State? The answers uncover a tale whose mix of legend and legitimacy ensures that Kidd's legacy will not soon be purged from the Jersey Shore.

Captain William Kidd, much like Robin Hood, has become a larger and more influential character than his biography genuinely merits. Kidd was born in 1645 in Scotland, worked as a ship captain carrying goods between the Caribbean and Britain, and in his forties, relocated to the colonies where he continued his highly successful merchant vessel business. When seeking a commission in the British Royal Navy, he returned to England. Kidd failed to gain the commission, but he nonetheless received a royal license to become a "privateer," seizing French and pirate ships on behalf of the British government.

In 1696, Kidd set off from England to New York in his newly outfitted ship, the *Adventure Galley*. However, before he got very far, the British navy stopped and "impressed" (drafted, that is) most of Kidd's crew and forced Kidd to find new crew mates; to them he promised an impossibly large share of his profits, given his commitments to his private backers.

Kidd sailed off to the Red Sea, where he ostensibly forgot his charge to corral pirates and instead became one. On the high seas his crimes and Ahab-like ruthlessness form, however, the stuff of speculation. Little evidence exists that Kidd was the evil, scavenging madman later generations of fiction writers have portrayed. He was, it seems clear, involved in some acts of thievery on the high seas, although his defenders claim he was simply fulfilling his mandate to capture other pirates' ships. Moreover, the historical record counters images of his alleged murderous nature; testimony of career military officers and merchants in England and New York claims Kidd was, in the words of King William, "Trusty and Well-Beloved." But historical record holds little sway in forging legend. Willard Hallam Bonner points out in his book, *Pirate Laureate: The Life and Legends of Captain Kidd,*

An anonymous seventeenth-century woodcut showing
the infamous pirate Captain Kidd burying a Bible.

The many ways in which Captain Kidd touched the imagination of America are little known, yet the sum total cannot be described otherwise than as an important contribution to the nation's culture. Around Kidd's name grew a whole mass of lore—beliefs, tales, legends—of interest in itself, of course, but serving a higher purpose for writers to come later. A fine old ballad was not only refined on American tongues, but its tunes entered the service of revival hymnology. The Kidd legend furnished themes and background for many pieces of nineteenth-century fiction and played a dominant part in fixing the character of the conventional buccaneer and the conventional buried treasure tale through Washington Irving and Robert Louis Stevenson. It came to life in the minds of the superstitious and naïve, in prose fiction and in lurid lives of criminals, on the stage, in the concert hall, and in moral tales for the young. All in all, it was inextricably associated with the American scene.

Especially the New Jersey scene. But Kidd was not, by any means, the first pirate to discover the strategic value of the Jersey Shore. In his study *Patriots, Pirates, and Pineys*, Robert Peterson explains the pirate-Jersey connection:

In old South Jersey, the mouth of the Delaware was a general rendezvous for merchantmen with their riches from the East and West Indies, making this area prime hunting ground for pirates. The merchantmen's cargoes were destined for New York, New England, and Burlington (then West Jersey's capital), but often found their way into a pirate's treasure trove. This area was made even more conducive to pirates due to Philadelphia's lack of naval and military strength and the reluctance of the peace-loving Quakers to hang such rascals. Delaware Bay and the barrier islands off Atlantic and Cape May counties became something of a resort for these outlaw vessels and were used for repair of their ships.

Kidd was known to have arrived in New Jersey shortly after he and his crew captured an Indian ship called the *Queedah Merchant*, a vessel reportedly filled with silks, spices, gold, and weapons. The captain scuttled the *Adventure Galley*, giving a good part of the newly seized loot to his crew. Kidd can be defended against piracy charges: he seized other ships only to be able to pay his own crew and continue his work for the British government. Kidd captained the *Queedah Merchant* to the Caribbean. When he landed, he discovered that he had been charged with "the crime of piracy." Immediately taking to the seas, he headed to New York in the hope that one of his well-heeled and influential colonist friends would intervene with the British government and arrange to have the charges dropped. During this trip, Kidd stopped several times in and around New Jersey in the *Queedah Merchant*, a ship still brimming with treasures. Ship logs indicate that he filled his water casks at Lilly Pond, a ten-acre fresh-water pond at Cape May, and dropped anchor in the Raritan Bay.

Unsuccessful in his attempts to clear his name, Kidd sailed up to Boston to ask the governor of Massachusetts for his assistance. Instead of intervening on his behalf, the governor had him arrested. The authorities demanded that Kidd turn over the wealth of the *Queedah Merchant*, but the unrepentant captain claimed to have hidden all but $10,000 worth of treasure (the total take was estimated to be near half a million dollars in 1700—a nearly inestimable fortune in today's dollars). The token amount Kidd handed over was sent to England and used as evidence in Kidd's trial. The rest, if Kidd is to be believed, was buried somewhere in or near the Jersey Shore.

In its "investigation" of the Kidd case, the editors of *Weird New Jersey* (Issue #14) cited the following four locations as having a particularly strong claim of "being the hiding place." These include Cape May, an island (now submerged) at the mouth of the Toms River, Sandy Hook, and "Money Island," another now-submerged island north of Sandy Hook near Whalen Creek, the current southeast border of Middlesex and Monmouth counties. Money Island was located off the coast where Cliffwood Beach is today. In addition to possible sites of Kidd's lost loot, the investigative article points out a number of landmarks and landscape features once thought linked to piracy:

NOT JUST FOR KIDDS

Although the notorious Captain Kidd is the figure most often associated with the reign of pirates who plagued the Eastern Seaboard during colonial times, Kidd himself was no match for the villain history has dubbed "Blackbeard the Pirate" (whose real name was Edward Teach). Kidd was, at one time, widely respected in polite society, even courted by legislators and wealthy businessmen.

But nobody liked Blackbeard. He is widely regarded as the meanest and most ruthless pirate ever to have prowled the high seas. He was also (if the stories are to be believed) quite a crackpot. The same man who used to braid his long black beard and then decorate the braids with colorful ribbons regularly enjoyed a sporting contest that involved filling pots in the hold of his ship with brimstone, lighting them on fire, closing all the hatches, and seeing how long he and his cronies could keep from suffocating.

Among the New Jersey locales frequented by Blackbeard were Burlington County, where he would stock up on foodstuffs for his transatlantic trips, and an unidentified island near the Mullica River, where he supposedly hid out when the authorities were seeking to corral him.

Eventually, the law did catch up to Blackbeard. In November 1718, after the pirate had terrorized the merchant trading ships off the Virginia and Carolina coasts for months, the governor of Virginia sent the HMS *Pearl* after Blackbeard. They got him. The governor's men attacked the ship, captured and killed Blackbeard, cut off his head, took it back to Virginia, and mounted it publicly on top of a pole.

What is not a legend, and cannot be disputed, was the existence of two gigantic elm trees, which were known as 'Kidd's Rangers.' One was at the mouth of the Matawan Creek, in Keyport, and stood until the turn of this century. The other was located at Fox Hill, now known as Rose Hill, which was thirty to forty feet higher than now (it is an interesting coincidence that Rose Hill became a cemetery in the early 1700s and is considered one of the most haunted cemeteries in New Jersey). These trees, according to legend, acted as range markers to guide Kidd back to his buried gold, and Cliffwood Beach is centered between these two markers when sailing west from Long Island. To this day, you can still see people occasionally searching for treasure at Cliffwood Beach using shovels and metal detectors. On occasion, some tiny bits of gold and silver are still found.

Edgar Allan Poe famously exploited this idea of certain trees being the key to the spot of the buried treasure. In his short story, "The Gold Bug," Poe sends his protagonist on a journey to "an enormously tall tulip-tree, which stood with some eight or ten oaks, upon the level and far surpassed them all, and all other trees which I had then ever seen, in the beauty of its foliage and form." One of Kidd's Rangers, perhaps?

New Jersey–born James Fenimore Cooper picked up the Kidd tales, which were circulating around the Jersey Shore, and turned them into a novel, *The Water Witch*. Cooper rhapsodizes about the shore's allure to pirates and law-abiders alike, romanticizing the inlets along the Raritan Bay:

A Happy mixture of land and water, seen by a bright moon, and beneath the sky the fortieth degree of latitude, cannot fail to make a pleasing picture. Such was the landscape which the reader must now endeavor to present to his mind. The wide estuary of Raritan is shut in from the winds and billows of the open sea by a long, low and narrow cape, or point, which by a medley of the Dutch and English languages, that is by no means rare in the names of places that lie within the former territories of the United Provinces of Holland, is known by the name of Sandy Hook. This tongue of land appears to have been made by the unremitting and opposing actions of the waves on one side, and of the currents of the different rivers that empty their waters into the bay, on the other. It is commonly connected with the low coast of New Jersey, to the south; but there are periods of many years in succession, during which there exists an inlet from the sea, between what may be termed the inner end of the cape and the mainland. During these periods, Sandy Hook, of course, becomes an island.

Such a romantic take on Kidd's stopping grounds is not at odds with the legends that arose in the wake of the famous pirate's Jersey Shore leaves. Local historian and author William McMahon, in his book *Pine Barrens: Legends and Lore*, relates an anecdote that reveals a slightly softer side of the notorious Captain Kidd:

It was in these waters awaiting repairs to his ship that he became infatuated of a farm lass identified only as Amanda, who lived in the vicinity of Barnegat. Because of this attachment, Kidd planned to abandon the wild, seafaring life of a buccaneer, trading it for the more peaceful one of a coastal fisherman. With this in mind he is said to have spirited away a great amount of stolen treasure from under the eyes of his crew with whom, according to pirate code, he should have shared it, and buried it in the vicinity of Oyster Creek. The love story could have had a peaceful and happy conclusion at this point save that some of Kidd's pirate crew became aware of their captain's amour and, believing they were being abandoned, they jumped ship and made their way overland to New York. Given the promise of full pardons, they informed authorities of the whereabouts of the pirate captain and his vessel. Kidd's ship was anchored near the mouth of the Little Egg Harbor river when three British armed vessels closed in on him. In a running battle he made good his escape into open waters. Amanda vanished into the vastness of the Pines. Whether she ever dug up the treasure and used it will never be known.

Kidd's fate was sealed—and his legend established—by the British Admirality Court, which found him guilty of piracy and murder. Kidd was accused of killing crew member William Moore by striking him in the head with an oaken bucket; Kidd countered that he was simply defending himself against the mutinous gunner's mate Moore. Kidd maintained his innocence to the bitter end, and it was bitter: Kidd was hanged, and his body was covered with tar, bound with chains, and left dangling from a support pole over the Thames River in London for more than a year as a deterrent to would-be pirates.

Prior to the pronouncement of guilt, Kidd told the court that he would be willing to return to the colonies, retrieve his treasure, and after paying back his backers, turn over the remaining spoils to the government. He never got the chance. But Kidd insisted that the treasure was out there, waiting for him; this secretly squirreled stash has left generations of weekend scavengers convinced that great wealth awaited them—if only they could find the right place to dig.

"Some thousands they will flock when I die / Some thousands they will flock!" goes a popular ballad from the early 1700s called "Captain Kidd's Farewell to the Sea." Three centuries later, along the Jersey Shore, they're still flocking.

FURTHER READING

Hinrichs, Dunbar. *The Fateful Voyage of Captain Kidd.* New York: Bookman Associates, 1955.

McMahon, William. *South Jersey Towns.* New Brunswick: Rutgers University Press, 1987.

Richie, Robert. *Captain Kidd and the War Against the Pirates.* Cambridge: Harvard University Press, 1986.

Roberts, Glenys. *Richard Knight's Treasure: The True Story of His Extraordinary Quest for Captain Kidd's Cache.* New York: Viking, 1986.

Burr, Hamilton, and the Duel of History in Weehawken

On the morning of July 11, 1804, Weehawken entered the annals of American history as the site of one of the country's most ignominious events: the fatal duel between Alexander Hamilton and Aaron Burr. Historian Joseph Ellis has written that the "duel has become an icon-event, like the Kennedy assassination, the liaison between Thomas Jefferson and Sally Hemmings, or the Salem witch trials."

Historians generally agree upon most facts leading up to the duel, yet some areas of inquiry remain maddeningly murky. For example, it has long been argued that the precipitating cause for the duel was some disparaging comment Hamilton uttered against his political rival and then-vice president Burr, but did that comment alone push Burr to his extreme response? The speculation on this point has ranged from the psychological (Burr was an egomaniac who could tolerate no public criticism) to the lurid (one celebrated contemporary author suggested Hamilton had accused Burr of an incestuous relationship with his daughter, Theodosia).

Even more vexing to historians is the question of what really happened on the palisades of Weehawken as the rivals stood ten paces (twenty feet) apart. Did Hamilton really fire into the air on purpose? Who fired the first shot? Were the pistols altered to give either participant an advantage? And why do the eyewitness accounts differ on some significant points?

There's no shortage of speculation on those points, much of it from established scholars of the period. In the last few years, a handful of book-length studies of the duel have appeared, though disagreements and discrepancies remain unresolved. Some authors have sought to crack the case through biographical studies that lean toward psychoanalysis while others have focused on reconstructing events, in the way modern commentators dissect televised debates. Still other scholars have focused on the now-anachronistic practice of dueling, a once-acceptable means of settling political disputes (with a complex set of codified rules to be strictly observed). The best studies of the face-off in Weehawken reflect an awareness of the period and its incongruities, shifting political alliances, and volatile personalities.

One area of agreement to emerge from this renewed study of the duel might surprise those whose notions of history were formed primarily before 1970. Almost all recent researchers who have waded into the confrontation emerge with a grudging respect for Aaron Burr; some even suggest that Burr deserves the accolades that Hamilton has usually received from posterity. Aaron Burr was, for much of the past two centuries, seen as a traitorous, murderous opportunist.

A drawing of the famous duel at Weehawken in 1804 between Aaron Burr and Alexander Hamilton.

Artist unknown. From the Collections of the
New Jersey Historical Society.

Most scholars today, however, accord him a much higher place: an effective, highly intelligent political operative who could have been one of the most influential figures in U.S. history if he hadn't been so consumed with embellishing his own reputation. (The most memorable description of Burr's character comes from historian Richard Brookhiser: "He was like a new refrigerator: bright, cold, and empty.")

A few major works have recently re-ignited interest in the duel. One of the most commented upon is Alex Rugow's *A Fateful Friendship: Alexander Hamilton and Aaron Burr* (1999, Hill & Wang). Rugow probes the personal relationship and dynamics that ultimately led to the duel. Not at all reluctant to plumb the psyches of the principals, Rugow theorizes about how the vastly different experiences each man had growing up made their collision course almost inevitable. He lays out their very different paths to the Palisades in the first paragraph of his first chapter, "Bastardy and Legitimacy":

> Alexander Hamilton's beginnings were as inauspicious as Aaron Burr's were promising. The dissimilarity between them could not have been put more succinctly, if somewhat crudely in respect to Hamilton, than by John Adams, who referred to Hamilton as "a bastard brat of a Scotch pedlar,"

whereas, in the case of Burr, he had "never known in any country, the prejudice in favor of birth, parentage, and descent more conspicuous."

Rugow's thesis—that dueling psyches really led to the Weehawken duel—requires him to do some armchair psychoanalysis. But from a distance of two hundred years, he's forced to make some rather large leaps. A critique in the journal *Reviews of American History* commented, "Much that Rugow wants to know about the private thoughts and unconscious urges of both men is highly conjectural." Sometimes these conjectures are hard to swallow, as when Rugow explores whether Hamilton's participation in the duel with Burr might have been the result of a subconscious duel going on within his own psyche:

> Had it not been that for Hamilton unacceptable negative and positive self-images were fused in the person of Burr, and that both, had he given them uninhibited expression, would have threatened to obliterate the image of himself he had created and presented to the world, probably there would have been no obsession leading to the duel resulting in his death.

Intriguing, if true. *A Fatal Friendship* puts a compelling spin on a critical historical episode, although it remains, in the words of the literary journal *Choice*, "engagingly written, if not always persuasive in its conclusions."

An antidote to such speculation is to inspect the original factual records of the incident. Plenty may be found in *Interview in Weehawken: The Burr-Hamilton Duel as Told in the Original Documents*, edited by Harold C. Syrett and Jean Cooke (1960, Wesleyan University Press). After a thirty-five-page introduction outlining the basic facts of the case, the editors lay out the extensive paper trail leading to the duel. It's all there: the vigorous exchange of letters between Hamilton and Burr as they taunt and countertaunt; the formal statement of agreed-upon ground rules for the duel ("The weapons shall be pistols not exceeding eleven inches in the barrel, the distance ten paces"); an account of the duel prepared for the newspapers by the seconds; even the coroner's inquest on the death of Hamilton. Couched amid the somewhat dry documents prescribing dueling behavior is a letter Hamilton wrote to his wife Eliza days before the duel. Its candor is disarming, its simplicity elegant:

> This letter, my very Dear Eliza, will not be delivered to you unless I shall first have terminated my earthly career; to begin, as I humbly hope from redeeming grace and divine mercy, a happy immortality. If it had been possible to have avoided the interview, my love for you and my precious children would have been alone a decisive motive. But it was not possible, without sacrifices which would have rendered me unworthy of your esteem. I need not tell you of the pangs I feel from the idea of quitting you and exposing you to the anguish which I know you would feel. Nor could I dwell on the topic lest it should unman me. The consolations of religion,

my beloved, can alone support you; and these you have a right to enjoy.
Fly to the bosom of your God and be comforted. With my last idea, I shall
cherish the sweet hope of meeting you in a better world. Adieu best of
wives and best of women. Embrace all my darling children for me. Ever
yours, A. H.

Most of the documents included in *Interview in Weehawken* are of a more pro-
saic, technical nature. If the specific questions about the sequence of events on
the Palisades engage your interest, check out *Hamilton II* (1976, Mason/Charter
Publishers), the second volume of a massive biography of Alexander Hamilton
by Robert Hendrickson. His most important contribution is his advancement of
the theory that Burr fired first (almost all historians have Burr holding his fire
briefly until after Hamilton takes his shot) and that "Hamilton had not fired
until Burr's bullet struck his body, and then his pistol discharged accidentally as
he fell."

This "Who-shot-first-and-what-was-he-aiming-at?" line of questioning
remains a real point of contention among Burr-Hamilton scholars. There are
roughly four different scenarios which have emerged over time:

1. Hamilton, wishing to appear magnanimous and charitable, fired his gun
   deliberately in the air, sending his opponent a signal to do likewise. Burr
   shot him anyway.

2. Hamilton fired first, but he was a bad shot, and he fired well over Burr's
   head. Burr returned fire and mortally wounded Hamilton in the stomach.

3. Simultaneous exchange of fire. It all happened too fast to sort out who
   fired first or what each was really aiming at.

4. Hamilton deliberately held his fire—perhaps as a sort of last-second
   pacifist stratagem—but Burr didn't care and fired away. As Hamilton fell,
   his gun discharged (Hendrickson falls into this camp).

Noting that Hamilton's shot reportedly severed a branch off a cedar tree "some
twelve and a half feet above the ground and four feet to the right of where Hamilton had stood," Hendrickson claims Hamilton could not possibly have fired first.
"No one's conscious marksmanship could be that rusty."

Though perhaps not handy with a dueling pistol, Hamilton was a master of
the quill, and as he prepared to meet Burr's challenge, he wrote an essay explaining his thoughts on the duel, a work historian Thomas Fleming said "might best
be described as a letter to the American Public." Fleming's *Duel: Alexander Hamilton, Aaron Burr, and the Future of America* (1999, Basic Books) not only provides
a clear and detailed account of the circumstances before, during, and after the
duel, but also recounts Hamilton's stated reasons for wanting to avoid the duel:
his religious principles, his love for his wife and children, his obligations to his

creditors, and his lack of malice toward Burr. Yet, "after this collection of seemingly overwhelming imperatives to shun the duel, Hamilton nevertheless maintained it was impossible to avoid it. He gave two explanations for this conclusion: One was the 'intrinsick' difficulties of the situation. The second was the 'artificial embarrassments' created by Burr's manner of proceeding."

Fleming suggests that Hamilton's public position as reluctant duelist was at odds with the real story:

> One suspects another darker motive in the divided Hamilton's moral posture. If he was killed, he wanted his death to destroy Burr as a political and military leader. It would have taken a year of prayer and fasting to scour hatred of Aaron Burr from General Hamilton's soul. The ongoing animosity is all too visible . . . no matter how often Hamilton declared he had no personal enmity toward Aaron Burr, the general's loathing for the man only becomes more apparent.

Fleming's book is filled with such provocative conclusions. His ability to prop up his psychological speculations with historical fact is impressive. In analyzing, for example, the significance of a meeting between Thomas Jefferson and Burr in January 1804 (Jefferson took detailed notes of the conversation), Fleming avoids the knee-jerk scholarly urge to simply annotate the discussion points; instead, he comments lucidly on the very fact of the meeting itself and finds it remarkable that "he asked President Thomas Jefferson for a private meeting to discuss his political future. Here, once more, we see evidence of a man who had become, without acknowledging the term, a professional politician."

DUEL PURPOSE

When Alexander Hamilton and Aaron Burr engaged in their infamous 1804 Weehawken duel, they were participating in a lethal, but quite common colonial tradition that stretched back several centuries. In fact, only three years before the Burr-Hamilton duel, Hamilton's son Philip was killed on the same dueling ground in Weehawken. Dueling was most common among the aristocratic classes—perhaps owing to the practice's origins in the Middle Ages when knights often dueled at courtly functions and coronation fairs.

From the late eighteenth century on, this antiquated, deadly form of conflict resolution gradually fell into disfavor, although some southern states permitted the practice well into the nineteenth century. At the time of the Weehawken duel, New Jersey and New York had outlawed the practice, and Burr had to flee the Northeast to avoid murder indictments issued by both states. For more information about the practice of dueling in early America, see Joanne B. Freeman's *Affairs of Honor: National Political Culture in the New American Nation* (New Haven, Conn.: Yale University Press, 2001).

Many worse things have been said about Burr. Fleming offers a portrait of the usually reviled Burr that often impresses: he was learned, thoughtful, doggedly determined, capable of great compassion, a loving father, and a cagey survivor of multiple political intrigues at the highest level. Fleming's Burr seems more credible than the one-dimensional assassin/traitor image bequeathed to posterity and widely accepted by most nineteenth- and twentieth-century historians. Fleming's Aaron Burr comes off as a man who got excited by the political process itself, the rough-and-tumble of Revolution-era plots and counterplots. He was the first American to fully grasp the dynamics of the smoke-filled-room approach to politics. Whether or not he believed in what he was preaching appeared to have been irrelevant as his imagination and ambition often led him into some fairly outrageous schemes. For example, early in 1804,

> Colonel Burr was doing something far more explosive than weighing the advantages and disadvantages of attacking Thomas Jefferson. The vice president was continuing to talk to New England federalists about the plan to create a secessionist Northeast confederacy . . . exactly what Burr thought about this idea is hard to pin down.

Those interested in knowing more about what Burr thought—or rather, what novelist Gore Vidal thinks he thought—should read Vidal's *Burr* (Random

A bust of Alexander Hamilton marks the spot on the Palisades where the duel occurred.

Copyright 2002 Reena Rose Sibayan.

House, 1973), his best-selling novel presented in the form of a partial memoir by Burr. The book, a critical and commercial success, won raves for fleshing out this shadowy character and making Burr (in the words of *Newsweek*) "more than a political cartoon." If Vidal intended to fire the first shot in the war to restore Burr to his rightful place in the American pantheon, he scored a decisive victory while also claiming a few casualties from the roster of founding fathers. A review in the journal *Commentary* bluntly agreed:

> Given the circumstances of the nation's inception, it is not surprising, Vidal suggests, that American mythology has chosen to sanctify a social-climbing power-hungry bastard from the West Indies like Alexander Hamilton, and a slave-owning megalomaniacal satrap like Thomas Jefferson, while writing off a man of genuine greatness like Aaron Burr as an adventurer and a scoundrel. For Burr was a man of moral imagination and intelligence far too refined and subtle for the American herd, which has always been inhospitable to greatness of every sort.

And the duel? Vidal's Burr returns to the scene with his own Boswell-type follower and sets him—and his readers—straight. Burr re-creates the duel in mime for his biographer—with Hamilton firing first, but missing. Then Burr delivers the fatal shot. Burr's acolyte provides the rest of the account:

> He sat down at the edge of the monument. Rubbed his eyes . . . in a quiet voice, he continued. "As usual with me, the world saw fit to believe a different story. The night before our meeting Hamilton wrote a letter to posterity; it was on the order of a penitent monk's last confession. He would reserve his first fire, he declared, and perhaps his second because, *morally,* he disapproved of dueling. Then of course he fired first. . . ."
>
> We got into the boat. "You know, I made Hamilton a giant by killing him. If he had lived, he would have continued his decline. He would have been quite forgotten by now. Like me."

Two hundred years after the fact, the most famous face-off in American history—the duel in Weehawken—remains one of the country's most puzzling and tragic events.

FURTHER READING

Kennedy, Roger. *Burr, Hamilton & Jefferson: A Study in Character.* Oxford: Oxford University Press, 2000.

Knott, Stephen. *Alexander Hamilton and the Persistence of Myth.* Lawrence: University Press of Kansas, 2002.

Melton, Buckner, Jr. *Aaron Burr: Conspiracy to Treason.* New York: John Wiley & Sons, 2001.

The Lindbergh Baby Kidnapping

Seven decades have passed, but the "trial of the century" continues to unfold in the court of public opinion—and on the shelves of bookstores and libraries. The kidnapping of twenty-month-old Charles Lindbergh, Jr., from his home outside Hopewell, New Jersey, on March 1, 1932, stunned the nation. The trial, which ultimately found German immigrant Bruno Richard Hauptmann guilty, has been dissected minutely, beginning even before Hauptmann was led to the electric chair in 1936.

But interest in the case has never been greater. More books were published about the trial in the 1990s than in any previous decade. What's more, the publishing flurry has been marked by a ferocity of opinion—and even a personal animus—that ensures that the case, in some people's minds, will never be closed.

The remarkable details of this crime have even become fictionalized, inspiring everything from best-selling novels (the case was the model for Agatha Christie's *Murder on the Orient Express*) to off-Broadway plays and made-for-TV movies. There are additional books slated for publication, several websites dedicated to the case, and at least one fellow going around the country telling everybody that *he's* the Lindbergh baby.

The dividing line separating the writers who've explored the case is the degree of actual involvement of the convicted man, Hauptmann. Some see him as the sole perpetrator, the unquestionable kidnapper, and the only defendant that the evidence points to. Others thinks he was the innocent, railroaded victim of both an overzealous police department and a growing anti-German sentiment in the 1930s. Still others believe him to have been one of a larger group of kidnappers who escaped prosecution when the fall guy was caught.

The case continues to be problematic. When one looks past the screaming tabloid headlines that heralded Hauptmann's arrest, conviction, and execution, the discrepencies become almost irreconcilable. Despite what the conspiracy theorists say, Hauptmann was almost certainly involved to some extent. And despite what the police defenders say, there were some serious shortcomings in the investigation, and some highly questionable actions on the part of the investigating agencies—and Lindbergh himself.

The New Jersey connections to the Lindbergh case are significant. The Garden State was home to the crime, the trial, and most of its major players. Here's a short list:

The kidnapping took place from Charles and Anne's home in the Hopewell area, although the Lindberghs generally resided in Englewood, at a fifty-acre estate called Next Day Hill.

The first officers on the scene were from the Hopewell Police Department, and the entire investigation was overseen by Col. Norman Schwarzkopf, superintendent of the New Jersey State Police. Schwarzkopf, a West Point graduate and World War I veteran, helped organize the state police force in 1920. (His son was the celebrated commander of combat forces in Kuwait and Iraq during the Gulf War.)

The trial, which H. L. Mencken called "the greatest story since the resurrection," took place in Flemington in the Hunterdon County Courthouse, during January and February of 1935. The Union Hotel, across the street from the Courthouse, was the main gathering spot for reporters and spectators (the jury was housed in the upper floors). More than 700 news and camera people stuffed themselves into the courthouse for each day's session. (If you want to get a sense of what it must have been like, you can sit in on any of the annual summer re-enactments at the Courthouse as actors perform the trial as it occurred.)

New Jersey Governor Harold C. Hoffman, who was sworn in on the day Hauptmann's trial began, tried to reopen the case after the verdict was returned because of some lingering, unanswered questions. He enlisted the help of Detective Ellis Parker, of Mount Holly, who was called "The American Sherlock Holmes" because of his success both locally and with London's Scotland Yard.

Although it is still a subject of much critical commentary among legal scholars and a small conspiracy-minded contingent, most contemporary readers probably find the facts of the case a bit murky. Before wading into the flood of books that espouse one theory or suspect over another, here's a brief overview of the principal facts of the case: The kidnapping occurred between 8 p.m. and 10 p.m. on March 1, 1932. The Lindberghs would not normally have been in their Hopewell home on a Tuesday night, but little Charles was said to be suffering from a cold, and, as the weather was miserable, the family delayed returning to the Morrows' house in Englewood. In the house at the time were Anne Morrow Lindbergh, Elise and Oliver Whately (the cook and the butler), and the baby's nursemaid, Betty Gow. Charles Lindbergh arrived at about half past eight, from New York City, where he had been scheduled to give a speech but reportedly forgot the appointment and drove home.

Lindbergh and his wife ate a late dinner. At about 10 p.m., Betty Gow went into the nursery to check on Charles, Jr. When she couldn't find him, she informed Anne and Charles, Sr. Anne went into the nursery with Betty Gow, and then Charles entered the nursery and discovered an envelope on the window sill, which he insisted not be opened until the police arrived. Later that night, police discovered a homemade ladder on the property, whose wooden legs matched indentations in the ground below the nursery. Neither additional physical evidence nor usable fingerprints were found at the crime scene.

Charles Lindbergh, international aviation hero, shortly before
the focus of the world press turned from "Lucky Lindy's" feats
to the mystery of his son's kidnapping.
Courtesy of the Newark Public Library.

Two days after the kidnapping, the Lindberghs issued the following appeal:

Mrs. Lindbergh and I desire to make personal contact with the kidnappers of our child. Our only interest is in his immediate and safe return.
We feel certain that the kidnappers will realize that this interest is strong
enough to justify them in having complete confidence and trust in any
promise that we make in connection with his return. We urge those who
have the child to send any representative that they may desire to meet a representative of ours who will be suitable to them at any time and any place
they may designate. If this is accepted we promise that we will keep whatever arrangements may be made by their representatives and ours strictly
confidential and we further pledge ourselves that we will not try to injure in
any way those connected with the return of this child.

The next day, the Lindberghs received the following letter (misspellings
preserved):

Dear Sir: We have warned you note to make anyding Public also notify
the Police now you have to take the consequences. this means we will holt
the baby untill everyding is quiet. We can note make any appointment just

now. We know very well what it means to us. It is rely necessary to make a world affair out off this, or to get yours baby back as soon as possible. To settle those affair in a quick way will better for both seits. Don't by afraid about the baby two ladys keeping care of its day and night. She also will feed him according to the diet.

A week after the kidnapping, a retired teacher from the Bronx named John Condon received a message from the kidnappers (Condon had written a letter to a local newspaper offering to be a go-between). Police verified that the purported kidnapper was not a fraud; Condon received some of the abducted baby's clothing in the mail. Negotiations led to clandestine meetings in cemeteries and eventually an exchange of $50,000 in gold certificates as ransom. In return, Condon was given a letter that stated the baby could be found on the "Boad Nelly," an obscurity that neither the police nor Lindbergh were able to figure out. In April, some ransom money began circulating in the Bronx (the police had recorded the serial numbers of the mostly small denominations). In May, a truck driver passing through Hopewell reported the discovery of a small corpse in the woods a few miles from the Lindbergh house. Though it was badly decomposed, the Lindberghs positively identified the body (it was wrapped in little Charles's clothing). The investigation, mostly focused on the trail of the ransom money, continued for more than two years. In September 1934, Bruno Richard Hauptmann, a German immigrant living in the Bronx, was arrested and charged with kidnapping and murder.

During the circuslike trial, prosecutors argued that Hauptmann's handwriting matched the ransom notes, that wood from Hauptmann's attic floorboards had been used in the kidnapping ladder, that Condon recognized Hauptmann's voice from the cemetery meetings, and that Hauptmann had hidden the ransom money in his garage (the police found most of it stashed behind a fake shelf in his garage). Hauptmann was convicted on February 13, 1935, and executed in the electric chair at New Jersey State Prison at Trenton on April 3, 1936.

The most ardent supporter of the prosecution's case and the most fervid and prolific deflator of the Hauptmann-is-innocent crowd has been author Jim Fisher. His two books on the case—*The Lindbergh Case* (1987) and *The Ghosts of Hopewell* (1999)—argue forcefully that the case against Hauptmann was massive and airtight. Fisher, a former FBI agent, dismisses the Hauptmann-was-framed movement as a bunch of overly imaginative authors and weak-minded readers:

> Since Americans tend to be more interested in injustice than justice, it's hard for writers to resist turning cold-blooded killers into victims of heavy-handed prosecutors and cops. Since complicated, intrigue-filled mysteries are more fascinating than cases involving more straightforward, obvious explanations, revisionist true crime writers prefer conspiracies over lone-wolf criminals. Sometimes, in their eagerness to plug a new conspiracy into

---

THE DETECTIVE DETECTED?

Imagine if the twentieth century's greatest detective became involved in the century's greatest criminal case—and then found *himself* indicted and convicted.

That's precisely what happened when detective Ellis Parker, an internationally famous private sleuth from Burlington County, began investigating the Lindbergh kidnapping case as doubts swirled around the accused (and soon to be executed) Richard Bruno Hauptmann.

Brought in at the behest of the state's recently elected governor Harold Hoffmann, Parker, known widely as "America's Sherlock Holmes," followed his own leads to an attorney named Paul Wendell. When Parker produced a signed confession from Wendell, who claimed responsibility for the kidnapping, the state police grabbed him. But when Wendell told the authorities that it was *he* who had been kidnapped and beaten and forced to sign a confession by Parker's henchmen, the detective was promptly arrested.

The Ellis Parker trial was as remarkable for its theatrics and conflicting stories as the Lindbergh trial. The courtroom drama played out for months on the front pages of national newspapers. Parker was convicted and sent to state prison. After serving five years and nearing an imminent parole, Parker died in prison of a brain tumor. His family, and numerous conspiracy theorists, maintain his innocence to this day.

More information about the Lindbergh case in general, and Parker's involvement specifically, can be found at *www.Lindberghkidnappinghoax.com*. For a dated, but utterly fascinating, study of some of Ellis Parker's most puzzling cases, see *The Cunning Mulatto and Other Cases of Ellis Parker*, by Fletcher Pratt (1935, Harrison Smith).

---

a historic case, these writers, by ignoring the truth, deprive themselves of the more fascinating, truthful account. This is particularly true in the Lindbergh case.

Fisher doesn't mince words. He calls Anthony Scaduto, whose book on the case, *Scapegoat* (1976), initiated a revival of interest in the Lindbergh case, "ingenuous" and "a bitter critic of the Lindbergh case investigators." He assails authors Gregory Ahlgren and Stephen Monier, whose book *Crime of the Century: The Lindbergh Kidnapping Hoax* (1993) suggests Lindbergh himself might have been the kidnapper, for proposing "silly motives in support of stupid theories." He accuses Ludovic Kennedy, author of *The Airman and the Carpenter* (1985)— a book that became the basis of both the widow Hauptmann's lawsuits against the state of New Jersey and an HBO movie—of "factual misrepresentation," labeling Kennedy "a revisionist, like Scaduto."

Dismissing the whole corps of researchers who've raised questions about Hauptmann as irrational fantasists, Fisher asserts:

For people who need Hauptmann innocent, evidence to the contrary just gets in the way. Trying to change their minds with hard evidence and rational analysis is as futile as using dental charts to prove to certain Elvis Presley fans that the "King" is dead. In a world without science, Elvis Presley can live as long as his fans need him, and Bruno Richard Hauptmann can be transformed into the image created by his widow.

Although Fisher may be right on his facts, his critics charge that he's skewing those facts in support of the prosecution. They also claim he uncritically accepts much that is questionable, if not outright dubious. Even those readers who conclude Hauptmann was guilty must surely raise an eyebrow when confronted with the apparent discrepencies between the "official" version (Fisher's line) and the "revisionists" (Scaduto, Kennedy, Ahlgren and Monier, and a small army of anonymous contributors to the more than one dozen websites aimed at "exposing" the hoax). Here's a short list of those nagging questions and discrepancies:

1. How could Hauptmann, or anyone outside the immediate family, have planned a kidnapping from the Hopewell home on a night when the Lindberghs were expected to be at the Morrows' Englewood mansion?

2. How could someone unfamiliar with the house know which room was the nursery? And further, how could anyone know that the shutters in the nursery were the ONLY pair of shutters in the whole house that couldn't be locked because they were too warped for the latch to catch?

3. Why would someone attempt a kidnapping during a time when all the lights were on, the domestic staff—including nursemaid—was in residence, and the family was at home having dinner?

4. The notoriously excitable family dog was in the nursery when the baby was taken. Yet the dog didn't bark when an intruder broke in, walked past the dog, took the baby, and then climbed out with the child through the window. (Some investigators have said such uncharacteristic behavior on the part of the family pet suggests an inside job.)

5. Hauptmann's footprints were never found at the scene. The ladder contained more than 400 sets of fingerprints. Not one belonged to Hauptmann.

6. Why didn't Anne Lindbergh or Betty Gow find the ransom note when they first searched the nursery for the child? Charles Lindbergh "discovered" an envelope on the windowsill but demanded it not be opened, or even touched, for two hours while they waited for the police to arrive.

7. Why would a kidnapper leave a ransom note on a sill in front of open windows where it might easily blow away, rather than in the crib or on the nursery floor?

8. If Hauptmann took the baby—and killed it either accidentally or intentionally—why, in his haste to get away, would he drive three miles in the opposite direction from his home in the Bronx, bury the baby, retrace his route past the house (and possibly police), and then drive home?

9. Why did Lindbergh initially refuse to allow the police to interrogate his wife or his employees?

10. Why did Lindbergh refuse the assistance of the FBI?

11. Why is the thickness of Hauptmann's attic floorboard different from the thickness of "rail 16" (which police say came from the attic floor)?

12. Why did Hauptmann maintain his innocence even after he was offered a commutation of his sentence to life in prison if he would simply confess? This offer was on the table right up until the time he was executed.

Those who have looked into the case can cite dozens of similarly intriguing questions, and it's likely that such unresolved issues will provide the basis for future books on the case. From a literary standpoint, the ongoing feud makes for riveting reading. Whether it's Anthony Kennedy dramatically declaring Hauptmann's innocence:

. . . of kidnapping, extortion and murder, as ignorant, and innocent, as you or I . . .

or Fisher's rhetorical ripostes:

There is probably no such thing as enough evidence to convince true believing Hauptmannites that he was, in fact, guilty of a terrible crime . . .

the case shows no signs of waning interest. Newspapers and magazines continue to revisit the story. A recent issue of the bizarre but always highly readable *Weird New Jersey* (Issue #16) featured an extensive interview with a man named Lorne Husted who claims to be the Lindbergh baby. Anthony Scaduto also claimed the Lindbergh baby may still be alive and living under the name Harold Olson. Ludovic Kennedy disagrees; he endorses the theory that the baby was in fact murdered but that Hauptmann was certainly not involved. Author Noel Behn, in his book *Lindbergh, the Crime* (1994), argued that the child's aunt was the killer. He builds his case for an inside job on the non-barking dog, the kidnapper's knowledge of the un-lockable shutters, and the never-explained suicide of a woman named Violet Sharpe, a domestic employee at the Lindbergh residence in Englewood, shortly after the kidnapping. Ahlgren and Monier build a compelling-sounding case against Lucky Lindy himself, citing, for example, his penchant for practical jokes (he had, months before, hidden the baby in a closet and watched in amusement as his wife frantically searched for the child). They argue Lindbergh may have taken the baby as a joke, accidentally killed the baby during a fall from the ladder, and raced to bury it nearby. The kidnapping story, the authors claim, may have been concocted to cover for the real crime; thus, a national hero's unsullied reputation is preserved and Lindbergh has time to orchestrate an investigation to find the "real" killers.

No smoking gun exists in the Lindbergh baby case. All the evidence is circumstantial. Hauptmann has been dead for seven decades, but the case won't close so long as new avenues of inquiry—and new books on the subject—keep being opened.

FURTHER READING

Berg, A. Scott. *Lindbergh*. New York: G. P. Putnam's Sons, 1998.
Lindbergh, Anne Morrow. *Hour of Gold, Hour of Lead: Diaries and Letters of Anne Morrow Lindbergh, 1929–1932*. New York: Harcourt, 1973.
Radelet, Michael L., et al. *In Spite of Innocence: Erroneous Convictions in Capital Cases*. Boston: Northeastern University Press, 1992.
Waller, George. *Kidnap: The Story of the Lindbergh Case*. New York: Dial Press, 1961.

The *Hindenburg* Disaster

Certain historical events indelibly change the way we see the world—not only because of their enormity but also because someone recorded the impact firsthand. John Kennedy's assassination will never fade from consciousness; Ron Zapruder and his Super 8mm film saw to that. Depression-era poverty made government support for the poor a moral imperative: photographer Walker Evans and the pictures he took of sharecroppers in the 1930s saw to that. And the *Hindenburg* disaster, the spectacular in-flight immolation of the greatest zeppelin the world had ever seen, will never be considered just another aviation accident: Herbert Morrison saw to that.

Reporting for WLS Radio in Chicago, Morrison's words, which were being taped for broadcast the next day, captured more than the cold facts of the story. For the first time, Morrison articulated the essence of a phenomenon that would become more common in the future—the terror of airborne disasters:

> Here it comes, ladies and gentlemen, and what a sight it is, a thrilling one, a marvelous sight . . . the sun is striking the windows of the observation deck on the westward side and sparkling like glittering jewels on the background of black velvet. . . . Oh, oh, oh! It's burst into flames! . . . Get out of the way,

please, oh my, this is terrible, oh my, get out of the way, please! It is burning,
bursting into flames and is falling. . . . Oh! This is one of the worst . . . Oh!
It's a terrific sight . . . oh! . . . and all the humanity!

Morrison's sob-choked narration from that evening of May 6, 1937, in Lakehurst, New Jersey, still has the power to chill listeners. Sixty-five years later, those
words, along with the newsreel footage of the explosion, remain a vivid testi-
monial to one of history's most celebrated fall from grace. The passage of time,
and a string of other horrific tragedies in the jet age, might have muted the
impact of the *Hindenburg's* annihilation, but it has brought us no closer to a
definitive explanation of what caused the catastrophe. Several theories—from
"authorized" government-sponsored commission reports to various scientific
and conspiratorial explanations—have been floated in the six decades since the
disaster. Most theorizing can be lumped into one of two markedly different sup-
positions: either natural acts (electrostatic energy buildup, lightning, hydrogen-
cell reaction to external stimuli) or sabotage. Additionally, these theories have
been put forward in a wide variety of genres: scientific journals, nonfiction
books, novels, made-for-television documentaries, even Hollywood movies. The
controversy regarding the exact cause continues to spur investigations and
spawn a massive paper trail. The most recent *Hindenburg*-based novel (written by
a descendent of a crew member) was just published, and there's no reason to
think the subject won't continue to fuel new writings. This situation could perhaps have been predicted shortly after the disaster when the International
Board of Inquiry—which interviewed survivors, witnesses, scientists, and government officials from Germany and the United States—published its findings
in a several-hundred-page document. What was it that caused the explosion
leading to the death of twenty-two crew members and thirteen passengers? The
report states:

> In spite of thorough questioning of all the witnesses [and] thorough
> inspection and search of the wreckage . . . no completely certain proof can
> be found for any of the possibilities.

The report went on to cite as the "most probable" cause a buildup of an electrostatic charge caused by lingering thunderstorms in the area setting off a spark
and igniting a leak from the hydrogen cells that held the ship aloft. The wide
range of possibilities has led to some half-cocked theorizing and melodramatic
reimaginings, but among the more restrained and informed analyses of the *Hindenburg's* celebrated career and shattering demise is John Toland's *The Great Dirigibles: Their Triumphs and Their Disasters* (originally published in 1957 as *Ships in
the Sky*).

The book deals with the entire history of zeppelin development, the fascinating personalities who championed their design and use, and their spectacu-

Once a busy terminal for zeppelin flights, the main hangar
at the Lakehurst Naval Station was essentially abandoned
after the *Hindenburg* disaster in 1937.
Courtesy of the Newark Public Library.

lar early failures. But the *Hindenburg* casts its shadow over the entire book, framing the text in both the prologue and the lengthy final chapter, titled "Twilight
of the Gods." For the casual reader who might wonder what all the fuss was
about Toland re-creates the excitement of the general public as worldwide zeppelin travel got off the ground. The research is solid, although the narrative
occasionally groans under the weight of Toland's novelistic tendencies ("On
boarding the ship, almost everyone felt an unwilling sense of danger . . . ").
Toland's gift is his ability to tell a big story through a small detail. Several memorable vignettes effectively illustrate the larger issues on his mind, such as this
scene, which captures the frenzy and awe of the crash site and its impact on
those who were there:

> Murray Becker, the AP photographer, walked slowly to the front of the
> hangar. His first batch of plates had already been flown by an American Air-
> lines plane to Newark, and he wanted to steal a few moments rest before tak-
> ing more pictures. Becker was physically exhausted, emotionally washed
> out. He flopped to a sitting position with his back against one of the huge,
> 1350-ton hangar doors. He looked out at the still-smoking wreck. Then he
> cried.

Toland is noncommittal on the issue of what caused the *Hindenburg*'s explosion. He enumerates the various possibilities, but before positing the idea that the cause can never be definitively established, he adds a curious observation (for one so enmeshed in the details of the disaster) that "the true cause remains unknown—and has become unimportant." He does, however, weigh in with his opinion of some of the better-known books that have purported to solve the mystery of the explosion. In response to those authors who have suggested sabotage, Toland says he has "grave doubts" about that theory "and [I] reaffirm my original statement that the true cause remains unknown."

Not all researchers have been so hesitant to theorize. Michael Mooney, advancing and elaborating on theories first introduced in A. A. Hoehling's *Who Destroyed the Hindenburg?* (1962), builds an intriguing case for sabotage in his book *The Hindenburg* (1972). He speculates that a crew member named Eric Spehl was the saboteur. Mooney argues that Spehl, a "rigger" whose job it was to ensure the integrity of the fabric that covered and protected the hydrogen gas cells, had opportunity (no doubt) and motive (less definitively established).

As a storyteller, Mooney is terrific. The writing is clear, engaging, and vivid. Through his lucid style he weaves technical information into the narrative without overwhelming the reader. It is probably the best written of the books that address the subject. Partly because he's so good at drawing the reader in, it's easy to overlook the rather broad leaps of speculation that support his central thesis that crew-member Spehl's contempt for the growing German nationalist movement motivated him to destroy the blimp. This calls for some mind reading on the part of Mooney, who has only a scattered dossier of

---

HOVERING OVER THE PRESENT

Once an important docking area for zeppelins, Lakehurst Naval Air Station changed its mission after the *Hindenburg* disaster in 1937—though the mammoth airship's ghosts continue to haunt the large, mostly vacant tract of land. The dominant feature on the landscape is Hangar #1, which served as the home for the Navy's rigid airships and, for a time, the North American home for the *Hindenburg* (although the ship barely fit, leaving only eighteen inches in clearance).

The primary custodian of the *Hindenburg*'s legacy is the Navy Lakehurst Historical Society, which maintains an archive of material and a website and conducts a memorial service each year on May 6 "for those who lost their lives in the *Hindenburg* and all airship accidents through history."

Tours of the Naval Station are conducted on the second Saturday of each month. For those who can't make the trip, the historical society's website includes lots of vintage photos, background information, and even a gift shop, where one can order books, lithographs, mugs, and t-shirts.

hearsay and scant documentary evidence to rely on (Spehl was among those killed in the explosion). Still, Mooney puts forth a not-implausible argument that Spehl—prompted by his girlfriend's antifascist radicalism—became disenchanted with Nazi extremism and began to plot a way to strike a blow against the Fatherland. This mix of theorizing and psychological reconstruction reaches its nadir in a scene where Spehl and his girlfriend, Bernice, are visited by Bernice's former husband, an artist active in the new German resistance movement. Mooney's recounting of this event is bracing:

> Then Beatrice's first husband knocked on the door of the apartment in the early hours of the morning. The artist needed help very badly. The Gestapo had been at him for eight days. They had just let him go. . . . The Gestapo had crushed his fingers in a vise, one by one. Where his nails should have been, there was nothing but red pulp, oozing with yellow pus. At the knuckle on his left thumb, the shattered bone showed through. . . .
>
> It was that man's hands which were the central image in the nightmare of the farm boy from Goschweiler, the upholsterer from Markdorf, the sailmaker at Friedrichshafen, the rigger aboard the *Hindenburg*. Because of those hands Eric Spehl had decided for himself that "one act of genius was worth a lifetime of labor."

That "act of genius" would come shortly, with the disenchanted rigger setting a homemade time bomb within the folds of the material that separated the hydrogen cells from the blimp's infrastructure. Mooney's book was the basis of the Hollywood film *The Hindenburg*, starring George C. Scott as the airship's captain, Max Pruss. The movie faithfully captured the thesis of Mooney's book, but it is otherwise undistinguished and surprisingly plodding for such a naturally engrossing story.

For those readers who require no fidelity to truth in their historical fiction, the book of choice is Jeff Rovin's *The Hindenburg Disaster* (1975). The novel features, among other chestnuts of pulp fiction, a wisecracking reporter, a humorless, sadistic Nazi, double-agent deceptions, a life-threatening thunderstorm, a woman who gets knocked into the ocean by a chandelier, a mauling by a lion, a hijacking, suicide attempts, engine fires, burst water pipes, and lots of cliché-filled sex scenes ("Their mouths met in a hungry, passionate kiss").

Rovin's plot places the blame for the explosion on a German SS officer shooting at a Nazi defector hiding in the keel. In a novel which, perhaps as a tipoff to the savvy reader, actually starts during a dark and stormy night ("The rains fell hard, lashing the airfield with ferocity. A static crackle ripped the nighttime heavens. Thunder rumbled and echoed ominously across the land"), little information is added to deepen our understanding of the tragedy. Yet Rovin does reveal a few trivial details in the course of his narrative that don't show up in any other fictional renderings: for instance, the score of the Dodgers-Pirates game during the inning the *Hindenburg* flew over Ebbets Field on its way to Lakehurst. Still, there's almost no historical worth to this formulaic pulp paperback.

Of all the fictional renderings of the *Hindenburg* disaster, Henning Boetius's *The Phoenix* (2001) has the purest pedigree. Boetius is the son of Eduard Boetius, the man who was at the elevator wheel (the control that kept the craft steady in flight) at the time of the disaster in Lakehurst. His novel, written in German and translated into English, is an uneven work, almost schizophrenic in construction. He's really written two books and yoked them together. The first is a fairly mundane retelling of the fateful flight, loaded with detail and extensive, though not particularly interesting, conversation among the passengers. The main character is a crewman named Edmund Boyson who, like Boetius's father, operates the elevator controls. The second story is the far more absorbing narrative of a *Hindenburg* survivor, a newspaper reporter named Per Olson, who spends ten years searching for the real reason for the explosion. He explains his fixation to his reconstructive surgeon, a kind of Dr. Frankenstein named Hans Bernstein, who practices in a secret laboratory in the desert.

> My obsession? Yes. I'm going to stake everything on shedding some light into the darkness of the *Hindenburg* disaster. It's as if, by doing that, I might shed some light on myself. You know only too well, Bernstein, that I'm a man with a split identity. Even if the wounds from all your surgical work are healed, the emotional wounds remain. I'm persuaded that this affair, which I got involved in by chance, this airship catastrophe, was something like a scalpel that made a deep incision in my life. I want to solve the case for myself, as my own form of psychological healing. Maybe then at last I'll be whole again, a man who can lead a new life.

It's impossible to avoid thinking that the questions and uncertainties that plague the fictional Olson must have been the same that nagged at Boetius's father, who survived the accident. The aching to know what really happened gives the book its drive. Olson's unrelenting ten-year quest for the truth makes for great reading. The other half of the book, which reconstructs life aboard the airship, or in training for zeppelin service, seems flat by comparison. As a piece of historical fiction, the book succeeds when it diverges from history and embraces the devices of great fiction. The "authentic" parts of the book announce themselves in bundles of well-researched pages about zeppelin construction, the *Hindenburg*'s passenger list, how to read a meteorological isobar chart, and the impact of headwinds on dirigibles. Perhaps Boetius, who says he "drank my tea from *Hindenburg* teacups all my life" couldn't decide whether to write a fully-informed history/analysis of the *Hindenburg* or a page-turning mystery. So he wrote both.

His protagonist does eventually discover who was responsible for sabotaging the *Hindenburg*: Hitler himself.

> The ship was in Hitler's way. He reacted pathologically to competition, above all when it concerned symbols or visions of the future. For symbols and visions were Hitler's sole reality, and therefore Eckener's [the airship's principal designer] dream of a worldwide Zeppelin transport company must have been a nightmare for him. Even the swastikas on the great dirigible's fins troubled Hitler, because the effect they made up there was oddly decorative and inconsequential.

Intriguing, but one ends this book wishing Boetius had spent more time establishing the groundwork for this admittedly bizarre theory (which feels "tacked on" and is a bit of a disappointment after so much exposition) and less time chronicling the minutiae of the doomed flight.

The single most important piece of writing about the *Hindenburg* remains the report issued by the Board of Inquiry in 1937. Despite its ambiguous conclusions—and its status in some researchers' opinions as a propagandistic effort to quell suspicions about sabotage—it still serves as the primary source for the testimony of those present at the explosion. Though not the most accessible piece of writing, it nonetheless tells the story in a way that can never be trumped. The report contains reprints of memos from the field investigators to the FBI, press clips from international newspapers, and the transcript of all those who testified before the Board of Inquiry. Here's a sample:

> Lt. May states that at no time did he notice a glow or flame on board the *Hindenburg* prior to the outburst and that in connection with the noting of the structural outburst, he heard a sound that seemed to be the cracking of metal and also he is of the opinion that the structure was virtually shot out at the area of the outburst, and that flames seemed to follow this eruption of structure.

The report is available through libraries and it is also posted in its daunting entirety, on line, linked to most of the dozens of websites that deal with the disaster.

The destruction of the *Hindenburg* definitively ended zeppelin travel. Airship designers were ignored in their pleas to use nonflammable helium rather than the combustible hydrogen, which kept the *Hindenburg* aloft. The public turned a deaf ear to assurances of future safety. The fiery scene at Lakehurst had burned too deeply into the public consciousness. The era of airships was over.

FURTHER READING

Archbold, Rick, and Ken Marschall (illustrator). *Hindenburg: An Illustrated History*. New York: Warner Books, 1994.

Collins, Max Allan. *The Hindenburg Murders: A Novel.* New York: Berkley Publishing Group, 2000.

Tanaka, Shelley. *The Disaster of the Hindenberg: The Last Flight of the Greatest Airship Ever Built* (for grades 9–12). New York: Scholastic Paperbacks, 1996.

The Trials of Rubin "Hurricane" Carter

It was a highly combustible mix of race, murder, and celebrity, of prizefighting and political bosses, of media glare and shadowy backroom deals, of justice and vengeance. It involved individuals, neighborhoods, a whole town, and eventually the American society, even spilling over the U.S. borders. Divisive and exhausting, it tested the limits of the justice system. And its protagonist was a figure of Shakespearean complexity, alternately feared, despised, and deified. At the eye of the storm was a man glowering and defiant who howled in anger for decades, sometimes to thousands of rabid supporters, sometimes alone in a fetid concrete chamber. And New Jersey—its citizens, its politics, and its history— were all publicly cross-examined in this cinematic rumble through the criminal justice system. More than three decades later, much of the tension and animosity stirred up at the time remains.

The odyssey of Rubin "Hurricane" Carter, a world-famous middleweight boxer arrested in 1966 for a grisly triple murder in Paterson, almost defies credulity. Carter's life has been chronicled in an autobiography, a Hollywood movie, an authorized biography, a documentary film, and has been retold in academic studies of the justice system, websites, even novels and song lyrics (Bob Dylan's "Hurricane" is probably the best-known example). Writers, legal scholars, and social activists are drawn toward Carter's story perhaps because no other figure in the last half-century found himself at the nexus of so many overlapping large-scale social contortions: the shift in urban demographics, the rise of a media-driven celebrity culture, the civil rights movement, and the growing cynicism about government and politics.

What turned Carter into a social lightning rod was neither his boxing, although he contended for the middleweight championship, nor his arrest for murder in 1966. His twenty-year struggle to clear his name and win his freedom was the catalyst for notoriety: a jailhouse journey that played out in varying degrees of visibility and involved retrials, charges of framing, and multiple

Supreme Court decisions. In the end, Carter won his freedom, but he was not really exonerated; his murder convictions were overturned by a New Jersey Appeals Court judge on grounds somewhere between minor technicality and prosecutorial misconduct.

A quick review of the facts: In the early hours of June 17, 1966, two gunmen burst into the Lafayette Grill, a neighborhood bar in Paterson, and shot four people—three fatally. Later that morning, police picked up Carter and a friend, John Artis, and questioned them about the murder, which appeared to be racially motivated (earlier that night, a black tavern owner in Paterson had been shot by a white man; the four victims at the Lafayette Grill were white and the gunmen black). Released but later rearrested, Carter and Artis were tried and found guilty of the murders. Witnesses placed them at the scene and identified Carter's car as the getaway vehicle.

Carter and Artis continued to proclaim their innocence, and, after reports of key witnesses recanting their testimony in the mid-1970s, a retrial was granted. However, after a second trial in 1976 Carter and Artis were found guilty once again, and they returned to prison where they resumed their former protestations of innocence. Artis was paroled in 1981, but Carter remained imprisoned until 1988, when his lawyers succeeded in having the 1976 retrial verdict reversed by the Federal District Court in Newark on procedural grounds (the prosecution had not shared certain polygraph results with the defense). Carter's release was aided by the exhaustive research of a group of Canadians who lived in a secretive commune and had adopted Carter's cause as their own. A decade after his release, Carter's life became the basis of a major motion picture, *Hurricane*, starring Denzel Washington in the title role. The film received mixed reviews; some longtime spectators of the case, who felt the film was more fiction than fact, offered excoriating criticism. Carter's life, trial, quest for exoneration, retrial, and ultimate release have been the subjects of many high-profile books. A consideration of the most important of these books, starting with the most recent, follows.

The question of what kind of man is Rubin Carter—thug or martyr, victim or perpetrator—is problematic. There's enough in his life story to find both, and the kind of book one writes about him is likely to skew the agreed-upon facts of his life story in favor of that view of his character. The danger any researcher faces is aligning oneself too closely with any one version of events. That's the principal shortcoming of an otherwise excellent book by James S. Hirsch called *Hurricane: The Miraculous Journey of Rubin Carter* (2002, Houghton Mifflin). The book's sympathy for Carter leads a reader to question some of Hirsch's assessments. The author explains in a note that "this book is an authorized biography of Rubin 'Hurricane' Carter. He cooperated fully with the effort, but the interpretations and conclusions are my own."

Thus, the reader gets Carter's version of events, which though perhaps accurate, seem a touch phony; for example, Carter refused to wear his prison-issued uniform upon admittance to Trenton State Prison:

> Carter looked at the guard, looked at the striped pants, then looked again at the guard. He suddenly realized what he had to do. If he was going to maintain his self-respect, if he was going to live with dignity, he had to treat the system as if it did not exist. Of course! He would ignore the prison. Why should I be a good prisoner when I haven't been a bad civilian? That's the depth of insanity.
>
> "No," Carter told the guard. He pushed back the uniform. "I would like to speak to someone in charge."
>
> The guard became livid. "Oh, would ya? Well, people in hell would like a glass of ice water, too. C'mon, get those duds off. I ain't got all day to fuck around. . . ."

There's something suspicious in scenes such as that one, with the famously gruff and militant Carter speaking as if he were at the customer service counter at Macy's and the guards sounding as if they just stepped out of a Mickey Spillane novel.

However, Hirsch's book does offer two things not found in any other writing about the Carter affair. First, Hirsch provides an excellent in-depth explanation of the political climate of Paterson at the time of the murder. He's done his homework, and he displays a fine ability to convey the character of the town in clear, memorable aphorisms: "Since its founding, Paterson has been the Wild West on the Passaic, where bare-knuckled industrialists converged with brawny immigrants and infamous scoundrels."

Second, Hirsch delineates the members of the Canadian commune who helped secure Carter's release. There is no doubt that the Canadians were pivotal and deeply committed to the case; many of the members moved to Trenton to work round the clock for Carter's freedom. Yet, unlike the self-aggrandizing portrait one gets from the book *Lazarus and the Hurricane* (written by two commune members and the principal source for the film), Hirsch provides testimony to suggest that commune members were at times controlling, even suffocating, and that Carter himself had to break from the group after his release to finally taste freedom. Hirsch quotes Carter: "The only thing that mattered was to be dependent on that house, to learn to never be separated from the group. It's a process of learned helplessness, but I could not learn to be helpless." Hirsch's book stands as a compelling portrait of a truly "miraculous journey," but whether the book will stand as *the* record of the Hurricane Carter case is less assured.

Far more measured in tone and straightforward in the telling is Paul B. Wice's *Rubin "Hurricane" Carter and the American Justice System* (2000, Rutgers University Press). Although his focus is on the legal apparatus, Wice provides a clear overview of the facts of the case. He reserves his outrage for the failings of the "adversarial" system of U.S. justice and admirably refuses to convict or exonerate Carter because, for all that is known, one still can't be sure. That is not to say that Wice lacks either passion or a point of view:

> I cannot, of course, say conclusively that they are innocent because I was not in the Lafayette Bar that night. Only Carter, Artis, the four victims, and perhaps Al Bello [a witness] can definitively attest to what actually happened that evening. The greatest puzzlement in my final assessment of the case is

---

THE STRAIGHT STORY

The 1999 film *Hurricane* may have introduced some movie-goers to life in the cell blocks of Rahway State Prison, but it was not the first time a national audience had a chance to peer beyond that prison's walls.

In early 1979, a nationwide audience sat mesmerized as it watched a documentary called *Scared Straight*, an unflinching film that chronicled the encounters between groups of New Jersey "juvenile delinquent" teens and Rahway convicts serving twenty-five years to life. The documentary became the subject of widespread praise, argument, and commentary, with its unedited, vulgar, and violent language and content. The purpose of the "Scared Straight" program, conceived by a small group of inmates called the Lifers Group, was to expose potential young offenders to the realities of life behind bars.

Originally intended simply to open prison doors to would-be felons, the small-group "counseling" sessions with prisoners gradually turned into attempts to unsettle, shock, to "scare straight." As James Finckenauer noted in his book, *Scared Straight! and the Panacea Phenomenon* (1982, Prentice-Hall):

> Over a period of time, the Lifers' approach evolved into a form of shock therapy rather than a form of counseling. This occurred because the inmates felt that with the low-key, big brother approach, they were not really reaching many kids in the most effective way. There was no overt attempt to intimidate or terrorize youngsters at first, but this later became a more prominent and dramatic feature of the project.

Criminologists, lawyers, social workers, and newspaper columnists have debated the merits of the approach showcased in the Oscar-winning documentary. It spawned several sequels, and many other state prisons went on to adapt the "Scared Straight" model. To this day, the program's effectiveness as a deterrent to crime is still hotly debated. Summing up the feeling of many experts who work in the criminal justice system, the *Trenton Times* editorialized skeptically that "the reported 'success' led some people to believe a magic panacea for juvenile crime has been found." However, reviewer Jerry Krupnick of the *Newark Star-Ledger* reported that "if just one kid going through that routine is kept out of prison, it's a super accomplishment."

how two separate juries (totaling twenty-four jurors) could conclude in less than six hours of deliberation at each of the two trials that the defendants were guilty beyond a reasonable doubt.

As one looks back over the barely credible and often contradictory evidence presented by both sides, it seems that there are still more questions than answers at the conclusion of this perplexing case.

Wice, a professor of political science at Drew University, maintains an explanatory style throughout; bolstered by first-person asides, the book attains an air of authority; for example, Wice inserts this comment into one of his analyses: "The defense attorneys I interviewed doubted the spontaneity of these taped conversations." The book serves as a good primer for readers who might otherwise be put off by the legal complexities of the twenty-year-long case. If there's a liability to Wice's book, it's the insertion, late in the text, of a generalized discussion of the European system of justice. Though interesting, Wice doesn't dedicate enough pages to fully flesh out the distinction between U.S. courts and European courts; thus, whatever point he was trying to make about the need to reexamine the justice system lacks the punch of his earlier exploration of the Carter case.

Nevertheless, Wice has done an impressive job of taking the reader by the hand through the legal labyrinth, through briefs and appeals, trials and convictions; he serves as a learned guide for "a case that illustrates many of the strengths and weaknesses of our nation's criminal justice system and attests to the resilience of the human spirit."

The researchers who've explored the record disagree on numerous points about the specifics of Carter's case, but everyone seems to agree that the turning point in the case—and in Rubin Carter's prison life—was the involvement of a group of Canadians in trying to secure his release. The story of how the relatively secret commune happened to cross paths with Carter is told in *Lazarus and the Hurricane: The Freeing of Rubin "Hurricane" Carter* (1991, St. Martin's Press; updated and reissued in 1999), written by commune members Sam Chaiton and Terry Swinton. The book's preface promises "a story . . . full of unlikely meetings, curious parallels, and Dickensian twists." Hyperbole notwithstanding, the book almost rises to that level. The "Lazarus" of the title is a teenager from the Bronx named Lesra, who becomes a sort of ward of the Canadian commune after commune members convince his parents that they can get the illiterate teen ready for college. As part of Lesra's education, he's taken to a Canadian used-book depository where he happens to pick up Carter's autobiography for use as a reading primer. As he learns to decipher the work he is moved by Carter's plight, as are his tutors, who become determined to assist the incarcerated boxer. First contact was made by Lesra, who wrote to Carter at Trenton State Prison. This excerpt from the letter started it all:

All through your book, I was wondering if it would have been easier to die or to take the shit you did. But now, when I think of your book, I say if you were dead then you would not have been able to give what you did through your book. To imagine me not being able to write you this letter or thinking that they could beat you into giving up, man, that would be too much. We need more like you to set examples of what courage is all about!

Carter responded, and a correspondence began between the Canadians and the prisoner; soon the commune was focused on helping find evidence and doing the legal legwork that might exonerate Carter. Accepting the assistance of a group of strangers left the prisoner feeling ambivalent, according to the authors:

The act of reaching out, peeking over the penitentiary wall, made him feel the fact of his imprisonment even more keenly. His association with Lesra and the Canadians was now a constant reminder of his confinement. What if he should never be released? His appeal had been denied first by Judge Leopizzi and then by the State Supreme Court, when everything had pointed to his imminent freedom. What if he could no longer do the time? With hopes so raised, how could he not have been disappointed? He knew better—he had learned to protect himself so he *could* do the time. It was easier not to feel, not to care, not to interact, and above all, not to need. Now he was really fucked up. Now he was tormented by hope.

The rest of the book covers the mostly legalistic maneuvering, witness chasing, and late-night legal-brief writing by the Canadians—all of which energized Carter's legal defense team and helped build a strong appellate case for overturning the convictions. The 1999 reprint of the book contains a brief epilogue detailing what has happened to the principal players in the legal drama in the decade since Carter's release.

The book that started it all, written long before exoneration seemed possible, was Carter's autobiography, *The Sixteenth Round: From Number 1 Contender to Number 45472* (1974). In a literary style befitting a boxer nicknamed "Hurricane," Carter lashes out with ferocity at the injustice of his incarceration. Even before the book actually begins—on the "Acknowledgments" page—he comes out swinging:

On this page I would like to mention the least first—the ungodly nemeses in my life who have made it necessary for me to write this book: the corrupt and vindictive officials who played their roles to a T in this tightly-woven drama to bury me alive, aided and abetted by laws which simply do not protect the sovereign rights of the individual, as the Bill of Rights requires, but the blatant wrongs of a select few.

Carter's pervasive anger keeps the narrative tense and compelling, but he also manages to tell his story with lots of detail and memorable dialogue. He takes the reader through his upbringing in Paterson ("The kindest thing I can say about my childhood is that I survived it"), his life as an Army paratrooper, his rise as a prizefighter, and his arrest, conviction, and resistance to life in prison. Not unexpectedly, his descriptions of life as an inmate boil over with invective:

> Trenton State Prison is a nasty, stinking, Medieval cubbyhole that was built in 1849 for non-citizens and mules, eight years before the Supreme Kangaroo Court under chief racist Taney declared the black man in America should not be considered a citizen of these United States. . . .
>
> At the entrance gate I could sense the depravity, violence, and racial bigotry within. Everything about it was wrong: the whole place seemed plagued by faggotry and ravaged by deep pockets of corruption.

The Sixteenth Round is not for the faint of heart. As a reviewer for *Library Journal* noted bluntly, "This is a tough and brutal book." The book's undeniable appeal, however, is its pulse-pounding passion. Carter never simply notices—he dissects, assails, lashes out. The weight of an oppressive injustice bears down on every page. And his candor is disarming. At the end of the book, he displays an uncharacteristic vulnerability and pleads for help from the anonymous reader:

> I come to you in the only manner left open to me. I've tried the courts, exhausted my life's earnings, and tortured my two loved ones with little grains and tidbits of hope that may never materialize. Now the only chance I have is in appealing directly to you the people, and showing you the wrongs that have yet to be righted—the injustice that has been done to me. For the first time in my entire existence, I'm saying that I need some help.

FURTHER READING

Algren, Nelson. *The Devil's Stocking* (a novel inspired by Rubin Carter's story). New York: Arbor House, 1983.

Sammons, Jeffrey T. *Beyond the Ring: The Role of Boxing in American Society*. Champaign: University of Illinois Press, 1990.

Part Four

A Literary Miscellany

Mobbed in New Jersey

It's an odd thing, perhaps, to take pride in. Yet the undeniable connection, forged over the better part of a century, between the Mafia and the Garden State has engendered a sort of civic pride in the land of Dutch Schultz and Sam "The Plumber" DeCavalcante. Despite the admonitions of prosecutors, the protests of Italian antidefamation societies, and widespread public support for law enforcement, the allure of organized crime—factual as well as fictional—has burrowed deeply in the New Jersey psyche. When HBO's drama series *The Sopranos* issued a casting call at a northern New Jersey high school, thousands of residents descended on location, waiting all day for a shot at representing mafiosi with a genuine Jersey pedigree.

Historically, the link between La Cosa Nostra and New Jersey is no greater than that of other locales: Chicago, New York City, Philadelphia, Las Vegas. But, as luck and posterity would have it, some of the bloodiest mob hits, most colorful Mafia characters, high-profile defections, and entertaining fictional incarnations have emanated from New Jersey. Robert Rudolph, longtime chronicler of organized crime for the *Newark Star-Ledger*, has written, "While the state's professional image polishers are ever vigilant to defend New Jersey against such mob-ridden stereotypes, the state's reputation as a hotbed of organized crime is not entirely undeserved." Not surprisingly, there is an abundance of Mafia-generated literature related to the Garden State: first-person accounts of the "connected" life, nonfiction books about famous Mafia trials, biographies of New Jersey mob bosses, FBI reports, trial transcripts, and, of course, novels and screenplays.

The roll call of mobsters who've been indicted, jailed, or "relocated" over the past decade is extensive. Federal law enforcement agencies, their hand strengthened by the far-reaching RICO statute, have been bolstered in their attempt to eviscerate organized crime. So successful, in fact, that it may be easy to forget the failures of such zealous prosecution. Sometimes, the Mafia wins.

A most surprising and significant victory over federal prosecutors occurred in the late 1980s in a case that took several years to put together and another two years to try. The target: an entire crime family in northern New Jersey. The trial generated national interest and, when it was over, the prosecutors had to contend with the jeers of mafiosi, the scourge of legal experts who said the feds overplayed their hand, and the caustic tone of editorials and news accounts bearing banner headlines like "Mob Trial Down the Drain."

The remarkable story of the case, *United States v. Accetturo*, is documented in Robert Rudolph's *The Boys from New Jersey: How the Mob Beat the Feds* (Rutgers

University Press, 1992). The subtitle promises readers "The fantastic true story of how the Lucchese Crime Family escaped justice," but in fact the reader gets a lot more. Rudolph, veteran crime reporter for the *Star-Ledger*, focuses on the trial but freely and comprehensively explores such areas as the state's multiple connections to organized crime and the legacy of the botched Accetturo prosecution. He paints a clear, thoroughly unromantic picture of the New Jersey organized crime scene, although he's mindful of how that scene is often distorted for entertainment purposes:

> For decades, New Jersey has battled the reputation spread and perpetuated by movies, television shows, and magazine features that, among all its other attributes, it has served as a virtual breeding ground for organized crime. Hardly a program on the mob is aired without some reference to an "Uncle Louis from Jersey," or some such black sheep of the family. In fact, when CBS premiered its much-acclaimed crime drama *Wiseguy*, the setting for the first "cycle" of episodes was . . . where else but New Jersey. The fact that the show was filmed in Canada only seemed to add to the state's reputed ambience. Obviously unfamiliar with New Jersey geography, the show's writers included references to "dumping a body in the Jersey River" (there is no such body of water) and to Newark State Prison, a fictitious institution, which, given all its other ills, the city of Newark is undoubtedly glad it does not play host to.

The bulk of the book comprises a play-by-play account of the trial. Rudolph's critique of the personalities, his ability to read between the lines of formal legal discourse and his surprisingly fast-paced narrative (the trial dragged on for almost two years) combine for a truly engrossing story. Some reviewers noted a "novelistic" quality to the work, and certainly much of the book seems as colorful, humorous, and chilling as any work of fiction. For example, consider this exchange, where defendant Giacomo DiNorscio complains to the judge Harold Ackerman about a federal prosecutor: "Next time he calls me a fat motherfucker, I'm going to kick his fuckin' ass. Mr. O'Malley called me a fat scumbag motherfucker. Did you say it? You yellow motherfucker. He called me a fat scumbag motherfucker, Judge . . ."

The outline of the case can be stated somewhat less colorfully. In the summer of 1985, the U.S. Attorney's office decided to move against the New Jersey faction of the Lucchese crime family, headed by Anthony Accetturo. Relying on informants, wiretaps, and video surveillance, the feds indicted the entire ruling hierarchy of the Jersey Luccheses, from the boss to the soldiers. U.S. Attorney Thomas Greelish acknowledged the case's importance when he stated before the trial, "It is the first time in the history of New Jersey where virtually an entire organized crime family has been indicted in one prosecution." The FBI issued a report stating that the case, "if successful, will result in the removal of the current management structure of the Lucchese Family in New Jersey, which should prove devastating to its operations."

Instead, after dragging on for twenty-one months, the verdict of "not guilty"—all defendants, on all counts—was announced. Legal analysts attributed the verdict to the jury's resentment of the length of the case, the unreliability of the criminal informants, and the difficulty of establishing the guilt of more than twenty individuals charged in the indictment. Rudolph quotes trial judge Harold Ackerman's analysis of the verdict: "Too much was charged against too many, which took too long and resulted in jury nullifications."

In a postscript, Rudolph points out that, despite the case, the Lucchese family's clout—in fact, its very existence—began rapidly to erode. New prosecutions, some highly placed mob defections, and deadly power struggles occurred within the family during the next five years. In 1993, Accetturo was convicted on a new set of racketeering charges. In exchange for a lighter sentence—instead of life in prison, he'll be eligible for parole in 2004—he agreed to turn informant. Rudolph interviewed him shortly before sentencing:

> "Years ago," he said, "people had honor. You sat down and gave a man your word." Now, he said, things have changed: "Honor, discipline . . . all these things are out the window. This was a thing of respect," he added. "Now, it's become a thing of money."

Some organized crime experts have suggested that Mafia books, movies, and television shows offer readers and viewers a vicarious thrill. Few people can walk into a restaurant and get the best table in the place, but a well-connected mobster can. Few people can get even with an inconsiderate neighbor, a dishonest businessperson, or even a rude sales clerk. Mobsters can, and do—in real life as well as fiction. (When John Gotti's neighbor accidentally struck and killed Gotti's son with a car while the youngster was riding his bike, the neighbor soon "disappeared.") This feeling of power—an almost omnipotent exercise of persuasion born of other people's fear—helps make stories of life in La Cosa Nostra so appealing. It's no wonder that so many books that have popularized the image of Mafia life have been insider accounts by mobsters-turned-authors. Readers crave an authentic peek behind the curtain that seals off the Secret Society. The oaths, the hits, the colorful dialogue—is it all true? Only an insider can answer that question.

Mobster George Fresolone and crime writer Robert Wagman wrote one of the best inside accounts to emerge in recent years, *Blood Oath: The Heroic Story of a Gangster Turned Government Agent Who Brought Down One of America's Most Powerful Mob Families* (1994).

Fresolone's account of life in the Bruno-Scarfo crime family in northern New Jersey is mesmerizing. Although he wasn't a "made man" until the very end of

his tenure in the mob—and even then he was already working for the feds, tap-
ing his own "initiation" ritual—Fresolone saw plenty as he worked his way up,
from his start as a kid growing up in Newark. One strength of Fresolone's
account of mob life in New Jersey is its ring of authenticity. He was surrounded
by these guys from the time he can remember. He can tick off mob bosses and
their territories the way a trucker knows Turnpike rest stops:

> Organized crime has become very much a cooperative effort. Members
> from one family work with members of another, so everyone makes money.
> In northern New Jersey, for example, things were laid out pretty carefully.
> The Genoveses ran the Port of Newark. The Luccheses had lucrative opera-
> tions in the "bedroom" communities of Bergen, Essex, Morris, Passaic, and
> Union. The DeCavalcantes had the unions, the building trades, the contrac-
> tors, and the construction sites. The Gambinos were heavily into both drugs
> and gambling. The Columbos had a major share of the loan sharking. And
> the Philadelphia-based Bruno family controlled much of Newark, and espe-
> cially "Down Neck."

TONY SOPRANO GETS BOOKED

Though a relative newcomer in the family of Mafia entertainment, *The Sopranos*,
the HBO series about a New Jersey mob boss and his assorted troubles, has
become one of the most popular fictions ever produced about the Mafia. The
series has spawned fan clubs, websites, Soprano-themed CDs, Off-Broadway plays,
a full range of licensed merchandise, and, of course, lots of books.

One of the best is *The New York Times on the Sopranos* (ibooks, 2001), a compilation of critical overviews and feature stories from the pages of the *Times*.
Though heavy on review-style reprints, the book provides a great introduction for
the uninitiated as well as some thoughtful exploration of the show as a cultural
phenomenon. The highlight of the book is the reprint of a feature story called
"Location, Location, Location: The Sopranos Tunes In to a New Jersey Nobody
Knows (Except for the Millions Who Call it Home)" by Charles Strum.

For the doting fan, there is *The Sopranos: A Family History* (New American
Library, 2001). It features all the things one would expect in an "authorized"
series companion: biographies, interviews, behind-the-scenes anecdotes, and a
brief season-by-season episode guide. Despite the not-terribly-clever conceit of
being presented as a dossier on a real-life crime family, the book is the best
single source of information on the show—a sure-fire hit with the "Bada-bing"
crowd.

For those who wish to indulge their Soprano fix on a daily basis, several websites are dedicated to the show; the best is Sopranoland (*www.Sopranoland.com*),
which offers useful information about the show's history, trivia, a lively chat area,
and a searchable database of names and places mentioned in the series.

A film crew for the HBO series *The Sopranos* prepares to shoot a scene
at the Green Hill Retirement Community in West Orange.
Much of the show's filming takes place in and around northern New Jersey.
Photo by Jerry McCrea. Courtesy of Star-Ledger Photographs.

Down Neck, also known as the "Ironbound section," is where Fresolone grew
up; he wanted to be a mafioso because "next to the parish priests, they were the
most respected guys in the neighborhood."

Blood Oath tells the story of Fresolone's rise through the ranks to become a
prime source of income for the Bruno-Scarfo family, a bookmaker who at twenty-
seven found himself "running one of the largest and most profitable bookmaking operations in New Jersey." But his meteoric rise was offset by a federal sting,
which earned him two years at Riverfront State Correctional Institute in Camden
and Rahway State Prison, "New Jersey's hellhole." He went in, he says, believing
his "associates" would help take care of his wife and three kids. In fact, Fresolone
re-creates a "farewell dinner" scene in which Nicholas "Turk" Cifelli assures
Fresolone and his wife Ann that they will be taken care of: "While George is
gone, you and the kids will never want for anything," Turk announces. Months
later, his wife visits him in prison and sets him straight:

> Completely in tears, Ann finally told me the truth. She was living hand to
> mouth. In a nutshell, she and I were just about broke. "I got food stamps,"
> she said. "And I'm going to have to apply for welfare. It's so degrading going
> down there, but the kids have to eat and I have got no choice. As far as your
> damn friends are concerned, I guess it's out of sight, out of mind."

The anger Fresolone felt at the betrayal of the "family's" promise to take care of his wife and children continued gnawing at him; upon his release a year later, he was searching to find a way to get even. Shortly after his release, and despite his best efforts to succeed in "legitimate" business, he finds himself drifting back into his old lifestyle, attracted by the money and the difficulty of starting at the bottom anywhere else. "At this point," he muses, "I just couldn't picture myself living a straight life or moving away to some faraway place. I could never go straight in New Jersey, or where they could find me. I knew too much."

What he knew became known to the feds after another sting operation in which prominent Lucchese family members were wiretapped, and Fresolone faced another indictment and a probable lengthy jail sentence. He saw his chance to get his revenge and secure his freedom at the same time. As an informant, he agreed to wear a wire and record more than four hundred conversations with fellow mafiosi on topics from bookmaking to rub-outs of fellow gang rivals. Fresolone's testimony and tapes formed the heart of what was called "Operation Broadsword."

Fresolone's account of what it's like to wear a wire during these casual conversations about killing and other violent crimes is gripping. The narrative is by turns comic and pathetic. The patina of honor that surrounds La Cosa Nostra slowly dissipates as one hears members of the same "family" defaming each other and as petty criminals fight over the dwindling spoils of such romantic Mafia enterprises as car theft and crooked carnival games. The story would perhaps have become unbearably seedy if it weren't for Fresolone's frequent use of gallows humor and his ability to find some significance in even the most debased mob transactions. Here he tells the story of the day he became a "made man":

> When I look back on that Sunday, one of the things that sticks in my mind is how hot it was in that house. John had money, big money, but he was too cheap to buy whole house air conditioning. All the house had was dinky window units, and I was sweating in part because the lone window unit in the living room couldn't compensate for the July heat. But a lot of the sweat was being caused by the weight of the two recording devices I had hidden on my body, including a very uncomfortable one secreted in my crotch. . . . I was burdened with the sure knowledge that if I slipped up and was found out, if somehow the tape recorder in the special pouch fell out, I likely would never be able to leave the house alive.

Fresolone, his wife, Ann, and his three children now live in a suburban home in an unidentified state, courtesy of the Witness Relocation Program. He is grateful for a second chance to "go straight." In the book's epilogue, he writes, "Despite what these guys might think, organized crime is not a thing of honor"— a point *Blood Oath* makes clear on every page.

Early in the movie *Casino*, a glitzy, violent film about the influence of organized crime in Las Vegas gaming, there's a scene where a local Teamster's Union pension-fund supervisor, played by Alan King, stands before a press conference announcing the pension fund's participation in the funding of a new casino. "On behalf of the Teamster's Union, it's my pleasure to present you this check for sixty-two million dollars," he says to the casino's chairman, a know-nothing real estate developer who's a front man for a sham corporation run by the mob. Bulbs flash and the local pols applaud.

Scorsese's film gets it exactly right, say the experts. The gaming industry presents an image of polish, professionalism, and legitimacy. Gaming commissions hold public hearings, politicians crow about job creation and vow to maintain strict oversight, and the mob laughs all the way to the cashier's window.

Ovid Demaris begins his study of Mafia influence in Atlantic City, *The Boardwalk Jungle* (1986), with New Jersey Governor Brendan Byrne's celebrated pronouncement in 1977, the year he signed the state's Casino Control Act: "I've said it before and I will repeat it again to organized crime: Keep your filthy hands off Atlantic City! Keep the hell out of our state."

Four hundred pages later, Byrne's warning stands in almost-comic contrast to the record of organized crime's role in Atlantic City's rise to gambling prominence. The mob's reputed involvement in the gaming industry even became familiar campaign-trail fodder for the state's political aspirants. Demaris quotes Robert Del Tufo, former U.S. attorney and candidate for governor during the mid-1980s:

> "We have two governors in New Jersey, two state governments, and two administrations. The one administration is that elected by the people. The other administration is that designated by the leaders of organized crime." He accused the [then-Governor Thomas] Kean administration of being soft on the Mob. "It is a government that lives off blood money and drug money and rules from the alleys and back rooms and the shadowy places you and I never go. No party—and no candidate—can lay legitimate claim to the first government of New Jersey until it deals with the second."

Demaris spends the first few chapters exploring the history of Atlantic City and its cheek-by-jowl relationship with both the corrupt political machine bosses in New Jersey and the increasingly powerful mob bosses in Philadelphia. As the resort business gained a foothold in Atlantic City in the first few decades of the twentieth century, the various corrupt entities all operating around the area naturally moved in, well positioned to run things. It didn't take long for Atlantic City to become the playground for mob bosses as well as tourists:

> The country's top racket bosses decided to use Atlantic City as the site for an underworld conference. Arranged by Al Capone and Lucky Luciano, the

conference was an attempt to restructure the rackets on a nationwide basis. "Seated in a rolling chair at Kentucky Avenue and the Boardwalk yesterday afternoon, puffing on a big black cigar and surrounded by half a dozen henchmen, 'Al' took in the sights of the famous strand and breathed deeply and freely of the ozone with apparently not a care in the world," the local press reported. None of the visiting mobsters seemed to have a care in the world. They were spotted cavorting on the beach in the daytime and in the local nightclubs at night. The way they acted it was as though Atlantic City had been declared a DMZ for the week of the conference.

Once in, they never really left, despite several decades' worth of counter-claims by law enforcement officials and elected representatives. As Demaris demonstrates, just too much money was up for grabs; it was too hard to keep track of all of it and to keep clever crime bosses from finding a way to capitalize. The Mafia families knew that entry into the casino business as "legitimate" casino operators was problematic so they passed by the front door and came in through every other entrance: the hotel unions, the Teamsters, the construction unions, the concessionaires, local prostitution rings, loan sharking—any area likely to realize an influx of cash from the lure of the casinos. Demaris explains,

> More casinos meant more street crimes, more prostitutes, more loan sharks, more mobsters working the edges, more workers joining corrupt unions, more drugs on the streets, more high-school students trading their allowances for gambling chips, more shoplifting, more burglaries and rob-beries and more arson.

Demaris's research into the corruption that turned Atlantic City into the "Boardwalk Jungle" is prodigious, although the book frequently gets bogged down in a dizzyingly detailed chronicle of names, dates, meetings, dollar amounts, and excerpted dialogue from wiretap transcripts. He makes his case thoroughly, though often at the cost of derailing the momentum the narrative sometimes generates. Still, better to get one's facts straight in a story this complex, and with the stakes so high, "a boom big enough to satisfy the greediest of entrepreneurs."

FURTHER READING

Gosch, Martin, and Richard Hammer. *The Last Testament of Lucky Luciano*. Boston: Little, Brown, 1974.

Pileggi, Nicholas. *Wiseguy: Life in a Mafia Family*. New York: Simon and Schuster, 1985.

Puzo, Mario. *The Godfather*. New York: Fawcett Crest, 1969.

Sifakis, Carl. *The Mafia Encyclopedia*. 2d ed. New York: Checkmark Books, 1999.

On the (Paper) Trail
of the New Jersey Devil

There's a serpent lurking in the Garden State. Winged, hooved, fanged, it has terrorized hikers and motorists, small-town residents and city dwellers, tourists and lifelong New Jerseyans.

Sound sensational? It's been sighted by police chiefs, doctors, even foreign dignitaries and military officers. Books, magazine articles, poems, and movies have been made about this creature. Documented by eyewitness testimony, it has roamed the state freely for three centuries. There are websites dedicated to tracking its movements, and "hunters" who pursue the beast to its very lair. There's even a Stanley Cup–winning hockey team named in its honor.

New Jersey may be the birthplace of Sinatra and Springsteen, baseball and the Sopranos, but much more ink—and blood, if you believe the tales—has been spilled on the trail of a misshapen, cranelike creature with a goat's head and a serpent's tail known quasi-affectionately as the Jersey Devil.

So is there anything to all of this?

Although some disagree about the record of physical evidence, the Jersey Devil has left quite a paper trail in his wake during the last few centuries. The major texts tracing his origin and movements have been penned by the venerable New Jersey authority Henry Charlton Beck and a pair of dogged devil researchers—James F. McCloy and Ray Miller, Jr.—whose book, *The Jersey Devil* (1976), was the first book-length treatment of the diabolic dissembler.

Beck, in his book *Jersey Genesis: The Story of the Mullica River* (1963), dedicates a chapter to the Jersey Devil; he focuses mostly on the origins of the legend and related folk tales as they have been passed from one generation of Pinelands dwellers (the Pinelands is the reputed birthplace of the fiend) to the next. Beck also explores the connection between mass hysteria and the rise of the Jersey Devil myth:

> Since they were first aware, Jersey ears have heard grim whisperings about The Jersey Devil. Newspapers used to carry little stories and sometimes long feature articles concerned with certain inexplicable happenings in queer places, odd noises strangely linked with swamps and salt marshes . . . with reputable folk telling and repeating shuddersome anecdotes lacking what old-fashioned mortals call common sense. If a man's hen house happened to be invaded with nothing in the way of a clue left behind except a misshapen hoofprint in the mud, if a group of friends boisterous in some moonlit country house became suddenly transfixed by uncanny howls that descended from the roof peak, if some romantic pair driving along an

equally romantic lane was tossed unwarned into a ditch because a horse reared and dashed away—"it must have been The Jersey Devil!"

The devil's first appearance in print was in 1859, in a full-length feature story in the *Atlantic Monthly* ("In the Pines"). But the devil, by that time, was already a centenarian. Most devil stories place his birth date around 1735 (though the first reports of a devil-like creature date back to the time of the Lenape Indians, who called the area of South Central New Jersey "Popuseeing"—"Place of the Dragon"). Most tales of his origin follow a similar pattern: Somewhere near Leeds Point, deep in the Pine Barrens, a "Mrs. Shourds," matriarch of an already-too-large family, learned she was pregnant with child number thirteen. Despondent (to say the least), she cursed the unborn child. "Let it be the very devil himself!" she howled in contempt.

When the child was finally born, its humanlike form at birth rapidly morphed into the malformed creature of modern legend. The rap sheet on the Jersey Devil reveals a gruesome, hideous beast, generally endowed with a head like a dog, goat, or cow; wings (sometimes like a bat, sometimes like a giant swamp crane); hooves like a horse; long, pointed serpentlike tail; eyes which glow bright, either bloody red or fiery golden; a screeching, squealing, high-pitched nasal growl; a low, awkward flight when airborne and a rapid, kangaroolike hop when grounded.

His manners are even less attractive. He's been accused of killing dogs, chickens, and livestock. He knocks down fences, smashes windows, thumps on roofs, frightens campers, chases cars, and wakes people up in the middle of the night by screaming and flapping outside their bedroom windows. He's even been accused of cannibalism. And, for good measure, he turns milk sour. According to the *Atlantic Monthly* piece of 1859, he was a menace from the moment of birth:

> No sooner did he see the light than he assumed the form of a fiend, with a horse's head, wings of a bat. And a serpent's tail. The first thought of the newborn Caliban was to fall foul of his mother, whom he scratched and bepommelled soundly, and then flew through the window out into the village, where he played the mischief generally. Little children he devoured, maidens he abused, young men he mauled and battered.

Is there the slightest possibility that any of this is even remotely connected to reality? Could there *really* be a Jersey Devil? Authors McCloy and Miller leave the door open:

> Belief in the Jersey Devil is quite real, and based on records going back through the years detailing concrete occurrences of this being, times when he terrorized populations, ran down city streets and through lonely woods, when he attacked animals and was seen assuming a great variety of forms

before many sorts and kinds of people. The Devil's activities have been witnessed by reliable people, including police, government officials, postmasters, businessmen and many others, whose integrity is beyond question.

How could so many rational people be so deluded? Even the well-heeled have been among its witnesses; one of the devil's observers was Joseph Bonaparte, former king of Spain and brother of Napoleon. McCloy and Miller offer several theories:

1. Citing a theory first advanced by Jack Boucher in his book, *Absegami Yesteryear*, the authors suggest that the Jersey Devil could actually have been a deformed human being. Perhaps Mrs. Shourds, sometimes called "Mother Leeds," kept the unfortunate child locked away to protect it, and when she died or became too ill to care for it, the being fled into the woods and began frightening strangers and killing for food.

2. The devil, a personification of the abstract concept of evil, turns the supernatural but unknowable Prince of Darkness into a real presence. The presumed existence of an actual devilish creature gives people someone to blame when things go wrong. The idea of a devil lurking "just beyond the trees" helped early Pine Barrens colonists maintain a daily vigilance against evil.

3. The devil could be a bird, albeit a really ugly, noisy bird, such as the sand hill crane, which weighs about twelve pounds, has a wingspan of more than six feet, and is known to be ferocious when cornered. It has a loud, screeching "whoop" and has also been known to hop across large distances during mating season.

Citings of the devil continue to appear in the police blotter of various Garden State municipalities. In their second book about the devil, *Phantom of the Pines* (1998), McCloy and Miller list some of the more recent reported encounters with the Jersey Devil:

1993, Winslow Township: For a number of years up to 1993, a woman says, she heard and saw the Jersey Devil on her property. He usually arrived in the fall.

1995, Pompton Lakes: A strange creature is seen along Route 287. It has an armadillolike face and is hopping in a manner similar to a kangaroo.

1995, New Gretna: A number of moving lights are seen just above the tops of pine trees.

1996, Sayreville: A motorist claims he saw the Jersey Devil flying over his car at night.

A HANDSOME DEVIL

Although no photographs of the Jersey Devil exist (the CIA, however, reportedly examined a suspicious devil photo in 1975), he has been portrayed throughout the years in a mind-boggling array of postures and media. Most artists who've tried to capture his essence usually focus on his dominant features: bat wings, serpent's tail, red glowing eyes, and so on. The devil's dramatic profile has made him a favorite of painters, cartoonists, and illustrators. He was the sole subject of a 2001 retrospective at the Walt Whitman Cultural Center in Paterson, where paintings and sculptures of the devil were on display in the main gallery. Perhaps the most "artistic" incarnations come from Michael Dorofee, of Dorofee's Glassworks, near Tuckerton, who has fashioned devil figurines, Christmas ornaments, even swizzle sticks.

The devil's image would be even better known if the Citizen's Advisory Committee on Postage Stamps hadn't refused a 1966 petition to put the demon on a stamp for the "American Folklore" series of commemorative stamps.

Still, the fiery fiend gets the last laugh, gaining national attention every year from sports fans who cheer on the Jersey Devils hockey team, which relocated in 1982 from Colorado to gain a new identity—and a couple of Stanley Cups—to go with all that legend and history.

It's one thing to be surprised by a sighting of this menacing demon. It's quite another to go looking for it. Of the many websites dedicated to the Jersey Devil one (*www.nj.com/jerseydevil*) features the tales of honest-to-goodness devil hunters. You can even download an application to join the Jersey Devil Hunting Team. According to the site,

> The Jersey Devil Hunters prowl the Pinelands searching for the legendary Jersey Devil. They haven't yet come face to face with the beast, but they have found artifacts and strange footprints that they say prove the Jersey Devil exists.

What should one do if he or she actually encounters the beast? That answer can be found in the "Jersey Devil" chapter in *The Field Guide to North American Monsters* (1998) by W. Haden Blackman:

> Unfortunately, encountering the Jersey Devil is a frightening prospect. If you do search for it, do so in the Pine Barrens. Always travel with a bright lantern, which a handful of researchers insist can dissuade the monster from attacking. Others claim that holy items, such as the Bible and a crucifix, might ward off the creature. Most important, never forget that the Jersey Devil has a wide array of incredible powers and abilities. It can lift you into the sky and rip out your throat with its teeth. Or it could stalk you and spit fire into your face. If threatened by your presence, it will momentarily become invisible, only to reappear as its claws pierce your belly.

Blackman further warns would-be pursuers that "the Jersey Devil is fond of kid-napping children and travelers who stray too close to its home in the New Jersey Pine Barrens."

Though occasionally dormant, the devil has never gone into permanent hibernation—only dropping out of sight when it seemed expedient. For instance, the devil had several slow decades after an infamous rampage one week in 1909, when he was seen in at least thirty different towns in New Jersey and Pennsylvania. Currently, by most estimates of his activity, the devil is in something of a

The infamous Jersey Devil.

slump, generating nowhere near the terror and mayhem that have generally marked his salad days.

Has he finally been dispatched? Has the legend run its course? Have all those devil hunters frightened him out of the Garden State? Or is suburban development to blame for the quietus?

Russell Roberts, in his book *Discover the Hidden New Jersey* (1995), takes an historical view:

> In recent years, civilization has nibbled at the corners of the Pinelands, and it's the opinion of some that the Jersey Devil is dead, killed by the encroachment of concrete and asphalt. This, however, seems like a premature obituary. The wily creature has been considered dead before (most notably in 1925, when its "carcass" was put on display by a Gloucester County man who supposedly shot the beast), but has always turned up again. It seems like it would take a lot more than urbanization to kill so cunning a creature.

But "urbanization" does seem to affect the beast. A curious geographical mutation of the devil takes place the farther north you go in the state. In the Pine Barrens and south, the devil maims, destroys, kills, and terrorizes. By Hudson County northward, according to devil trackers, the creature changes into a rather benign specter, leaping around the Parkway, leaving footprints along the Palisades, and even lending his image to tattoo parlors and bars. There's even a Jersey Devil cocktail (first concocted by the cranberry growers of Ocean County):

Jersey Devil Punch

1½ quarts	Apple Jack
1 quart	Cranberry Juice Cocktail
⅓ quart	Triple Sec
½ quart	lemon juice

Combine the ingredients, stir briskly, and serve over crushed ice. Serves eight.

A documentary film was made in the early 1970s, produced by New Jersey Public Television, but the devil has yet to achieve the profile of such folkloric beasts as Bigfoot or the Loch Ness Monster. However, his traits have been grafted onto other monstrous beings whose reign of terror extends beyond New Jersey. In Texas, in the 1970s, a number of people reported seeing the "Texas Big Bird," an oversized pelicanlike creature with glowing eyes and the face of a bat. Wilmington, Delaware, was the site of several devil-type sightings in the first decade of the twentieth century, prompting the Jan. 27, 1909, headline in the *Wilmington Morning News*, "The Monster Has Arrived." Creatures matching the Jersey

Devil's description have been spotted as far north as Canada and as far west as California. There can be little doubt, however, that the Jersey Devil is a local boy. He's even been given the state's official imprimatur: named "Official State Demon" in 1939.

Unlikely ever to be caught, less likely ever to be forgotten, the devil seems destined to inhabit the imagination of New Jerseyans just as surely as he's inhabited the bogs and lowlands of his haunting homeland, the Pine Barrens. Perhaps he's even itching for a return to prominence. It has been a while since he's been up to his old tricks. As Henry Charlton Beck put it,

> By now it may be that New Jersey's most celebrated of all unwanted children has come back as he or she or it was supposed to long ago. Perhaps there have been unexplained flutterings of ghostly wings at Leeds Point, unearthly cries at midnight down a Pleasantville chimney, or even a clumsy clutter of cloven foot-prints, neither human nor animal, in the snows of an Estellville dooryard. For in his old haunts further afield The Jersey Devil has long been overdue.

FURTHER READING

Brown, Tom, and William Jon Watkins. *The Tracker*. Englewood Cliffs: Prentice-Hall, 1978.

Hodge, F. W., ed. *Indian Notes and Monographs: Religion and Ceremony of the Lenape*. New York: M. R. Harrington, 1921.

McMahon, William. *South Jersey Towns*. New Brunswick: Rutgers University Press, 1973.

Skinner, Charles. *American Myths and Legends*. Philadelphia: J. B. Lippincott, 1903.

Dodge Poetry Festival

For the uninitiated, the scene must be a little puzzling: thousands of people suddenly pouring into an historic village in New Jersey, some having traveled from overseas, some hiking over from nearby towns . . . children and senior citizens, side by side on lawns, around ponds, in tents . . . hoots, cheers, and roars of laughter at 9 a.m., 9 p.m. . . . high school kids sharing stages with Nobel Laureates . . . a dozen languages, countless regional accents . . . barefoot hippies, soccer moms, and insurance salespeople mingling with philanthropic titans, TV reporters, and librarians . . . and all the while, the air is filled with words—spoken or shouted, memorized and made up, whispered in secret or broadcast with megaphones.

Since 1986, the Village of Waterloo in Stanhope, New Jersey, has been host to the largest public poetry event in North America. Every two years, the most eminent names from the roll call of regional, national, and international poetry join thousands of poetry enthusiasts for a four-day celebration of poetry in all its incarnations: written, spoken, academic, public, personal, in translation, and in a dozen different tongues.

Featuring readings and workshops, conferences, social events, and concerts, the festival has been supported since its inception by the Geraldine R. Dodge Foundation, as an extension of its stated mission to be "an encourager, backing persons, ideas, and institutions which serve a purpose that transcends self-interest and may contribute to sustain human society and the environment which shelters it." For ninety-six hours, Stanhope becomes the host site of a word circus as acrobatic linguists dazzle listeners with virtuoso performances of scripted and impromptu readings.

"The trees and horses make New York City feel much farther than an hour away," wrote Elizabeth Lund in her review of the 2000 festival for the *Christian Science Monitor*. "But that's part of the attraction for festival goers—there's an air

The historic Morris Canal as it flowed past the locks
of Waterloo Village, shortly before the waterway
was officially abandoned by the state in 1924.
Courtesy of the Newark Public Library.

of adventure in the long admission lines. People speak of the Dodge Festival (nicknamed 'Wordstock') as if it were a modern-day pilgrimage."

Book magazine, calling the festival "Heaven in New Jersey," adds that "many people have learned of the festival through Bill Moyers's television programs about poetry. But no recorded footage can capture the energy generated by this unlikely community of poetry lovers." And poet Kurtis Lamkin calls it "a carnival—and you're the ride."

The carnival gets bigger every year. Held in September in the restored colonial village surrounded by tree-lined hills and abandoned shipping canals of the nineteenth century, it attracts more than fifteen thousand people every two years to hear poets such as Billy Collins (poet laureate of the United States), Gwendolyn Brooks, Stanley Kunitz (former poet laureate), Chinua Achebe, and Yusef Komunyakaa. Musicians have included the Paul Winter Consort, Jenny Bray and her band, and hip-hop performers The Roots. Festival organizers say the music isn't merely background noise, separate from the mission of bringing poetry to the masses: it's a reminder of the musical nature of language and the historic linkage between the two arts.

For those who have never attended the festival, a number of videos and books have featured aspects of the four-day program. These include:

"Poets in Person." A one-hour documentary, originally aired on PBS, features the 1986 Poetry festival, with interviews of Allen Ginsberg, Sonia Sanchez, and Derek Walcott.

"The Power of the Word." A six-hour television series, hosted by Bill Moyers, focuses largely on the 1988 festival and features readings and interviews with Robert Bly, Octavio Paz, Lucille Clifton, and Mary Tall Mountain.

"A Life Together—Donald Hall and Jane Kenyon." A one-hour program, originally broadcast as part of the *Bill Moyers Journal* television series, features footage from the 1992 festival, as well as readings from Hall and Kenyon.

"The Language of Life." An eight-hour television series, taped at the 1994 festival, offers readings and interviews with eighteen poets, including Adrienne Rich, Victor Hernandez Cruz, and Gary Snyder.

"Poetry Heaven." A three-hour television special about the 1996 festival includes an overview of the festival's history and development and looks at the variety of workshops, lectures, readings, and social activities that make up the biennial gathering.

"Fooling with Words, with Bill Moyers." A two-hour overview of the 1998 festival features Amiri Baraka, Coleman Barks, and former U.S. poet laureate and New Jerseyan Robert Pinsky.

THE GARDEN STATE'S MOST FAMOUS DITCH

One of the greatest engineering marvels of the nineteenth century could be found wending its way through New Jersey: the once famous but now nearly forgotten Morris Canal.

The canal, dredged in the 1820s, linked the coalfields of Pennsylvania to the markets of New York City. In the era before railroads, canals provided a cost-effective—though slightly cumbersome—means of conveyance. The trip between Pennsylvania and New York City could take five days, proceeding along a series of twenty-three water-powered inclined planes and running through thirty-four locks.

The canal was necessitated by economics: until its development, it was actually cheaper to bring coal from England to New York than to transport it from eastern Pennsylvania. Traffic went both ways, with high-grade iron ore regularly transported to the iron furnaces of Bucks County and the Lehigh Valley. Competition from railroad companies crippled the canal in the 1880s, and by the early twentieth century the canal no longer handled commercial traffic. It was officially abandoned by the state in 1924.

Glimpses of the canal can still be found, however. The stone entrance archway is still visible on the New Jersey shore across from the guard lock of the Delaware Canal. The Village of Waterloo, now a restored historic village and site of the biennial Dodge Poetry Festival, originally sprouted up around an important lock on the canal. One of the largest surviving sections, on a 4,300-foot ridge in Montville, attracts speed skaters in the winter. And throughout the state, hundreds of isolated sections range from just a few feet in length to several thousand.

There is a surprisingly abundant amount of literature available to canal enthusiasts. A good place to start would be Barbara Kalata's *A Hundred Years, A Hundred Miles—New Jersey's Morris Canal*, published by the Morris County Historical Society in 1983. Additional information about both the Morris Canal and the role of canals in the industrialization of the United States can be found at the website of the National Canal Museum at *www.canals.org*.

Festival organizers, poets, and reviewers all say that the marquee names who are featured in the videos about the event take a back seat to the real stars of the gathering: the audience. "At the heart of the festival are the series of readings which remind us that poetry is, historically, an oral/aural art in which the audience plays a critical role," state's the festival's website (*www.grdodge.org/poetry*).

Many first-person accounts about the poetry festival published in newspapers and magazines have focused on the "pleasant surprise" of finding so many casual fans of poetry, neophytes who respond to the playfulness of words rather than the obscurities of academic dissection. The atmosphere at Stanhope is about as far from a typical academic conference on poetry as can be imagined. As Ginger Murchison wrote in the *Cortland Review* after her first visit to the poetry festival in 2000,

Most of us slept too little, ate too much, found out that people we've known on-line and in print for years are real, and forever changed the way we will read and enjoy poetry. I lost my digital camera and three days' worth of memories on disk, but I still have the image of that high school girl, a wad of bills in her hand, chasing a man who had bought a drink and dropped his money (not a wallet, but a wad of bills), and I'm still grateful to the young couple in the red jeep who drove me, in the near-dark and cold, to find a parking lot that had somehow relocated itself since morning. It was, as Marie Howe put it, "Wordstock." The Dodge is poetry that, on or off the page, like poet Jane Kenyon's fish, "astonished the air."

The poetry festival is the most public event of the Dodge Poetry Program, which sponsors a wide range of public and small-group workshops, seminars, readings, and contests throughout the year. The program spends most if its energy and resources reaching out to teachers, offering in-service workshops that last from two hours to six weeks. All workshops and seminars are led by "Dodge Poets," who also visit schools to meet with teachers and to host one-day "Mini Poetry Festivals."

The poetry program also sponsors the New Jersey High School Poetry Contest. Each year twenty students are chosen to read their award-winning work at a ceremony at Rutgers University–Newark. The winners of the contest are also invited to read from the main stage during a special session at the Dodge Poetry Festival.

The poetry program is run by the trustees of the Geraldine R. Dodge Foundation, a philanthropic group established in 1974. According to the foundation's mission statement, the trustees seek to "encourage imaginative proposals" that are likely to further interest in the arts and "promise to have impact, be replicable, and to effect systemic change."

Change has certainly come to the Village of Waterloo, which was an important lock on the Morris Canal in the nineteenth century. Since 1964, it has traded on its past as an established historic village, featuring a working blacksmith shop, a gristmill, a sawmill, a pottery barn, and an assortment of colonial and Victorian homes.

And, every two years, a bunch of people who really love poetry.

FURTHER READING

Haas, Robert, and David Lehman, eds. *The Best American Poetry 2001*. New York: Scribner's, 2001.

Lewis, Joel, and Anne Waldman, eds. *Bluestones and Salt Hay: An Anthology of Contemporary New Jersey Poets*. New Brunswick: Rutgers University Press, 1990.

Moyers, Bill, ed. *Fooling with Words: A Celebration of Poets and Their Craft*. New York: William Morrow & Co., 1999.

The New Jersey
Literary Hall of Fame

Roughly every two years, for the last quarter-century, a ceremony has taken place that affirms the world-class literary contributions of New Jersey writers. The ceremony—official induction into the New Jersey Literary Hall of Fame—may be largely unknown among the state's residents (though it's held in the very public venue of the PNC Bank Arts Center), but the inductees have been among the most important voices in the American conversation. Scientists, philosophers, children's book authors, nature writers, politicians, and essayists have all been honored by the Hall of Fame, which is maintained by the New Jersey Institute of Technology (NJIT) in Newark and governed by a board of trustees that includes writers, academics, and corporate leaders. Inductees have ranged from Princeton's Albert Einstein (a charter inductee in 1976) to former New York mayor Ed Koch (who was originally from Newark). Metuchen's Paula Danziger (*The Cat Ate My Gym Suit*), Summit's Arthur Vanderbilt II (*The Challenge of Law Reform*), and Montague's Paul Zindel (*The Effect of Gamma Rays on Man-in-the-Moon Marigolds*) comprised the class of 2002.

Many inductees are familiar to readers worldwide, such as Joyce Carol Oates and James Fenimore Cooper. Others are more obscure—at least outside their areas of expertise (such as Madison's Robert Chapman, author of the *New Dictionary of American Slang*, or Princeton's Jesse Williams, author of *Why Marry?*, the first play to receive a Pulitzer Prize). All inductees have satisfied at least one of the four main criteria for inclusion: (1) sold one million copies or more of their books; (2) made the best-seller list of the *New York Times*; (3) received nominations or awards of national or international literary recognition; (4) made a marked contribution to American literature.

The New Jersey Literary Hall of Fame was the brainchild of Herman Estrin, of Scotch Plains, an educator for more than sixty years and emeritus professor of English at NJIT. Estrin, who died at the age of eighty-three in 1999, received the "Distinguished Teaching Award" from the

NEWARK HAS WRITERS' BLOC

The New Jersey Literary Hall of Fame has no official website, but there is an exhibit about the Hall on the campus of the New Jersey Institute of Technology in Newark, in the Kupfrian Hall building. The family of the Hall's founder, Herman Estrin, donated his extensive collection of papers to the institution upon his death in 1999. The Estrin collection can be viewed at the Van Houten Library. A biography of Estrin and a roster of the Hall's inductees can be accessed at *www.library.njit.edu/archives/lit-hall*.

New Jersey Council of Teachers and was also honored by the New Jersey Scholastic Press as "an outstanding faculty advisor" to NJIT's school yearbook and literary magazine. His legacy of promoting great writing and encouraging wide reading across the disciplines still informs the New Jersey Literary Hall of Fame, whose board of trustees meet quarterly to consider potential inductees. More than one hundred writers have been inducted into the Hall, reflecting the immense range of interests, periods, geography, and learning among the state's native crop of authors. Some inductees have been chronicled elsewhere in this volume, so here's a look at a half-dozen other highly regarded authors whose achievements have merited inclusion not only in the New Jersey Literary Hall of Fame but also in the ranks of important men and women of American letters.

JIM BISHOP (Jersey City)—A well-regarded journalist and historian, Bishop's sharp eye for the telling reportorial detail was put to use most effectively in his landmark book, *The Day Lincoln Was Shot* (1955). The book is an hour-by-hour account of the lives of Lincoln, Booth, Mary Lincoln, and those in the presidential circle. Bishop's comprehensive approach covers everything from the agenda of the day's cabinet meeting to Lincoln's dream the night before his death. Reviewers hailed the book as suspenseful and historically accurate. Bishop employed a similar approach in books dealing with the Kennedy assassination and even the crucifixion of Jesus Christ. Bishop not only records the history of the day, but he gets inside the heads of the protagonists; for example, in his Kennedy book he reveals just how eccentric—insane, almost—Oswald's mother Margarite was and paints a mental picture of a truly squirrelly Jack Ruby. The strength of Bishop's narratives lies in his ability to integrate small details other writers might omit into the larger historical context. He was inducted in 1985.

JUDY BLUME (Scotch Plains)—It's impossible to know just how much aid and comfort Blume has provided for girls on the cusp of adolescence. What is known is the degree to which she rewrote the rules for writers who address themselves to a newly-pubescent audience. The frankness of works like *Are You There God? It's Me, Margaret* (1970), though offensive to some critics at the time, has earned her the deep-seated affection of a generation of readers bolstered by her candor about topics such as menstruation and teenage sexuality. Blume has brought that same frankness to all her fiction, including the novel *Wifey* (1979), which is perhaps her best-known work for adults. Still, it is for her contribution in opening up the young adult novel to concerns ranging from masturbation to trying to understand death that Blume has made her biggest mark. Blume becomes, through her books, a confessor-friend rather than an omniscient narrator, with a writing style—to quote critic Naomi Decter—that "consciously or perhaps not, evokes the awkwardness of a fifth-grader's diary." She was inducted in 1976, the year her controversial novel *Forever* (with its detailed description of a first-time sexual encounter) was published.

NIKKI GIOVANNI (Piscataway)—Critic William J. Harris once made the following observation: "What is most striking about Giovanni's poetry is that she has created the charming persona of 'Nikki Giovanni.' That persona is honest, searching, complex, lusty, and above all, individualistic and charmingly egotistical." Missing from that list are "political," "radical," and "provocative"—words that would surely have dominated the discussion of Giovanni if she hadn't expanded beyond the idioms and ideas of her groundbreaking early works *Black Feeling, Black Talk* (1968) and *Black Judgement* (1968). Once allied firmly with the writers and activists of the Black Nationalist Movement (such as Newark's Amiri Baraka), Giovanni's poetic reach has extended to issues such as loneliness and parenthood. The impressive breadth of her work resists easy classification, although fans of Giovanni list her candor, passion, and restless, anxious search for truth as unifying themes. She was once a popular presence on college campuses; her public readings were often compared to revivals, and she has recorded many of her poems to Gospel music accompaniment. Giovanni has also written essays and children's books and edited literary anthologies. She was inducted in 1982.

ROBERT LUDLUM (Leonia)—This writer of books about international intrigue, corrupt global cabals, and cold war cat-and-mouse maneuvers could be considered a late bloomer. He didn't publish his first novel until he was in his mid-forties; he arrived at the creative world of writing through the creative world of acting (including appearances on Broadway and in more than two hundred early television dramas). However, once he segued from the stage to the page, he quickly made up for lost time. Ludlum has become a one-man publishing phenomenon, with sales of more than two hundred million copies of his books to date. His novels have been translated into more than thirty languages, and he recently signed a three-book deal said to be worth $4 million per book. Ludlum's commercial success has never quite translated into critical success, however. His books are often dismissed as formulaic pot-boilers, built around one-dimensional characters who find themselves engulfed in often unbelievable situations. Many of Ludlum's readers—and the writer himself—disagree. He told *Writer's Digest* in a 1977 interview, "I try to find something with an underpinning of reality" as a premise for his books. Indeed, one of his best-known villains, Carlos "the Jackal" from *The Bourne Identity*, was based on an Argentinian terrorist named Ilich Ramirez Sanchez, who was captured in the Sudan fifteen years after *The Bourne Identity* was on the best-seller list. Ludlum was inducted in 1976.

NORMAN MAILER (Long Branch)—There are as many different assessments of the work of this "notorious" (to use William F. Buckley's phrase) American writer as there are areas of achievement on his resumé. Should he be thought of as a two-time Pulitzer Prize–winning author? Or as a man who was once charged with assault with a knife on his own wife and committed to Bellevue Hospital? Or as a cofounder of New York's *Village Voice*? Or as a public gadfly, taking issue—loudly—with feminists, politicians, and fellow authors such as Gore Vidal and Tom Wolfe? Then there is the brilliant prose stylist whose works, like *The Executioner's Song* (1979), meld the best of journalism and fiction. And the man who once ran for mayor of New York City on a platform of secession from the rest of the state. Should readers care that he's been married six times, roughly once for every two books? Who's the real Norman Mailer? The one who won the National Book Award for the brilliantly-rendered *Miami and the Siege of Chicago* (1968) or the one arrested for disorderly conduct at a New York jazz club because he wouldn't pay an $8 bar bill? Mailer has been a lightning rod for his admirers and detractors ever since the publication of *The Naked and the Dead* (1948), and he continues to write his massive, thoroughly reported books concerning everyone from Marilyn Monroe to Jesus Christ to Lee Harvey Oswald. He was inducted in 1980.

GAY TALESE (Ocean City)—An important writer and one of the originators of the "New Journalism," Talese has trained his eye on some of the most significant trends, institutions, and people in contemporary society. From his portrait of the *New York Times* (where he was a reporter for ten years) in *The Kingdom and the Power* (1969) to his dissection of the Bonanno crime family in *Honor Thy Father* (1971), to his celebrity profiles of Frank Sinatra and Joe DiMaggio for *Esquire,* Talese knows how to tell a story from the inside out. Eschewing fiction for the style of new journalism, Talese once said that his work "may read like fiction, it may give the impression that it was made up . . . overdramatizing incidents for the effect those incidents may cause in the writing, but without question, there is reporting." Talese's most controversial—and popular—book was his report from the front lines on the American sexual revolution, *Thy Neighbor's Wife* (1980). He was inducted in 1991.

FURTHER READING

Holland, Laurence B., et al. *The Literary Heritage of New Jersey*. Princeton: Van Nostrand Co., 1964.

Roberts, Russell. *Discover the Hidden New Jersey*. New Brunswick: Rutgers University Press, 1995.

Stages of Greatness:
A Survey of the History of Theater
in New Jersey

First, a few firsts:

Fred Astaire made his professional dancing debut in New Jersey, at Keyport's Old Palace Theater.

Actor and Singer Paul Robeson graduated first in his class at Rutgers University.

The first drive-in theater in the world opened on June 6, 1933, in Camden.

T. S. Eliot wrote his first play, *The Cocktail Party*, while he was living in Princeton.

The list of New Jersey's notable theatrical firsts could go on, of course. The Garden State has played a prominent role in the pageant of American theater since colonial times. Because of its geographical location, New Jersey has often been a fertile testing ground for Manhattan-bound productions or a convenient temporary stage for itinerant theater companies en route to or from Philadelphia. In its own right, New Jersey has contributed significantly to dramatic literature as well as the development of regional and "little" theaters, and it has become a recognized leader in musical theater and the production of Shakespeare.

The roots of legitimate theater in New Jersey stretch back to the mid-eighteenth century, when traveling acting companies crisscrossed the state, usually presenting lighter fare but often mounting respected productions of the classics. A British-based theater troupe of some renown, calling itself the "American Company of Comedians," presented a highly successful series of Shakespeare plays in Perth Amboy in 1752. The eighteenth-century American playwright William Dunlap (1766–1839), also from Perth Amboy, was an important figure in the development of American theater. His works were performed nationally throughout the latter part of the eighteenth century, and his *History of the American Theater*, published in 1832, is considered the first authoritative study of the development of American drama.

Little is known of Dunlap's boyhood in New Jersey. His father, a former Irish soldier-turned-importer, moved the family to New York when the budding playwright was in his teens. When he was eighteen, Dunlap went to London to study painting with Benjamin West, but he neglected his studies and spent most of his time frequenting the theaters. Three years later, he returned to New York to begin a tumultuous career as a playwright, theater manager, itinerant portrait painter, editor, and theater reviewer. Among the prolific but mostly forgettable products of his pen must be included a fair number of then-successful dramas that captured the romantic American spirit and earned him the title "Father of American Drama" by later biographers and theater historians. Dunlap also seems to have been among those far-sighted entrepreneurs who sensed a growing appetite for theater among a public increasingly interested in native-born drama.

In the early nineteenth century, traveling acting troupes began facing competition from newly established resident theater companies in Newark, Trenton, Jersey City, and Camden. Following the national tastes, spoken drama on New Jersey stages was gradually supplanted by musical fare, minstrel shows, and a wealth of popular romantic operas and operettas. To accommodate this trend, a number of music halls and opera houses were built throughout the state in the mid-nineteenth century, such as the Concert Hall in Newark and Greer's Hall in New Brunswick.

After the Civil War, patriotic and sentimental melodramas established a foothold, which brought such noted Victorian-era thespians as Emma Waller and

Productions such as Chekhov's *Three Sisters* from the 2001 season have helped establish the New Jersey Shakespeare Festival's nationally respected reputation.
Photo by Gerry Goodstein. Courtesy of New Jersey Shakespeare Festival.

Joseph Jefferson to stages in Newark, Trenton, and Hoboken. Thrillingly obvious but popular melodramatic works, such as *The Poor of New York* by Irish playwright Dion Boucicault, were performed to packed houses. The dramatization of Harriet Beecher Stowe's *Uncle Tom's Cabin*, with all its obvious and sentimental splendor, attracted enthusiastic audiences in New Brunswick, Bordentown, and Burlington (preceded by an eight-horse gallop-through-town to publicize the production). New theater companies continued to spring up throughout the state; permanent troupes, residing in Morristown and Passaic, performed the works of such respected New Jersey playwrights as William Gillette and Augustus Thomas.

In the 1890s, burlesque and broadly comic vaudeville-type revues became popular. These shows, replayed several times nightly in music halls in such places as Freehold, Asbury Park, Bridgeton, and Jersey City, generally featured scantily-

---

ILLEGAL ALIENS

One of the most celebrated events in twentieth-century drama took place in New Jersey—sort of.

When Orson Welles's Mercury Theater went on the air on October 30, 1938, few listeners could have guessed that theater history was about to be made. Welles's radio dramatization of the sci-fi classic "War of the Worlds" remains one of the most bizarre and remarked-upon episodes in the history of that medium. Instead of simply retelling H. G. Wells's story of a Martian invasion, Welles (whose radio program was engaged in a ratings battle against the popular Edgar Bergen and Charlie McCarthy on Sunday nights) took a more dramatic tack.

For his Halloween show, Welles created a façade of a radio program, ostensibly broadcasting "the Music of Ramon Raquello and his Orchestra" from the Meridian Room in the Hotel Park Plaza in New York City. The sounds of the ballroom were created in Welles's radio studio, with the dance music regularly interrupted by "special bulletins," each becoming increasingly alarmist in nature. (The first bulletin teasingly reported that a professor at the Mount Jennings Observatory in Chicago had reported seeing explosions on Mars.)

Subsequent bulletins reported a huge shock in the Princeton area "of almost earthquake intensity." A Princeton professor suggests it might be a meteorite. A reporter is dispatched to Grovers Mills, New Jersey, a real locale, a few miles east of Route 1, near Princeton Junction (a small memorial now stands where the actual "landing" took place).

The meteor—reporter Carl Phillips tells us in breathless radio verité—turns out to be a huge metal cylinder whose top begins "to rotate like a screw." The drama builds, the invaders are described, they take out a weapon, some sort of heat ray, and . . . silence.

When the broadcast resumes, the announcer states that the New Jersey State Militia is now mobilizing—so was much of the listening area. Some residents who clad chorus girls, popular music, and coarse physical comedy. During this time, several vaudeville "circuits" ensured a steady stream of touring vaudeville talent, from pigeon acts to strippers, jugglers to comics. The eastern circuit, in which New Jersey played a key role, was the most profitable and longest running.

The dawn of the twentieth century saw the state's vibrant theater scene splinter into several discrete, highly successful avenues of performance. The most important development during this period was the rise of the Atlantic City musical theater scene. Already popular as a seaside resort town and accessible by rail from Philadelphia, Atlantic City became the summer tryout spot for major Broadway-bound musical extravaganzas.

The overwhelming success of the premier of Ziegfeld's first *Follies* in Atlantic City in 1907 led to a surge of interest by Broadway producers in mounting productions there; three theaters were built in Atlantic City in the year after the

---

were tuned to WABC, which carried the broadcast, reacted with panic suitable for an alien invasion. Press accounts the next day indicated the following:

—In Newark, more than twenty families in the Hawthorne Avenue neighborhood bolted from their homes with wet towels and handkerchiefs over their faces, fearing a poisonous gas raid.

—Thousands of calls flooded into the Jersey City Police Department.

—At St. Michael's Hospital in Newark, fifteen people were treated for shock.

—In Caldwell, a parishioner reportedly rushed into the First Baptist Church, announcing a meteor had landed, destroying much of New Jersey. The congregation immediately began praying for the safety of the state.

—In West Orange, a tavern was closed and patrons sent home so the bartender could rescue his wife and children.

The panic was widespread. San Francisco, Chicago, St. Louis, and Baltimore all reported varying degrees of mass hysteria. Many listeners ignored, or weren't listening closely to, the announcement at the beginning of the program that the broadcast was "based on a novel." There were also select reminders throughout the broadcast that the whole production was the work of the Mercury Theater of the Air.

That seemed to matter little to panicked residents near Grovers Mills. To this day, one can still see the remains of the water tower that was shot up by a posse of Martian hunters. For those who can't make the trip, the local historical society maintains a website at *www.waroftheworlds.org*.

Numerous books about Welles contain information about the infamous broadcast. The best comprehensive account is *The Complete War of the Worlds: Mars Invasion of Earth, from H. G. Wells to Orson Welles* (with audio CD), edited by Brian Holmstein and Alex Lubertozzi, and published by Sourcebooks of New York (2001).

Follies debuted. New York theater giants such as David Belasco routinely mounted productions in Atlantic City, with other New York producers booking spots in Asbury Park and Long Branch as well.

Another noteworthy theatrical spin-off at this time was the development of motion pictures. New Jersey's position as a crossroads of theatrical culture made it a natural location for the growth of movies. Fort Lee, the silent movie production capital of the world in the first two decades of the century, attracted such talents as Mary Pickford and "Fatty" Arbuckle, among other performers who were already popular on the state's vaudeville circuit.

A development of extreme importance, and directly related to the development of movies, was the rise of so-called "little theaters" in New Jersey. As radio, movies, and vaudeville moved into center stage in popular culture during the 1920s, fewer and fewer theaters presented serious drama. Those that did were generally smaller, often subscriber-run or associated with an academic institution. Led by the Theatre Intime at Princeton University, the state's colleges increased the number of theater courses and workshops available and elevated the quality of dramatic training. Little Theaters in Newark and New Brunswick presented sophisticated, thoughtful works by Eugene O'Neill, Lillian Hellman, and Clifford Odets.

Derailed by the Depression, many commercial theaters for both movies and plays closed down, though the local theater scene soon received an infusion of life from the New Deal's Federal Theater Project. In New Jersey five counties established Project-funded theater companies: Essex, Bergen, Hudson, Camden, and Monmouth. These companies, performing classic or experimental works for little or no admission charge, traveled throughout the state. Although short-lived—and mired in controversies regarding the "political" nature of some of the Project-sponsored plays—the experiment continued to build on the foundation of the Little Theater and helped spawn the development of first-class regional theaters still in operation today.

Since the end of the Second World War, New Jersey has been home to some of the most widely respected theater companies in the nation. Notables include:

The McCarter Theater in Princeton. Founded in 1930 and incorporated in 1972 as a professional performing arts center, its various troupes play to more than 200,000 patrons a year. The theater presents a mix of classics (Thornton Wilder's *Our Town* premiered there in 1938), concerts, musical theater, and dance.

The Paper Mill Playhouse in Millburn. Established in 1934, with the active support of Eleanor Roosevelt, it became the "official state theater" in 1972. Its stage has seen the talents of Helen Hayes, Douglas Fairbanks, Jr., Jerome Hines, and countless numbers of A-list performers. More populist than artistic, Paper Mill has established a niche as northern Jersey's Broadway lite by attracting nationally-known actors and singers (often in the twilight of their careers, it must be admitted) and building musical revivals around them. The Playhouse is regularly lauded for its professional production values and solid directorial talent.

The New Jersey Shakespeare Festival, in Madison, is a permanent company-in-residence at Drew University. Offering a mix of public performance and professional training programs, NJSF has become one of the most respected repertory Shakespeare companies in the United States.

As home to more than twenty not-for-profit professional theaters, New Jersey continues to nurture audiences and artists alike. The New Jersey Theater Group, a formal organization whose members are drawn from the state's dramatic arts community, helps promote theater throughout the Garden State. In 2003, each of the following professional theater companies was continuing to bring live drama to the state's footlit corridors:

American Stage Company (Teaneck)
Cape May Stage
Centenary Stage Company (Hackettstown)
Forum Theater Company (Metuchen)
Foundation Theater (Burlington County College)
George Street Playhouse (New Brunswick)
The Growing Stage Theater (Netcong)
Luna Stage Company (Montclair)
McCarter Theater (Princeton)
New Jersey Repertory Company (Long Branch)
New Jersey Shakespeare Festival (Madison)
Paper Mill Playhouse (Millburn)
Passage Theater (Trenton)
Playwrights Theater of New Jersey (Madison)
Pushcart Players (Verona)
TheatreFest (Montclair State University)
12 Miles West Theater Company (Montclair)
What Exit? Theater Company (Maplewood)

Several other theater companies in the state doing interesting, often groundbreaking, work deserve an audience. Usually smaller, these eclectic groups have carved out a permanent niche in the state's dramatic landscape:

African Globe TheaterWorks (Newark)
The Bickford Theater at the Morris Museum (Morristown)

The Celtic Theater Company at Seton Hall University (South Orange)

Dreamcatcher Repertory Theater (Bloomfield)

John Harms Center for the Arts (Englewood)

Palistage (Tenafly)

Surflight Theatre (Beach Haven)

Tri-State Actors Theatre (Hamburg)

Union County Arts Center (Rahway)

Women's Theater Company (Madison)

FURTHER READING

Alter, Judy. *Vaudeville: The Birth of Show Business*. Danbury, Conn.: Franklin Watts, 1998.

Dunlap, William. *Diary of William Dunlap, 1766–1839: The Memoirs of a Dramatist*. New York: New-York Historical Society, 1930.

Webb, Michael. *New Stage for a City: Designing the New Jersey Performing Arts Center*. Mulgrave, Vic., Australia: Images Publishing, 1998.

Reaching Critical Mass in the Garden State

The function of a critic has been the subject of debate from the very beginnings of literature. Among the questions that have engaged critical minds from Aristotle to Harold Bloom are "How should we judge a work of art?" and "Does art imitate life—and should it?" Less ambitiously, many modern literary "critics" simply concern themselves with reviews of best-selling books—that is, they offer a "thumbs up or down" recommendation. Although the actual influence of literary criticism is itself the subject of discussion among critics, there's little doubt that much of what gets published and discussed—in lecture halls or radio call-in shows—is determined, in part, by critics.

Some literary critics have exerted an influence that extends far beyond any particular book or author. These critics have influenced *how* we read a book by forcing us to think about whether the work is "well made," whether the plot has "structure," or whether the narrator is "reliable." A good critic can enhance the experience of reading by providing a mental road map of that reading; the critic forces us to ponder, for example, the impact of our own culturally determined assumptions on our reading experience or asks us simply to think about what voices, or points of view, are absent from a text. Or a critic can deepen the reading experience by calling one's attention to certain patterns of symbolism or distinctive linguistic styles that might otherwise go unnoticed. Literary critics have helped shape modern productions of Shakespeare, "discovered" neglected authors, rescued "classics" (such as *Moby-Dick*, which lapsed into obscurity for a half-century after it was published), and even named literary periods (nineteenth-century authors didn't know they were creating "romanticism," ditto the "modernists" of the early twentieth century).

Though ranking critics in importance is as futile and reductive as ranking authors, painters, or musicians, there have been a handful of critics who have provided the talking points for modern discussion of literature. Three of the most influential have been connected to New Jersey—by birth, education, or professional affiliation, or as a cradle of inspiration. Here is an overview of the work and life of three giants of the modern critical era who cultivated their insights in the Garden State: Edmund Wilson, Kenneth Burke, and Elaine Showalter.

There are a few modern critics who share Wilson's passion for literature and a few who emulate his intellectual rigor. There are journalists who have written for as wide a swath of publications and novelists who embrace his social conscience. And there are public intellectuals who discourse on as broad a range of subjects and essayists who ruminate as deeply as Wilson did on the state of the world. And there are scholars who are as enmeshed in arcana or as schooled in dead languages or disappearing cultures as Wilson was. But no one in the twentieth century has combined all of the above in such a forceful, articulate, and prolific manner as the man from Red Bank, New Jersey, the Princeton-educated Edmund Wilson.

From the jazz clubs of Greenwich Village to Freudian psychology, from the Dead Sea Scrolls to Marx, Wilson seemed to know about it all. Scholars of literature long ago gave up trying to characterize the subject matter or intellectual bent of this peripatetic critic. The adjective that perhaps best suits Wilson, who died in 1972 but continues to exert critical influence, is "widely recognized." He achieved the status of expert in almost every area he applied his mind to, although he once disagreed with such a characterization: "I am far from an authority in any of these subjects, but, out of volatile curiosity and an appetite for various entertainment, I have done some reading in all of them; and I have been working, as a practicing critic, to break down the conventional frames, to get away from the academic canons, that always tend to keep literature provincial."

Wilson's "volatile curiosity" took him from the rarefied lecture halls of Princeton to the trenches of World War I. He began his career as a reporter and a sort of roving cultural journalist after the war, writing about American expatriates in Paris, modernist poetry, jazz, and politics for publications such as *The Dial* and *The New Republic*. He wrote moving and thoughtful essays about the plight of the unemployed during the Depression, flirted briefly with the ideology of socialism (he visited the Soviet Union in 1936), and wrote reviews and short stories about Manhattan life in the 1940s for *The New Yorker*. In the last decades of his career, he turned his mind to major scholarly endeavors: he translated and interpreted the Dead Sea Scrolls and produced an influential work on the literature of the Civil War period. The unifying theme in Wilson's work is probably his belief in a detached, historically informed perspective. Wilson was largely distrustful of intellectual fads and literary innovations. His scientific temperament gave his criticism a certain authority and his theories were usually illustrated with lots of relevant and historical examples. As the critic Charles Glicksberg once noted, "Mr. Wilson has no patience with mystification in criticism."

His first major work, *Axel's Castle: A Study in the Imaginative Literature of 1870–1930* (1931), established his reputation as a serious thinker. His overview of the development of writers such as Joyce and Yeats was hard-nosed and clearly articulated. While many other critics were hailing modernism (or Dadaism, or imagism) for its radical nature, unpredictability, and sheer innovation, Wilson was aiming to establish the movement as a logical outgrowth of naturalism and symbolism. In *Axel's Castle*, he stated bluntly that a critic should concern himself with "a history of man's ideas and imaginings in the setting of the conditions which have shaped them."

Wilson was also a strident defender of literature as relevant. He bristled at the suggestion of books as "mere entertainment" and felt it was up to serious readers to maintain certain aesthetic standards. Such exhortations opened him up to the frequent charge of elitism. Wilson *was* implacable in the defense of "quality," as he defined it, as can be gleaned from his famous lecture of 1941, "The Historical Interpretation of Literature":

> This relief that brings the sense of power, and, with the sense of power, joy, is the positive emotion which tells us that we have encountered a first-rate piece of literature. But stay! You may at this point warn: are not people often solaced and exhilarated by literature of the trashiest kind? They are: crude and limited people do certainly feel some such emotion in connection with work that is limited and crude. The man who is more highly organized and has a wider intellectual range will feel it in connection with work that is finer and more complex. The difference between the emotion of the more highly organized man and the emotion of the less highly organized one is a matter of mere gradation. . . . When I was speaking a little while back of the genuine connoisseurs who establish the standards of taste, I meant, of course, the people who can distinguish Grade A and who prefer it to other grades.

Many of Wilson's books and collections of essays, journals, and reviews are still in print, and his ideas are still discussed in academic journals, in college classrooms, and on the World Wide Web. The man who once claimed that "the spirit of artistic and intellectual adventure has, as I say, been deadened" might be surprised to find himself at the center of so much robust debate decades after his death.

It's almost a comic picture: A man who spends his days in a cabin, with no electricity or plumbing, growing vegetables and chopping wood, spending his nights by lantern writing books that will change the landscape of twentieth-century literary criticism. But such was the case with Kenneth Burke, who dropped out of Columbia University at age twenty, wandered around Greenwich Village for a few years soaking up ideas, and then retired to a small farmhouse he built himself in Andover, New Jersey.

IN THEORY

The number and complexity of theories that have arisen in the twentieth century under the heading "literary criticism" is daunting—if not outright mind-numbing. Keeping track of the trends has been the business, largely, of graduate English faculties and the competing theorists themselves. For those who wish to sort out the various strands themselves, here's a sampling of the most important approaches in contemporary literary criticism, but determining who's up and who's down at any given time is a dicey and uncertain parlor game:

FORMALISM—Based on the theory that a work of literature creates meaning largely through the deliberate artistic arrangement of its constituent parts. Formalists mostly dismiss the idea that aspects "outside" the work—for instance, the time period in which the work was created—are relevant to the work's impact.

PSYCHOLOGICAL CRITICISM—Owing much to the theories of Sigmund Freud, this style of analysis seeks to discover either how the author's own psychic temperament is revealed in a work or how a reader's reaction to a piece of literature may be impacted by the employment of certain psychological triggers (the most famous being the guilt-inducing "Oedipus complex").

STRUCTURALISM—An attempt to analyze the "sign systems" of human interaction and how these systems convey meaning through cultural communications, including literature. Structuralists rely largely on the language of linguistics to help differentiate between the components of these sign systems. Of all the schools of criticism, this is among the most jargon-ridden and complex.

READER-RESPONSE CRITICISM—A theory built on the idea that the reader plays a key role in the conveyance of meaning of any literary work. The text merely provides a set of stimuli for the readers, who often react in wildly different ways, explaining why some works of literature can engender divergent, even contradictory, interpretations.

From that bucolic retreat, Burke issued a remarkable number of significant works, studied today by some critics almost as sacred texts. Books such as *Attitudes Toward History* (1938), *The Philosophy of Literary Form* (1941), and *The Rhetoric of Religion* (1962) are required reading in many graduate programs. The college dropout who called New Jersey home for the better part of his life (he died in 1993) still puzzles, frustrates, and inspires would-be literary critics. As more of his correspondence and private papers have become available in the decade after his death, scholars have reevaluated Burke; his reputation has risen to the upper ranks of the lit-crit pantheon. Once seen as something of an iconoclast, Burke is now considered a visionary for his theoretical dissections elucidating some very contemporary critical concerns: the use of language as power, the formation of culture and identity, and literature as an "action." Probably, that equation of writing with action has garnered Burke the most critical accolades.

In a series of books and essays he developed his theory of language, which argues that writing something is akin to doing something and that the motivations for literary expressions are the same as those underlying the motivation for any human action. Writing a poem, for example, isn't an attempt to translate an action into words—it is an action. This notion seems less radical today, especially in the wake of structuralism, which views literature as a "speech act," part of a larger culturally conditioned set of behaviors. But at the time it caught most critics off guard. Burke claimed that "pure literature" does not exist: stories and poems are "strategies for selecting enemies and allies, for socializing losses, for warding off evil eye, for consolation and vengeance . . . implicit commands or instructions of one sort or another."

Burke's way of reading hinges on reducing any text to a scene and then dissecting that scene as if it were actually being performed in front of the reader. Rhetoric, then, becomes action. The method he created to "discover" the action involves a five-pronged filter Burke called the "pentad." The development of the pentad is without doubt Burke's most significant contribution to literary criticism.

The pentad is comprised of these five parts: agent, act, scene, agency, and purpose. Although all writing can be parsed for these five components, the relationship, or "weight" of each factor varies, depending upon the specific work. Burke's advancement of this theory led naturally to his idea that every piece of writing has a purpose, that it seeks to "do" something. In his famous essay, "Literature as Equipment for Living," Burke explored the real purpose behind several types of writing, from proverbs to historical novels, and suggested that each encodes or embodies an "action," not merely an aesthetic reflection or a desire to entertain:

Examine random specimens in *The Oxford Dictionary of English Proverbs*. You will note, I think, that there is no "pure" literature here. Everything is "medicine." Proverbs are designed for consolation or vengeance, for admonition or exhortation, for foretelling.

Or they name typical, recurrent situations. That is, people find a certain social relationship recurring so frequently that they must "have a word for it." The Eskimos have special names for many different kinds of snow (fifteen, if I remember rightly) because variations in the quality of snow greatly affect their living. Hence, they must "size up" snow much more accurately than we do.

Few critics of the twentieth century could claim to have "sized up" the act of writing more accurately than the thoroughly original Kenneth Burke.

One of the most important critical approaches to emerge from the stew of theories and "isms" in the latter part of the twentieth century was feminist criticism—an approach that has helped reinvigorate the study of some unfairly neglected literary works as well as cast important new perspectives on the established canon. Perhaps the single most important figure in the development of feminist literary theory is Elaine Showalter, a longtime Princeton professor and former member of the faculty of Douglass College, Rutgers, where she began her trail-blazing career. Since the publication of her seminal work, *A Literature of Her Own: British Women Novelists from Brontë to Lessing* (1977), Showalter and feminist literary criticism have taken off. She has received a plethora of high-grade academic honors, including a Guggenheim Fellowship and a Rockefeller Humanities Fellowship.

But Showalter is no highbrow. She once defended her work on hysteria, which she addressed in her 1997 book *Hysteries: Hysterical Epidemics and Modern Culture*, against an angry corps of "hysteria victims" on the decidedly lowbrow daytime television program, *The Rolanda Show*. And, perhaps taking a cue from her Princeton colleague and friend Joyce Carol Oates—who has written for such populist outlets as *TV Guide*—Showalter served a brief stint as television critic for *People* magazine. Her range has made her somewhat difficult to characterize, but *Mirabella* magazine took a shot at pinning her down: "Elaine Showalter is Camille Paglia with balls."

Born and raised in Boston, Showalter received her bachelor's degree from Bryn Mawr, her master's at Brandeis, and her doctorate at the University of California at Davis in 1970. She then took a position at Douglass College, Rutgers, and in 1984 she became a professor of English at Princeton University, where she remains today. Her work has raised the ire of some academics and stoked the intellectual embers of others. Showalter is often credited with founding feminist criticism—or, more specifically, a concept Showalter calls "gynocriticism." She has put forth her theories in a number of books, and she was the editor of the groundbreaking *Women's Liberation and Literature* (1971), the first textbook specifically focused on women in literature. Other important works include *These Modern Women: Autobiographies of American Women in the 1920s* (1978) and *The New Feminist Criticism* (1985). But her best-known and still widely discussed book was her first, *A Literature of Their Own*, which helped erect the underpinnings of feminist literary theory. Showalter's ideas may be complex, but her writing is a model of clarity and concision. Tackling what in many other academics' hands might be head-pounding, thickly-layered jargon, Showalter moves from point to point with ease. Here's an example:

> Feminine, feminist, or female, the woman's novel has always had to struggle against the cultural and historical forces that relegated women's experience to the second rank. In trying to outline the female tradition, I have looked beyond the famous novelists who have been found worthy, to the lives and works of many women who have long been excluded from literary history. I have tried to discover how they felt about themselves and their books, what choices and sacrifices they made, and how their relationship to their profession and their tradition evolved.

Some colleagues and critics of Showalter, while endorsing her aims, feel that she occasionally lapses into the sins she herself excoriates—namely, adopting an ideologically driven posture that prevents a broader, more comprehensive view of gender roles. As David Richter put it in *The Critical Tradition* (1989):

> Obviously in Showalter's program there is some danger of overestimating the extent to which the female tradition and the male tradition are separable and (as Kenneth Ruthven has put it) of feminist critics "repeating exactly the same mistake for which they take male critics to task, namely an exclusive preoccupation with the writings of one sex."

Regardless of these quibbles over the comprehensiveness of her critical embrace, Showalter remains a major force in shaping contemporary discussions of literature.

FURTHER READING

Culler, Jonathan. *Literary Theory: A Very Short Introduction*. New York: Oxford University Press, 2000.

Tyner, Lois. *Critical Theory Today: A User Friendly Guide*. New York: Garland Publishing, 1998.

Stoned in New Jersey

Where an artist chooses to live might reveal a great deal about him or her. For many writers the sense of "place" is central in their oeuvre; it feeds their creative energies and offers a refuge from the harsh, larger world. For others, perhaps, the connection is accidental—make of it what you will.

But what about an eternal resting place? Is that significant in helping understand an artist's life and work? Many famous writers have turned their thoughts toward their own death while they were still very much among the living. John Keats wrote his own epitaph. William Butler Yeats wrote a poem musing about the view from his eventual resting place and selected the final stanza from that poem for inscription on his tombstone. Few, though, have been as involved as Camden's Walt Whitman, who not only dictated meticulous plans for a final resting place but also visited the site regularly to supervise construction of his memorial tomb.

More generally, however, burial sites retain cultural significance. And just as the Garden State has attracted creative artists of the first rank through the centuries, so too does it cradle the remains of countless wordsmiths whose work lives on today. Though many people have visited the gravesites of famous Jersey authors, such as Whitman, they may have been unaware that scattered throughout the state are the burial sites of other, significant contributors to the world of letters. Here's a small sampling of those women and men in the word trade who helped change the course of literature.

SYLVIA BEACH—Literary history records this indefatigable supporter of writers and readers as a force behind the effort to publish James Joyce's modernist masterpiece *Ulysses*. Indeed, Beach's commitment to making books available through her shop Shakespeare and Co., and her support of the many international writers who visited the bookstore in Paris, are legendary. So was her courage. She once refused to sell the store's only remaining copy of *Finnegans Wake* to a German officer who threatened to confiscate her entire inventory if she refused; he made good on his threat and shut down the entire shop. In the case of *Ulysses*, Beach bravely stepped in after Joyce, who called her shop "Stratford-on-Odeon," was unable to find a publisher for his book, which had already earned a reputation for its "obscene" content.

Born in Baltimore in 1887, Beach spent much of her adolescence in Princeton in a Presbyterian parsonage overseen by her minister father. She escaped her rather circumscribed life in New Jersey, fled first to Florence, then Spain, and finally settled in Paris. Her bookshop, which functioned more like a lending library than a traditional retail bookstore, was a frequent gathering place for writers such as T. S. Eliot, Ernest Hemingway, and André Gide.

She remained abroad until her death in 1962. Her body was returned to New Jersey for burial in the Princeton Cemetery.

MEYER BERGER—If there is one figure who came to embody the "golden age" of journalism, with its bustling newsboys and hard-boiled reporters in cheap fedoras breathlessly shouting "Get me re-write!"—it was Meyer "Mike" Berger, a New York–based journalist who rose from the ranks of copy boy to Pulitzer Prize–winning *New York Times* reporter.

Berger was born in 1898 to Eastern European Jewish immigrant parents. His keen eye and immense heart helped him bring to life the harsh realities of existence for many New Jerseyans and New Yorkers, from the Depression through World War II. In 1950, he won the Pulitzer Prize for his story about Howard Unruh, a WWII veteran who went on a rampage in Camden, shooting thirteen people.

Berger's writing holds up well today, a model of clarity and detail. Equally notable was his range, from prize-winning crime reporting (his series on Al Capone's 1931 trial was nominated for a Pulitzer) to his feature stories in the *Saturday Evening Post* and *Readers' Digest*, to his serious scholarship, including his history of the New York Public Library.

Berger died in 1959. He is buried in Riverside Cemetery in Saddle Brook.

ISAAC KAUFFMAN FUNK—Fans of television's once-popular game show *Password* might remember host Allen Luden somberly intoning that all disputes regarding definitions of words would be resolved by referring to *Funk & Wagnalls Standard Dictionary*. The first partner in the esteemed publishing house of Funk & Wagnalls—which aimed to put high-quality literature in the hands of readers of modest means—Isaac Funk was a linguist and editor of legendary zeal. Originally drawn to publishing through his desire to serve ministers' reading needs and fueled by his own campaign to promote temperance and Christian values, Funk later expanded into general literature; he published the reference work that bears his name in 1894.

His dictionary, produced with longtime friend and former schoolmate Adam Willis Wagnalls, spawned one of Funk's most widely embraced reform movements (he was involved in lots of reform movements) called "Simplified Spelling"—a cause promoted and underwritten by Andrew Carnegie. In addition to the dictionary, he helped write and edit a massive twelve-volume *Jewish Encyclopedia*, and he wrote religious and philosophical books as well. But he will always be remembered for his dictionary, a work he never stopped tinkering with. He was, in fact, revising the pages for the letter "S" when he was found dead in his home in Montclair in 1912. He was buried in Rosedale Cemetery, in Orange.

His work was carried on by his son, Wilfred, who joined the family business in 1909. After graduating from Princeton with a degree in English, he became a noted lexicographer in his own right. He also edited several magazines and literary reviews while continuing to produce works of etymology and revisions of the original Funk & Wagnalls dictionary. He was the author, from 1946 until his death in 1966, of the monthly *Readers' Digest* feature, "It Pays to Enrich Your Word Power." When he died, he was also buried in the family plot at Rosedale Cemetery.

RICHARD WATSON GILDER—Born in Bordentown in 1844, in his first twenty years Gilder showed little that would predict his future literary importance. The son of a minister, he attended schools run by his father, read a little, and hung out at newspaper offices; he left little impression on those around him. But in his early twenties, after being hired as a reporter on the *Newark Daily Advertiser*, Gilder came into his own. After cutting his journalistic teeth on the *Advertiser*, he cofounded his own newspaper with Robert Crane (Stephen's uncle) called the *Newark Morning Register*.

Simultaneous to his journalism, he also began a fruitful, lifelong association with Charles Scribner and Co., which hired him to run an in-house publication called *Hours at Home*. After a decade with the publishing company, he was

GRAVE CONSIDERATIONS

Anyone with a serious interest in the cemeteries of the Garden State should investigate Janice Kohl Sarapin's *Old Burial Grounds of New Jersey: A Guide* (1994, Rutgers University Press). Providing much more than a graveside gazetteer, Sarapin—a founding member of the New Jersey Graveyard Preservation Society—offers an entertaining, informative, and well-researched romp through the traditions, rituals, and geography of burial throughout the state's history. Covering everything from funeral customs to oft-repeated ghost stories, Kohl's book is a surprisingly engrossing read, with some oddly compelling curio on almost every page, as in her discussion of grave markers in Chapter Three:

> A common motif on pre-1750 grave markers (especially, but not exclusively, in Presbyterian churchyards) is a skull, with bones crossed beneath it. This piece of Puritan symbolism, more common in New England than in New Jersey, reminds the onlooker of the mortality of the body. . . . Between 1730 and 1770, another version of the skull became popular on the tombstones in central and northern New Jersey: the death's head, with its deep eye sockets, prominent nose bridge, and rectangular teeth. A downward slant to the eyes or mouth added to the gloomy aspect of these effigies. Wings to the sides of the death's head underscored the Puritan belief that flight from death, sin, and damnation was impossible.

named editor of Scribner's prestigious *Century* magazine, a national tastemaker boasting more readers than *Harper's* or the *Atlantic Monthly*. Gilder used this influential position to advance the work of established authors (he serialized Henry James's *The Bostonians*) as well as to promote new writers, such as Thomas Nelson Page and George Washington Cable. Gilder was also a prolific poet, and, though his work is unread today, it was quite popular with his contemporaries and went through several profitable editions during his lifetime. His commitment to literature moved beyond his work on periodicals to include his lobbying on behalf of copyright protection as well as the establishment of the Society of American Artists in 1877.

Gilder died in 1909 and was buried in the town of his birth at the Bordentown Cemetery.

FURTHER READING

Felson, Greg. *Tombstones: Final Resting Places of the Famous.* Kansas City, Mo.: Andrews McMeel Publishing, 1999.

Meyer, Richard, ed. *Cemeteries and Gravemarkers: Voices of American Culture.* Ann Arbor: UMI Research Press, 1989.

Index

Page numbers in italics refer to illustrations.

Accetturo, Anthony, 172, 173
Ackerman, Harold, 173
Adams, John Quincy, 11
adventure stories, 80
African American drama, 71–72
Ahlgren, Gregory, and Stephen Monier, *Crime of the Century,* 152, 154–155
airships, 160
Alcott, Louisa May, 31
American Revolution, 9–10, 11
Andover, 203
animals, 46–49, 127–128
"Annual Captain Kidd Treasure Hunt," 135
Artis, John, 163
Asbury Park, 43, 44, 196
Atlantic City, 177–178, 197–198
autobiography, 51, 167
avant-garde, 71

Baraka, Amiri, 71–75, *72;* "African Slaves/American Slaves—Their Music" [essay], 72; *Daggers and Javelins,* 73; *Dutchman* [play], 71–72; *The Legacy of Malcolm X . . . ,* 73; *Preface to a Twenty-Volume Suicide Note,* 71; *Raise Race Rays Race,* 73; *The System of Dante's Hell,* 73
baseball, 85
Bayonne, 111
Beach, Sylvia, 207–208
beaches, 109, 135
beach reading, 64, 83
Beat movement, 58, 61, 71
Beaver Brown Band, 108

Beck, Henry Charlton: *Jersey Genesis,* 179, 185; *A New Jersey Reader,* 3
Behn, Noel, *Lindbergh, the Crime,* 154
Benchley, Peter, 79–83; *The Deep,* 82; *Jaws,* 80, 83; *"Q" Clearance,* 82; *Time and a Ticket,* 81; *White Shark,* 82
Berger, Meyer, 208
Bishop, Jim, 191
Black Arts community, 72
Blackbeard [Edward Teach], 138
Black cultural nationalism, 72, 74
Blackman, W. Haden, *The Field Guide to North American Monsters,* 182
Black Nationalism movement, 74
black writers, 68, 71–72
Blume, Judy, 191
Boetius, Henning, *The Phoenix,* 160–161
Bonner, Willard Hallam, *Pirate Laureate,* 136
Bordentown, 196, 209–210
Boucher, Jack, *Absegami Yesteryear,* 181
Boucicault, Dion, *The Poor of New York* [play], 196
Bridgeton, 196
Broderick, James F., 217
Bruno-Scarfo crime family, 173–176
Bucke, Richard M., 25
burial sites, 207–210
buried treasure, 135–139, 140
Burke, Kenneth, 203–205; *Attitudes Toward History,* 204; "Literature as Equipment for Living" [essay], 204; *The Philosophy of Literary Form,* 204; *The Rhetoric of Religion,* 204
burlesque, 196

Burlington, 196
Burlington County, 138
Burr, Aaron, 141–147, *142*
Byrne, Brendan, 177

Cafferty, John, 108
Callow, Phillip, *From Noon to Starry Night*, 25
Camden, 21, *21*, 23, 25–26, 175, 194, 208
Camp Mills, 56
canals, 188
Cape May, 137, 138
"Captain Kidd's Farewell to the Sea" [song], 140
Capuzzo, Michael, *Close to Shore*, 81
caricature, *34*, 35
Carter, Rubin "Hurricane," 162–168; *The Sixteenth Round*, 167–168
cartooning, 32–36, 111
Casino [film], 177
Casino Control Act, 177
casinos, 177–178
cemeteries, 139, 207, 209
Chaiton, Sam, and Terry Swinton, *Lazarus and the Hurricane*, 166–167
Chapman, Robert, 190
character studies, 39, 52
children's literature, 28–31, 38, 86
Ciardi, John, 38
Cifelli, Nicholas "Turk," 175
Civil War, 22, 33
Clark, Joe, 117, 118; *Laying Down the Law*, 116–119
Clark, Mary Higgins, 62–65; *Aspire to the Heavens*, 62; *On the Street Where You Live*, 62; *Stillwatch*, 63; *Where Are the Children?*, 64
Cliffwood Beach, 135, 138, 139
College of New Jersey. *See* Princeton University
Cooper, James Fenimore, 12–16; *The History of the Navy . . .* , 14; *The Last of the Mohicans*, 15; "Leather-Stocking Tales," 14–16; *The Pioneers*, 14; *Precaution*, 14; *The Spy*, 14; *The Water Witch*, 139
Condon, John, 151

corruption, 177–178
Cosa Nostra, 171–178
Crane, Robert, 209
Crane, Stephen, 41–45; *Maggie*, 42; "The Open Boat" [short story], 42; *The Red Badge of Courage*, 44–45
Crane, Townley, 43
crime, 124–127, 148–155, 162, 163; in drama, 172; in fiction, 120–123; reporting, 208. *See also* organized crime
criminal justice system, 125, 165–166
criticism, literary, 68–69, 72, 200–206
critics, 38, 200–206
Cunningham, John, 3

Daily Princetonian [student newspaper], 69
Davis, Linda, *Badge of Courage*, 43
Daynor, George, 107
De Haven, Tom, 109–112; *Derby Dugan's Depression Funnies*, 111; *Funny Papers*, 111; *Jersey Luck*, 109–112
Delaware River, 137
Del Tufo, Robert, 177
Demaris, Ovid, *The Boardwalk Jungle*, 177–178
development, real estate, 103
devil. *See* Jersey Devil
DiClerico, James, and Barney Pavelec, *The Jersey Game*, 85
dictionaries, 208
dirigibles, 160
documentary film, 165, 184
Dodge, Mary Mapes, 27–32; *Hans Brinker*, 28, *29*, 31
Dodge Foundation. *See* Geraldine R. Dodge Foundation
Dodge Poetry Festival, 73, 185–189
Dodge Poetry Program, 189
dog stories, 46–49
Dorofee, Michael, 182
drama, 71, 194
Drew University, 199
duel, Burr-Hamilton, 141–147, *142*
dueling, 141, 145
Dunlap, William, 194–195; *History of the American Theater*, 194

Dwyer, William, *The Day Is Ours,* 122

Eddie and the Cruisers [film], 106, 108.
    See also Kluge, P. F.
Edison, Thomas A., 114
Edison [township], 114
editorial cartoons, 32–33, 35
educational system, 116
Englewood, 148
environmental movement, 102
essays, 14, 60, 72–74, 76, 86, 100, 201
Essex County Juvenile Detention Center,
    118
Estrin, Herman, 190
Evanovich, Janet, 120, 122–123; *One for
    the Money,* 120–123

FBI, 172
Federal Theater Project, 198
feminist literary theory, 205–206
Fernincola, Richard, *Twelve Days of Terror,*
    81
film, 106, 165. *See also* documentary film
Finckenauer, James, *Scared Straight! and
    the Panacea Phenomenon,* 165
Fisher, Jim: *The Ghosts of Hopewell,*
    151–153; *The Lindbergh Case,* 151–153
Fleming, Thomas, *Duel,* 144–146
Flemington, 149
Follies [theatrical revue], 197–198
form, poetic, 59
formalism, 203
Fort Lee, 198
Fox Hill, 139
Franklin Township, 17
Freehold, 196
Freeman, Joanne B., *Affairs of Honor,* 145
Freeman, Mary Wilkins, 37–41; "Criss-
    Cross" [short story], 40; *Pembroke,* 38
Freneau, Philip, 7–12, 8; "The American
    Village" [poem], 9; "The British Prison
    Ship" [poem], 10; "Neversink" [poem],
    12; "On the Civilization of the Western
    Aboriginal Country" [poem], 7; "A
    Political Litany" [poem], 9; "The Wild
    Honeysuckle" [poem], 10
Fresolone, George, and Robert Wagman,
    Blood Oath, 173–176

Friedel, Robert, Paul Israel, and Bernard S.
    Finn, *Edison's Electric Light,* 114
frontier tales, 14–16
Funk, Isaac Kauffman, 208–209
Funk, Wilfred, 209
Funk & Wagnalls Standard Dictionary, 208

gambling, gaming industry, 177–178
Gateway National Recreation Area, Sandy
    Hook, 109
Geraldine R. Dodge Foundation, 186,
    189. *See also* Dodge Poetry Festival
ghost stories, 65
Gilbreth, Frank, 91, *92,* 93–95
Gilbreth, Frank Jr., and Ernestine Gilbreth
    Carey: *Belles on Their Toes,* 93; *Cheaper
    by the Dozen,* 91–95
Gilbreth, Lillian, 93
Gilder, Richard Watson, 209–210
Gillette, William, 196
Ginsberg, Allen, 58–61, *72;* "Howl"
    [poem], 58, 59
Giovanni, Nikki, 192
Glen Ridge, 123–127
grave markers, 209
gravesites, 207
Great Depression, 93
Green, Martin, *New York 1913,* 52
Griffith, Mary, 17–20; *Three Hundred Years
    Hence,* 17–19
Grovers Mills, 196–197
Gunnison Beach, 109

Hamilton, Alexander, 141–145, *142, 146*
Harding, Ruth Guthrie, "The Old Wagon-
    Market" [poem], 1
Hasbrouk Heights, 46
Hauptmann, Bruno Richard, 148, 151,
    153
Hendrickson, Robert, *Hamilton II,* 144
Hillside, 45
Hindenburg [airship], 157, 158; disaster,
    155–162
Hindenburg, The [film], 159
Hirsch, James S., *Hurricane,* 163–164
historical fiction, 14, 159–160
historical narrative, 191
Hoboken, 85, 196

hockey, 129
Hoehling, A. A., *Who Destroyed the Hindenburg?*, 158
Hoffman, Harold C., 149
Hopewell, 148
horror/suspense fiction, 80, 82
Hudson County, 109
Hunterdon County Courthouse, Flemington, 149
Hurricane [film], 163
Hurricane Carter case, 162–168
Husted, Lorne, 154

ice skating, 30, 129, 188
illustrators, 34
International Board of Inquiry, report on the *Hindenburg*, 156, 161
Irving, Washington, 14, 36
Irvington, 28

Jefferson, Joseph, 196
Jersey Chronicle [newspaper], 11
Jersey City, 110, 111, 196
Jersey Devil, 179–185, *183*
Jersey Devil Hunting Team, 182
Jersey Devils hockey team, 182
Jersey Shore, 81, 104, 109, 135, 137–140
Jewish Encyclopedia, 208
Jones, LeRoi. *See* Baraka, Amiri
journalism, 11, 42, 44, 84, 129, 208, 209
justice system, 125, 165–166

Kabbalah, 130
Kalata, Barbara, *A Hundred Years, A Hundred Miles*, 188
Kalm, Peter, *Travels in North America*, 48
Kennedy, Ludovic, *The Airman and the Carpenter*, 152
Kenyon College, 107
Ketchum, Richard, *The Winter Soldiers*, 122
Key, Francis Scott, 11
Keyport, 139, 194
Kidd, William, 135–140, *136*
kidnapping, 148–155
Kilmer, Joyce, 53–58; "Trees" [poem], 53–54; "The Twelve Forty-Five" [poem], 56

Kilmer, Kenton, *Memories of My Father, Joyce Kilmer*, 55
Kluge, P. F., *Eddie and the Cruisers*, 1, 104–108
Kohl Sarapin, Janice, *Old Burial Grounds of New Jersey*, 209
Kramer, Jane, *Allen Ginsberg in America*, 59

Lakehurst, 105, 156; Naval Station, 157
language theory, 204
Lean on Me [film], 118
Leeds Point, 180
Lefkowitz, Bernard, *Our Guys*, 123–127
legal system, 166
legends, 139, 179
Lenape Indians, 180
Lindbergh, Charles, 149, *150*
Lindbergh, Charles, Jr., 148; kidnapping case, 148–155
List, John, 126
literary criticism, 13, 38, 200–206; theories, 203–205
literary journals, 71
literature, theories of, 202
Little Egg Harbor River, 140
"little theaters," 198
Livingston, 128
"local color" writers, 39
Lowell, Amy, 43
Lucchese crime family, 172
Ludlum, Robert, 192

McCarter Theater, 198
McCloy, James F., and Ray Miller, Jr.: *The Jersey Devil*, 179, 180; *Phantom of the Pines*, 181
McMahon, William, *Pine Barrens*, 139
McPhee, John, *The Pine Barrens*, 99–104
Madison, 199
Mafia, 171–178
magazine illustrations, 32–36
magazines, 28, 37, 154
Mahwah, 55
Mailer, Norman, 193
Mary Higgins Clark Mystery Magazine, 62, 64
melodramas, 195–196

Menlo Park, 114
"Mercury Theater of the Air" [radio program], 196
Metuchen, 38
Millburn, 198
Mitchner, Stuart, 113, 116; *Indian Action,* 113; *Let Me Be Awake,* 113; *Rosamund's Vision,* 112–115
Mitgang, Herbert, *Dangerous Dossiers,* 61
modernism, 43, 52
"Money Island," 138
Montclair, 91, 93, 208
Montville, 188
Mooney, Michael, *The Hindenburg,* 158–159
Morris Canal, *186,* 188
Morrison, Herbert, 155–156
Morrison, Toni, 65–70, *66; Beloved,* 68–69; *The Bluest Eye,* 67; *Memory, Creation, and Writing,* 65; *Song of Solomon,* 69
Morristown, 35–36, 55, 196
motion pictures, 198
motion study, 94
Mount Pleasant, 8
movies, 198
Moyers, Bill, 187
Mullica River, 138
murder, 126, 162, 163
Murray, Thomas C., and Valeria Barnes, *The Seven Wonders of New Jersey—and Then Some,* 114
musical theater, 195–197
music halls, 195–196

Nast, Thomas, 32–36, *34*
National Canal Museum, 188
National Parks and Recreation Act of 1978, 102, 103
nature poetry, 25, 54
naturists, 109
Navy Lakehurst Historical Society, 158
Newark, 44, 72, 95–97, *96,* 174–175, 190, 195, 196, 198; Public Library, *96,* 98–99
Newark Morning Register [newspaper], 209
New Brunswick, 195, 196, 198

New Jersey Devil, 179–185, *183*
New Jersey Graveyard Preservation Society, 209
New Jersey High School Poetry Contest, 189
New Jersey Institute of Technology, 190
New Jersey Literary Hall of Fame, 64, 190–191
New Jersey Public Television, 184
New Jersey Shakespeare Festival, *195,* 199
New Jersey State Police, 149
New Jersey State Prison, Trenton, 151, 164, 168
New Jersey Theater Group, 199
New Jersey writers, 190
newspapers, 11, 69, 106; cartoons, 111; columns, 86
New York Times, 84, 190
New York Times on the Sopranos, 174
novels, 42, 44, 62–65, 65–70, 76–79, 80, 86, 95–99, 104–113, 120–123, 127–131

Oates, Joyce Carol, 76–79; *The Barrens,* 77; *Them,* 78
Ocean County, 184
opera houses, 195
"Operation Broadsword," 176
Orange, 208
organized crime, 171–178
Oyster Creek, 140

PNC Bank Arts Center, 190
Paine, Thomas, 11
Palace Depression, 106–107
Palisades, 141, *146*
Pantoliano, Joe, 108
Paper Mill Playhouse, 198–199
Parker, Ellis, 149, 152
Passaic, 196
Paterson, 51, 52, 59, 116–119, 163, 164, 168
patriotic writers, 52
Peacock, Louise, *Crossing the Delaware,* 122
Perth Amboy, 194
Peter Benchley's Amazon [television show], 83

Peterson, Robert, *Patriots, Pirates, and Pineys,* 137
pets, 48
photo collections, 86
Pine Barrens, 77, 100–103, *100,* 179–185
Pinelands Commission, 103
Pinelands Protection Act, 103
Pinsky, Robert, 187
pioneer stories, 14
pirates, 136–139; and treasure, 135–139, 140
plays, 71, 194
Poe, Edgar Allan, "The Gold Bug" [short story], 135, 139
poetry, 20–21, 22–23, 37, 38, 42–44, 50–51, 54, 58, 61, 74; criticism, 85; festival, 185–189
political cartoons, 32–33, 35
Pompton Lakes, 48
pop culture, 129
Pratt, Fletcher, *The Cunning Mulatto,* 152
Princeton, 113, 115, 194, 198, 208, 209
Princeton University, 9, 69, 198
psychoanalysis, historical, 143
psychological criticism, 203
public libraries, 98
publishing, 208

Quindlen, Anna, 84–87; *Black and Blue,* 84; *Living Out Loud,* 87; *Naked Babies,* 86

radicalism, 52, 59–60
radio, 62, 83, 196–197
Rahway State Prison, 165, 175
Raritan Bay, 137, 139
reader-response criticism, 203
Red Bank, 201
reform movements, 208
regional theaters, 198
Reiken, Frederick: *The Lost Legends of New Jersey,* 127–131; *The Odd Sea,* 128–129
reviews, 202. *See also* criticism
Revolutionary War, 9–10, 11, 122
revues, 196
Ringe, Donald, *James Fenimore Cooper,* 13
Riverfront State Correctional Institute, 175

Roberts, Russell, *Discover the Hidden New Jersey,* 184
rock and roll, 104, 108
Rose Hill, 139
Roth, Philip: *Goodbye, Columbus,* 1, 95–99; *Portnoy's Complaint,* 97
Route 1, 77
Rovin, Jeff, *The Hindenburg Disaster,* 159
Rudolph, Robert, *The Boys from New Jersey,* 171–173
Rugow, Alex, *A Fateful Friendship,* 142–143
Rutgers University, 194; Rutgers University–Newark, 189

Saddle Brook, 208
St. Nicholas [magazine], 28, 30–31, 37
Sandy Hook, 109, 135, 138, 139
Santa Claus, 33, 36
Scaduto, Anthony, *Scapegoat,* 152
Scared Straight [documentary film], 165
Schwarzkopf, Norman, 149
science fiction, 17, 18
sea stories, 81–82
series fiction, 48, 120–123
shark attacks, 81
Shore. *See* Jersey Shore
Short Hills, 97
short stories, 39, 42, 48, 52, 76, 78, 202
Showalter, Elaine, 205–206; *Hysteries,* 205; *A Literature of Her Own,* 205–206; *The New Feminist Criticism,* 206; *These Modern Women,* 206; *Women's Liberation and Literature* [comp.], 205
"Simplified Spelling," 208
skating, 30, 129, 188
Smith, Rosamond. *See* Oates, Joyce Carol
social commentary, 17, 33, 35
Sopranos, The [television series], 174, 175
Sopranos, The: A Family History, 174
Spehl, Eric, 158–159
Spirit House Players, 72
spiritual enlightenment, 130
Spring Lake, 62
Stanhope, 186
state prisons, 151, 164, 165, 168, 175
Stowe, Harriet Beecher, *Uncle Tom's Cabin* [play], 196

structuralism, 203, 204
suburbs, 123–127
"Sunnybank," Pompton Lakes, 46, 48
supernatural stories, 40
suspense fiction, 62–64, 82
Syrett, Harold C., and Jean Cooke, eds., *Interview in Weehawken,* 143–144

Talese, Gay, 193
Tammany Hall, 35
Teach, Edward [Blackbeard], 138
television, 172, 184, 187
Terhune, Albert Payson, 46–49; *The Heart of a Dog,* 47; *Lad: A Dog,* 48
Terhune, Anice, *Across the Line,* 49
theater, 71–72, 194–200
theater companies, 196, 198–200
theories: of criticism, 203; of language, 204
Thomas, Augustus, 196
time travel, 18
Toland, John, *The Great Dirigibles,* 156–158
Toms River, 135, 138
Traubel, Horace, *With Walt Whitman in Camden,* 23
travelogue, 48, 99, 113
treasure hunters, 135
Trenton, 120–123, 151, 196
Trenton State Prison, 151, 164, 168
"trial of the century" [Lindbergh case], 148
Turtle Back Zoo, 127–128
Tweed, William Marcy, 35

United States Journal [magazine], 28
United States v. Accetturo, 171–173
Unruh, Howard, 208
urban landscape, 112
utopic fiction, 17

Van Gogh, Vincent, 34
vaudeville, 196, 197
Vidal, Gore, *Burr,* 146–147
videos, 187

Vineland, 107
Vineland Times-Journal [newspaper], 106
violence, 127; in fiction, 78. *See also* crime; horror/suspense fiction; murder

Waller, Emma, 195
Walt Whitman Cultural Arts Center, 23, 182
war fiction, 44–45
"War of the Worlds" radio broadcast, 196–197
war poems, 9–10, 23
Washington, George, 122
Waterloo Village, 186, *186,* 188, 189
websites, 161, 174, 182, 188, 190
Weehawken, 141, *142, 146*
Weird New Jersey [magazine], 154
Welles, Orson, 196–197
Westbrook, Perry, 39
westerns, 16
Westfield, 126
West Orange, 127–128, *175*
Whitman, Walt, 20–27, *24,* 207; *Franklin Evans,* 22; *Leaves of Grass,* 20–21, 22–23; "Patrolling Barnegat" [poem], 25; "When Lilacs Last in the Dooryard Bloomed" [poem], 26
Wice, Paul B., *Rubin "Hurricane" Carter and the American Justice System,* 164–166
Williams, Jesse, 190
Williams, William Carlos, 50–53, 59; autobiography, 51; *The Farmer's Daughters,* 52; *Paterson,* 51; *Pictures from Brueghel,* 52; *Spring and All,* 50; *White Mule,* 52
Wilson, Edmund, 201–203; *Axel's Castle,* 202; "The Historical Interpretation of Literature" [lecture], 202
Wilson, Woodrow, 69
women writers, 19, 27, 31, 37, 40
World War I, 56–57

zeppelins, 156–157, *157*
Ziegfeld's *Follies,* 197–198

About the Author

JAMES F. BRODERICK is an assistant professor of English and journalism at New Jersey City University in Jersey City. A former newspaper reporter and copy editor, he lives in Glen Ridge with his wife, Miri, and daughters Olivia and Maddy.